# Black Ships and
# Sea Raiders

# Greek Studies: Interdisciplinary Approaches

Series Editor: Gregory Nagy, Harvard University
Executive Editors: Corinne Pache, Emily Allen Hornblower, and Eirene Visvardi
Associate Editors: Mary Ebbott, Casey Dué Hackney, Leonard Muellner, Olga Levaniouk, Timothy Powers, Jennifer R. Kellogg, and Ivy Livingston

**On the front cover**: A calendar frieze representing the Athenian months, reused in the Byzantine Church of the Little Metropolis in Athens. The cross is superimposed, obliterating Taurus of the Zodiac. The choice of this frieze for books in *Greek Studies: Interdisciplinary Approaches* reflects this series' emphasis on the blending of the diverse heritages—Near Eastern, Classical, and Christian—in the Greek tradition. Drawing by Laurie Kain Hart, based on a photograph. Recent titles in the series are:

*Dramatic Action in Greek Tragedy and Noh: Reading with and beyond Aristotle*, by Mae J. Smethurst
*Greek Heroes in and out of Hades*, by Stamatia Dova
*Becoming Achilles: Child-sacrifice, War, and Misrule in the Iliad and Beyond*, by Richard Kerr Holway
*Chronos on the Threshold: Time, Ritual, and Agency in the Oresteia*, by Marcel Widzisz
*Disguise and Recognition in the* Odyssey, by Sheila Murnaghan
*Choral Identity and the Chorus of Elders in Greek Tragedy*, by U. S. Dhuga
*Light and Darkness in Ancient Greek Myth and Religion*, Edited by Menelaos Christopoulos, Efimia D. Karakantza, and Olga Levaniouk
*When Worlds Elide: Classics, Politics, Culture*, Edited by Karen Bassi and J. Peter Euben
*Archaeology in Situ: Sites, Archaeology, and Communities in Greece*, Edited by Anna Stroulia and Susan Buck Sutton
*The Philosopher's Song: The Poets' Influence on Plato*, by Kevin Crotty
*Under the Sign of the Shield: Semiotics and Aeschylus' Seven Against Thebes*, by Froma I. Zeitlin
*Metrical Constraint and the Interpretation of Style in Tragic Trimeter*, by Nicholas Baechle
*Diachronic Dialogues: Authority and Continuity in Homer and the Homeric Tradition*, by Ahuvia Kahane
*Fighting Words and Feuding Words: Anger and the Homeric Poems*, by Thomas R. Walsh
*The Visual Poetics of Power: Warriors, Youths, and Tripods in Early Greece*, by Nassos Papalexandrou
*Homeric Megathemes: War-Homilia-Homecoming*, by D. N. Maronitis
*A Penelopean Poetics: Reweaving the Feminine in Homer's Odyssey*, by Barbara Clayton
*The Poetry of Homer: New Edition*, Edited with an Introduction by Bruce Heiden, by Samuel Eliot Bassett
*The Other Self: Selfhood and Society in Modern Greek Fiction*, by Dimitris Tziovas
*The Usable Past: Greek Metahistories*, Edited by K. S. Brown and Yannis Hamilakis
*Tragedy and Athenian Religion*, by Christiane Sourvinou-Inwood
*Imagining Illegitimacy in Classical Greek Literature*, by Mary Ebbott

# Black Ships and Sea Raiders

## The Late Bronze and Early Iron Age Context of Odysseus' Second Cretan Lie

Jeffrey P. Emanuel

LEXINGTON BOOKS
*Lanham • Boulder • New York • London*

Published by Lexington Books
An imprint of The Rowman & Littlefield Publishing Group, Inc.
4501 Forbes Boulevard, Suite 200, Lanham, Maryland 20706
www.rowman.com

Unit A, Whitacre Mews, 26-34 Stannary Street, London SE11 4AB

British Library Cataloguing in Publication Information Available

**Library of Congress Cataloging-in-Publication Data Available**

ISBN 978-1-4985-7221-7 (cloth)
ISBN 978-1-4985-7223-1 (pbk.)
ISBN 978-1-4985-7222-4 (electronic)

# Contents

Acknowledgments     vii

1   Epic, Oral Tradition, and Archaeology     1

2   Structure and Methodology     11

3   Raiders, Traders, and Sea Peoples in the Late Bronze
Age and Beyond     25

4   Mycenae, Aḫḫiyawa, and the Collapse of the Late Bronze
Age Order     41

5   The Sea Peoples and the Egyptian Records     61

6   The Changing Face of War and Society     79

7   Hedgehog Helmets, Sea Peoples, and Ship-to-Ship Combat     97

8   Mariners and Their Ships: Vessel Types, Capacity,
and Rigging     117

9   Αἴγυπτόνδε: Life, Prosperity, and Health in the Land of
the Pharaohs     151

Notes     163

Bibliography     179

Index     211

About the Author     219

# Acknowledgments

My deepest gratitude goes to Gregory Nagy, a peerless teacher, friend and mentor whose guidance helped achieve the convergence of Homeric and archaeological scholarship that resulted in this book. Without his support and inspiration, the project would neither have gotten off the ground nor reached its current state.

I am also indebted to Shelley Wachsmann, a giant in the field of Mediterranean seafaring and ship construction. For several years now, I and my research have benefited from his encouragement, insightful feedback, and willingness to share information.

I would also like to thank Kevin McGrath and Jacob Damm for several years of formal and informal conversations about many of the topics presented in this book, which have influenced its direction and progress more than they know. Likewise, the constant encouragement and unflagging support provided by Shaughn Casey and Jim Anderson has been more valuable to this project than I could ever express.

Reaching farther back in time, the introduction to Classical Archaeology as a discipline that I received from Naomi Norman as an undergraduate at the University of Georgia, and the love of history that was imparted in me by my high school World History teacher, Joseph Jarrell, were foundational experiences that many years ago helped set me on my present course.

Finally, and most importantly, I offer my love and gratitude to my family: my parents, Paul and Gail, who have been a source of unwavering encouragement throughout my life and academic career; Katie Emanuel, my wife and the love of my life, who has not only endured the years of research and scholarship that culminated in this book, but who has provided steadfast support and inspiration every step along the at-times-tortuous path; and my children, Jack, Kristen, and Connor, who have been as patient and supportive as possible throughout (not to mention endearingly excited that some of the illustrations in this volume are my own artwork!).

As with any work that whose creation and evolution spans several years, more debts of gratitude have been incurred than I could possibly repay. To everybody who has provided support, feedback, or constructive comments, or who has served—knowingly or unknowingly—as a sounding board for the ideas presented in this book, I am sincerely grateful. As always, the content itself, including any remaining errors or omissions are solely my own.

# Chapter One

# Epic, Oral Tradition, and Archaeology

ἄνδρα μοι ἔννεπε, μοῦσα, πολύτροπον, ὃς μάλα πολλὰ
πλάγχθη, ἐπεὶ Τροίης ἱερὸν πτολίεθρον ἔπερσεν:
πολλῶν δ' ἀνθρώπων ἴδεν ἄστεα καὶ νόον ἔγνω,
πολλὰ δ' ὅ γ' ἐν πόντῳ πάθεν ἄλγεα ὃν κατὰ θυμόν,
ἀρνύμενος ἥν τε ψυχὴν καὶ νόστον ἑταίρων.
ἀλλ' οὐδ' ὣς ἑτάρους ἐρρύσατο, ἱέμενός περ:
αὐτῶν γὰρ σφετέρῃσιν ἀτασθαλίῃσιν ὄλοντο

Tell me, O Muse, of the man of many devices, who wandered full many ways after he had sacked the sacred citadel of Troy. Many were the men whose cities he saw and whose mind he learned, aye, and many the woes he suffered in his heart upon the sea, seeking to win his own life and the return of his comrades. Yet even so he saved not his comrades, though he desired it sore, for through their own blind folly they perished. . .

*Odyssey* i, 1–7[1]

So begins the Homeric epic about the hero Odysseus, the πολύτροπος 'many-sided, much-traveled, versatile, ingenious' man, and his decade of wanderings following the Achaean sack of Troy. These wanderings took the hero to places like the city of the Kikones, the land of the Cyclopes, Phaiakia, and even Hades itself, with myriad stops in between—including, via false *ainos*, Crete, Egypt, Lebanon, and Libya—before finally returning him to Ithaka, ten years after he first set sail for home and twenty after his initial departure.

Trials like these were not unique to Odysseus: other tales of suffering in the aftermath of the Trojan War can be found amidst the "framework of heroic portraits" that make up the epic tradition, from Menelaos' eight-year journey home (*Odyssey* iv, 81–85) to Agamemnon's murderous reception at the hands of his wife's lover, Aigisthos (*Odyssey* xi, 409–411).[2] A major aim of this

1

study is to chip away at one such individual story—Odysseus' Second Cretan Lie—for the purpose of shedding light on the interplay between a Homeric individual and the historical and archaeological background. As we shall see, at least some of the wanderings and sufferings of Homer's epic heroes in general, and of Odysseus in particular, are not out of place when viewed against the larger tapestry of the chaotic transition from the Late Bronze Age to the Early Iron Age in the years surrounding the beginning of the 12th century BCE.

## TWO TAPESTRIES: EPIC AND HISTORY

Before we begin, it is necessary to cover some background on epic and oral tradition, and on their tangled relationship with that modern invention which we call "history." Unfortunately, the largest and most tantalizing question—when and where did the characters and events of epic originate, and what relationship do they have with people that actually lived and events that actually happened?—is, on the whole, unanswerable. Myth and oral tradition occupy a unique space within human communication, vested as they are with motifs, artifacts, content, and meaning that is simultaneously reflective both of years long past and of the present.

However, epic and oral tradition also can—and almost certainly do—transmit some measures of historical truth within the received fiction. This does not mean that exact historical connections should be sought between characters, events, and descriptions contained in myth, and it certainly does not mean that epic works should be treated as historical texts. Such a search is bound to end in futility, in no small part because epic is the product of such a lengthy compositional process that single characters, events, or even objects can simultaneously represent analogues that are centuries apart in historical time. A classic example of this is the shield of the Trojan hero Hektor, which Homer first describes as a tower shield of the type seen in iconography from the Bronze Age shaft graves at Mycenae (Fig. 1.1):

**Figure 1.1.    Battle depicted on the "Warrior Krater" from Shaft Grave IV at Mycenae**
Blakolmer, F. 2007. "The Silver Battle Krater from Shaft Grave IV at Mycenae: Evidence of Fighting 'Heroes' on Minoan Palace walls at Knossos?" In Morris, S. P. and Laffineur, R., eds. *EPOS: Reconsidering Greek Epic and Aegean Bronze Age Archaeology*. Liège. Plate LVII1.

ἀμφὶ δέ μιν σφυρὰ τύπτε καὶ αὐχένα δέρμα κελαινὸν
ἄντυξ ἣ πυμάτη θέεν ἀσπίδος ὀμφαλοέσσης

. . . the black rim of hide that went round his shield beat against his neck and
his ankles

*Iliad* VI, 117–118[3]

Scarcely one scroll later, this object has leapt forward in time nearly half a
millennium, becoming the circular shield known from the end of the Bronze
Age and the succeeding Iron Age (Fig. 1.2):

**Figure 1.2. LH IIIC 'Warrior Vase' from Mycenae, fea-
turing parallel processions of armed men in 'hedgehog'-
style helmets and in helmets with horns and plumes**
Tsountas, Ch. and Manatt, J. I. 1897. *The Mycenaean Age: A Study
of the Monuments and Culture of Pre-Homeric Greece*. London.
Plate XVIII.

Αἴας διογενὴς προΐει δολιχόσκιον ἔγχος,
καὶ βάλε Πριαμίδαο κατ᾽ ἀσπίδα πάντοσ᾽ ἐΐσην

Then Ajax threw in his turn,
and struck the round shield of the son of Priam

*Iliad* VII, 249–250

As archaeologist Susan Sherratt asked, "So where is history in all this? I have no doubt that something (or perhaps many things) that we might just call real history in some sense of the word is there, lurking in the palimpsest of Homeric oral prehistory. But the question of whose history, and when and where, is something we can probably never untangle."[4]

Whatever measures of truth may be contained in the Homeric epics cannot truly be accessed without peeling back the layers of the received text. These layers are abundant: a characteristic of oral tradition is composition-in-performance, which lends itself, over time and a broad geographic area, to many slightly different versions of a single story.[5] Add to that the agglutinative nature of epic poetry, which has among its progenitors "a vast reservoir of inherited myths, legends, and tales, the conflation of which has left traces and sometimes, at least by literary standards, rather glaring anomalies of structure and detail."[6] A potential example of such an "inherited myth" is the set of false *ainoi* in Homer's *Odyssey* known as the "Cretan Lies." The length and detail of these micronarratives, writes classicist Steve Reece, combined with "the remarkable contrast of our poet's vague notion of the topography of the Peloponnese to his quite detailed knowledge of Crete," may mark these false *ainoi* as remnants of an alternative version of the epic in which they were presented as truth rather than fiction.[7]

While this is probably the case, as other studies have also shown, the specific circumstances of the composition and incorporation of this and other variants will never be fully understood.[8] It *is* clear, though, that Homeric poetry overall is simultaneously *expressive* of Indo-European themes that predate the Greek language itself; *reminiscent* of the earliest phases of Greek prehistory and before, like the 16th century BCE Shaft Grave culture of Mycenae and the settlement of Akrotiri; and *reflective* in many aspects of the beginning of the watershed Archaic period in the eighth century (and beyond).[9] This is compounded by the necessary disconnection, or poetic distance, between the performance of Homer's epics and the age(s) and events they purport to recount, which further precludes simple one-to-one identifications of these passages with archaeological remains or other material evidence of historical peoples and events.[10]

These issues begin to illustrate the problematic nature of attempting, in the words of one scholar, "to create a serious history out of fantasy and folklore."[11] However, interwoven into this complex tapestry are details of varying size and import which can be seen as reflecting the world of the Late Bronze Age and the early years of the Iron Age, or roughly the 14th through 12th centuries BCE. Familiar personal names and toponyms like *Alaksandu, Attarissya, Mopsos, Wiluša,* and *Aḫḫiyawa* peek out at us from ancient texts, reminding us, respectively, of Alexander, Atreus, Mopsus, Ilios, and Achaea. The general geopolitical makeup of the world described in the *Iliad* also seems to accurately reflect the historical presence of a Mycenaean coalition on the western side of the Aegean and an Anatolian power to the east, with whom they had frequent tension.[12] However, the eastern power at this point in history was not Trojan at all; instead, it was the Hittites who ruled much of Anatolia and northern Syria from their seat at Ḫattušas (modern Boğazköi). Interestingly, documentary evidence shows that some of the historical tension between Mycenaeans and Hittites in the Late Bronze Age did, in fact, focus on Troy.

Homer's lack of awareness of the Hittites seems troubling at first blush, particularly when it comes to efforts to draw even modest parallels between the narratives of the *Iliad* and *Odyssey* on one hand, and our current information about the events and individuals of the Bronze Age on the other. This may be partially explained by the "bricolage" nature of the epic composition, of course, but it may also result from the radical changes that swept the Eastern Mediterranean in the years surrounding 1200 BCE. The chaos and disorder of the *Odyssey* also seem reflective of this late second millennium transition from the Late Bronze to the Iron Age, which was characterized by the threats, marauding, and rending of the social fabric governing society itself. Each of these is a hallmark of the Late Bronze Age's *terminus* in the years surrounding 1200 BCE in the Aegean and Eastern Mediterranean, with its palatial collapses, movements of peoples, and disruption of the international trading networks that had fostered widespread communication and fueled generations of elites' conspicuous consumption and display. As we shall see further below, the collapse of civilizations at the end of the Bronze Age did not just affect Greece, where the palatial system and Linear B writing were permanently lost and a post-Mycenaean "Dark Age" several centuries long was ushered in. The Hittite empire was also largely extinguished at this time, and seems to have been lost from memory in the Aegean region altogether—perhaps part of the reason for its absence from the world of Homer.[13]

Not all events in the years surrounding the Late Bronze–Early Iron Age transition were negative, particularly if one considers the situation from the point of view of those outside Eastern Mediterranean society's topmost stratum. Among the positive, forward-looking developments at this time was an acceleration in maritime innovations—particularly tactics and technology. Groundbreaking developments in ship design and construction provided sailors with an engine of raiding, warfare, and transportation the likes of which had never been seen, allowing naval operations to be conducted more effectively than ever before. This is among the more granular topics that will be addressed in this study, along with the conduct and expansion of piracy and coastal raiding, as well as the movements and experiences of specific peoples associated with these actions.

## ODYSSEUS' SECOND CRETAN LIE

ἀλλ᾽ ἄγε μοι σύ, γεραιέ, τὰ σ᾽ αὐτοῦ κήδε᾽ ἐνίσπες
καί μοι τοῦτ᾽ ἀγόρευσον ἐτήτυμον, ὄφρ᾽ ἐὺ εἰδῶ:
τίς πόθεν εἶς ἀνδρῶν

But come . . . tell me of thine own sorrows, and declare me this truly, that I may know full well. Who art thou among men, and from whence?

*Odyssey* xiv, 185–187

This question, posed to Odysseus by Eumaios the swineherd, prefaces the portion of Homer's *Odyssey* that will serve as the lens for this study. The hero's 'Second Cretan Lie,' found in *Odyssey* xiv, 191–359 and retold in part at xvii, 424–441, will be analyzed here with a focus on interpreting the details and identifying parallels to this myth within the historical and archaeological records. We shall consider three elements of Odysseus' story in particular within the setting of the Late Bronze–Early Iron Age transition (the late 13th and early 12th centuries BCE). My aim is to demonstrate these elements' consistency *generally* with the historical reality of this period, and *specifically* with the experiences of the so-called *Š3rd3n3 n p3 ym* 'Sherden of the sea' (fig. 1.3), one of the groups identified with the so-called 'Sea Peoples' who are best known from their portrayal in Egyptian records as foreign invaders who laid waste to empires across the Near East during this tumultuous period.

These elements are:

1. Odysseus' declaration that he led nine successful maritime raids prior to the Trojan War (*Odyssey* xiv, 229–233);
2. His ill-fated assault on Egypt, separately recounted to Eumaios (xiv, 245–272) and to Antinoos (xvii, 424–441); and
3. His claim not only to have been spared following his disastrous Egyptian raid, but to have spent a subsequent seven years in the land of the pharaohs, during which he gathered great wealth (xiv, 285–286).

A secondary purpose of this study, carried out in service of the first, is to examine these tales of Odysseus and the evidence for the Sherden within the context of the Late Bronze–Early Iron Age transition and the Sea Peoples phenomenon, with particular emphasis on the development, spread, and utilization of maritime tactics, technology, and capabilities at this time.

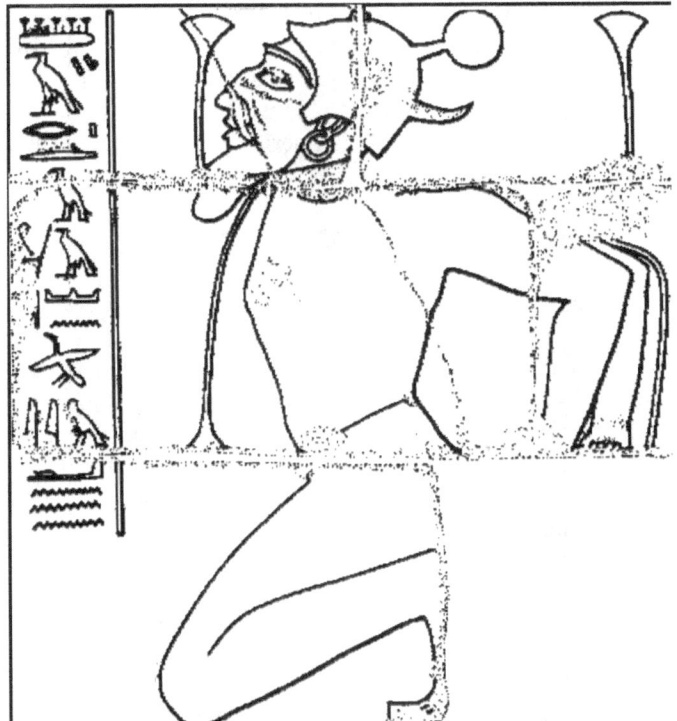

**Figure 1.3.   Captive from the front pavilion wall at Medinet Habu.
The figure serves as the determinative for the caption, which reads
*Š3rd3n3 n p3 ym* 'Šrdn of the Sea'**
Emanuel, J. P. 2013. "Šrdn from the Sea: The Arrival, Integration, and Acculturation
  of a Sea People." *Journal of Ancient Egyptian Interconnections* 5: 14–27. Figure
  2. (after *MH* VIII plate 600b)

The transition from the Late Bronze to the Early Iron Age was a period of
rapid and radical maritime innovation in the Aegean and Eastern Mediterranean. Changes in ship design and rigging revolutionized seafaring in the region,
allowing for greater freedom of movement on the seas and beginning a process
of development and innovation that would eventually spawn divergent lines of
ship development in the Aegean and on the Phoenician coast, thus setting the
stage for the great maritime powers of the first millennium BCE.

The role that seagoing ships and maritime acumen play in their respective
narratives is a key commonality between Odysseus' Cretan avatar and Sherden
warriors. The term "narrative" has two distinct meanings here: for Odysseus,
that narrative is the tale he tells to Eumaios and to Antinoos, which within
the larger narrative of Homer's epic is, of course, false. For the Sherden, on
the other hand, the narrative in question is conveyed through external sources

(primarily Egyptian), from which a "true" history can, at least in principle, be gleaned. In this case, I also argue that a close examination of the evidence for the ships of this period can help us better understand the connection between the 'Cretan' Odysseus and the Sherden, as well as their ultimate place in the events that marked this transformational period in the ancient Mediterranean.

## STRUCTURE AND CONTENT

The intent of this study is to explore the relationships between Odysseus' 'Second Cretan Lie' and related passages from the Homeric epics, and the literary, iconographic, and material evidence from the Late Bronze–Early Iron Age transition.[14] This introduction is followed by a chapter addressing the chronology, methodology, and approach, with particular emphasis on the interpretation of documentary evidence and material remains. Chapter 3 then uses *Odyssey* xiv, 229–233 as a point of departure for an evidence-based discussion of maritime interconnections, piracy, and raiding in the internationalist Late Bronze Age and the chaotic transition to the age of Iron that followed it, with particular emphasis on the evidence for an increase in coastal threats. This chapter also addresses "piracy" and "warfare" as definable and differentiable concepts, and leverages primary sources from Ḫatti, Ugarit, and 18th and 19th dynasty Egyptian records to explore the roles of piracy, raiding, and the mariners who carried out these activities in the Late Bronze Age and the Late Bronze–Early Iron transition.

Chapter 4 discusses the role of Mycenaean Greece in the Late Bronze Age Eastern Mediterranean, including the "Aḫḫiyawa Question," evidence both for direct trade and foreign contacts in the 13th century BCE (the Late Bronze II/Late Helladic IIIB), and the possibility that female workers listed in the Linear B tablets as *ra-wi-ja-ja* were human plunder of the type mentioned several times over in both *Iliad* and *Odyssey*. This chapter also addresses the collapse of the Late Bronze Age order in the Eastern Mediterranean, and discusses the wide range of interactions between those peoples who were on the move at this time and their indigenous hosts. The slow build and final palatial collapse in the Aegean is examined, as well, with specific focus on the evidence for the so-called "state of emergency" in the last days of Pylos on the southwestern Peloponnese, and on three sets of much-discussed Linear B texts from this site known as the "Rower Tablets."

Chapter 5 is dedicated to considering the inscriptional evidence for the arrival and activities of the Sea Peoples in the Eastern Mediterranean. The most prominent of these records come from three Egyptian pharaohs, Ramesses II (1279–1213 BCE), Merneptah (1213–1203), and Ramesses III (1184–1153), whose reigns span the vast majority of the roughly 125-year period between Ramesses II's ascension to the throne early in the 13th century BCE and the assassination of Ramesses III in the middle of the 12th century. This chapter examines the interactions between each of these pharaohs and elements of the Sea Peoples, beginning with the voluminous references at Ramesses III's "mansion of a million years" at Medinet Habu. From there, the discussion moves backward in time to the 13th century BCE, where it touches on Ramesses II's defeat of Sherden raiders at sea and his line of forts along the Nile delta and Mediterranean coast, which may have been established in part as a defense against further seaborne threats, and on Merneptah's battle against migratory Libyans who were accompanied by some Sea Peoples groups.

Chapter 6 reviews the circumstances surrounding the palatial collapses in the Aegean and Ancient Near East at the end of the Late Bronze Age, the corresponding establishment of "refuge settlements" on Crete and Cyprus in particular, and changes in the iconography of warriors and warfare in both the Aegean and the Eastern Mediterranean,[15] with particular emphasis on possible self-representations from Cyprus and the Levant and what those can tell us about the integration, mobility, and status of at least some individuals among these groups. Chapter 7 continues the exploration of these new warriors, who are shown on Aegean-style pottery and in Egyptian relief taking part in battles on land and sea. These warriors' appearance in Eastern Mediterranean iconography (painted pottery, glyptic, and relief) is examined in detail, with particular emphasis on the comparative representational methodologies of Mycenaean pictorial pottery and painted Egyptian relief. This chapter also addresses Submycenaean "warrior burials" from around the mainland, Aegean islands, and on Cyprus which have been connected in the past to Homer's "returning heroes," and discusses post-palatial society in the Aegean, with particular emphasis on shifts in social organization and the lack of darkness in this "Dark Age."

Chapter 8 is the most comprehensive and technically involved section of this study. It addresses the Helladic oared galley, a revolution in maritime technology—and ancestor to the sailing vessels of the first-millennium maritime powers in Greece and Phoenicia—that makes its first appearance in the years surrounding 1200 BCE as an instrument of naval warfare.[16] This chapter explores the background of this vessel type and the development and use of its constituent parts, and analyzes the impact of both crew and fleet sizes on its role in both piracy and naval warfare, both through primary sources and in the context of Odysseus' fictive piratical activity, where a close reading of Homer's narrative can serve as a case study in its use. Visual evidence plays a central role in this portion of the study, with iconography from the Aegean, the Levantine coast, Egypt, and the East Aegean-West Anatolian Interface,[17] providing comparative examples of the development and representation of this vessel type around the region.

Chapter 9 concludes the study by revisiting the initial discussion of oral tradition, visual language in the Late Bronze Age, and the search for historicity in epic poetry. This chapter also further surveys the Sherden and their roles in Egyptian society, which included being conscripted into the Egyptian army, participating in raids, and acquiring material wealth in the service of the pharaoh.[18] In conclusion, this chapter also notes where the stories of the Sherden and Cretan Odysseus diverge, with the latter departing Egypt after seven years to continue his wandering, while the former became increasingly integrated and acculturated into Egyptian society, creating new lives for themselves in the land of the pharaohs, complete with wives, children, and ownership of land that could be passed down through generations.

This study is not intended to serve as an argument for the supposed historicity of the Homeric epics, nor is it intended to be an exhaustive survey of historical parallels between the Odyssey and the archaeological data we currently possess on the periods reflected in these myths. These have been subjects of scholarly inquiry on various levels for many years now, and the debates surrounding them are unlikely to end any time soon. Instead, the analysis presented here focuses on the development and spread of the oared galley, the possible role of the Sea Peoples in this transfer, and parallels between the actions and experiences of Odysseus' Cretan avatar and one Sea Peoples group about whom a close reading of the textual, iconographic, and material evidence can tell us a great deal: the "Sherden of the Sea."

# Chapter Two

# Structure and Methodology

This analysis deals with three major categories of evidence: *documentary*, in the form of texts; *iconography*, primarily in the form of relief, painted pottery, and seals; and *material remains*. The contents of these categories will by necessity span the Aegean and Eastern Mediterranean, from the Greek mainland to Crete, the Cyclades, Cyprus, Egypt, the Levant, the Hittite empire, and the East Aegean-West Anatolian Interface.

## CHRONOLOGY

Before beginning a discussion of methodology, it is important to briefly address chronology, as it weighs heavily not only on the events and evidence discussed in this study, but also on the terms we use to describe them. The broad terms "Late Bronze Age" and "Early Iron Age" (or the synonymous "Iron I") are frequently used with respect to chronological horizons in the Near East (terms and concepts, incidentally, which we owe to the Greek poet Hesiod). Matters only become more complicated from there, beginning with the application of the term "Late Bronze III" to the period that has traditionally been called the Iron Age IA, in recognition of the continuity now recognized between the last years of the Late Bronze Age and the earliest years of the Iron Age I (Fig. 2.1).

There also exist frameworks of absolute chronology within which we can situate both long-term processes and specific events. Radiocarbon dating, dendrochronology, and other modern scientific methods are providing more date-related data points, and are becoming more useful as their strengths and weaknesses alike are better understood. However, synchronisms between records of events in ancient Egypt, Assyria, and Babylonia have long allowed

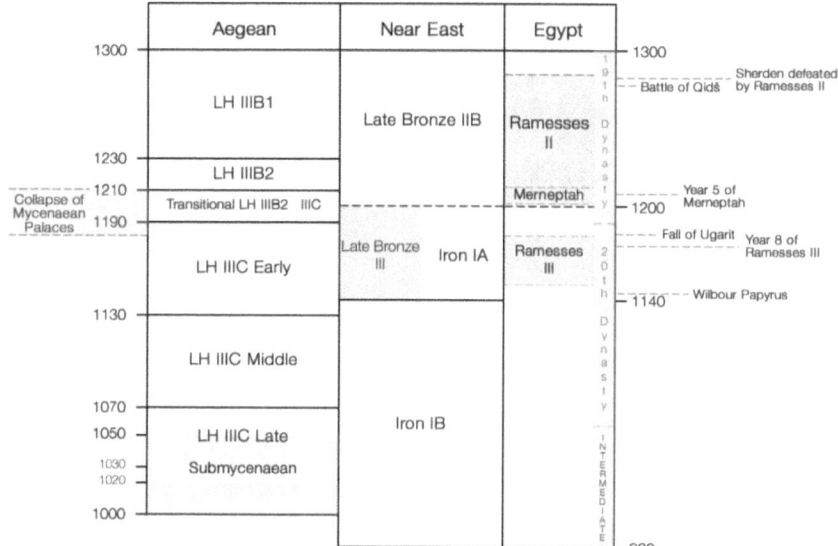

**Figure 2.1.   Comparative chronology of the Aegean, Near East, and Egypt**
Illustration by the author.

chronologies to be drawn with remarkable specificity based on documentary evidence alone.

This situation, and the tension between a reliance on documentary evidence and other methods like scientific and ceramic analyses, is reflected in a characteristically entertaining paper by Egyptologist Kenneth Kitchen, which is titled "Egyptian and Related Chronologies—Look, No Sciences, No Pots!"[1] Though the quality of the available documentary evidence allows us to cite regnal dates for Egyptian pharaohs, and the years of events within their reigns, with high confidence, this study still includes a *circa* when citing regnal years to denote the level of uncertainty surrounding those dates (even though this can, in some cases, be as small as a decade or less). Relative chronology, on the other hand, can be more important than absolute chronology when it comes to joining events that took place across civilizations:

> The discovery of the absolute dates is not as important as the question of the relative chronology. For historical conclusions, moving an event a hundred years forward or back in time is not as important at our present level of knowledge as understanding its relevance to other events from approximately the same time.[2]

Of course, where absolute dates are largely nonexistent (in contrast to Egypt's well-documented history), relative dates are all we have. It is in these cases that objects like pots are necessary for developing chronologies. The Aegean is an example of the latter: given that we generally lack absolute dates for the Minoan and Mycenaean periods, our chronology for the region is relative, and depends on pottery sequences. The Aegean Late Bronze Age (*circa* 1700–1100 BCE) is divided into the Late Minoan (LM) I, II, and III for Crete, and Late Helladic (LH) I, II, and III for the mainland, each of which is based in large part on changes in pottery forms and decoration. This ceramic sequence establishes a relative internal chronology whose periods are further divided based on seriation, with suggested chronologies that are best-guesses based on the estimated length of human generations or of the settlement phases at a given site.[3] Additionally, the terminology for these subdivisions is not always uniform: for example, Late Helladic IIIA (roughly the 14th century BCE) is divided into LH IIIA:1 and IIIA:2, while Late Helladic IIIC, the period following the collapse of the Mycenaean palaces (early 12th century to early 11th century BCE), is divided into LH IIIC Early, Middle, and Late (or Final), with LH IIIC Early and Middle each being divided into two further phases: 1 and 2, and Developed and Advanced, respectively. Regional differences in pottery forms and motifs further complicate efforts to impose an overarching chronological framework on the Aegean region.

As noted above, these periods and subphases are entirely relative—that is, their only intrinsic chronological value is in relation to each other.[4] We are only able to attach absolute dates (or, more correctly, date ranges) when these ceramics are found in contexts that are anchored through other sources. Generally, these contexts are datable Egyptian settings: for example, a Mycenaean pot that is found either alongside objects inscribed with pharaonic cartouches, or at securely datable sites like the 18th dynasty capital of Akhetaten (el-Amarna), whose brief occupation, spanning only the second half of the 14th century BCE, provides a temporal context for the ceramics found there. Other examples include the *terminus post quem* for the end of LH IIIB and the beginning of LH IIIC, which is anchored by the presence of LH IIIB:2 pottery in the destruction of the Syrian *emporion* of Ugarit, and a stirrup jar from Beth Shean that long served as the only anchor for the absolute dating of the LH IIIC Middle period.[5] Because of these limitations, references to dates in the Aegean in this study will necessarily reference pottery-based periodization, though they are presented in concert with absolute date ranges wherever possible. To this end, we are fortunate to be able to lean on the truly masterful work that has been done on the classification, analysis, and chronology of Aegean ceramics from the Late Helladic and Submycenaean periods for several decades now, despite the aforementioned obstacles.[6]

## TEXT, ILLUSTRATION, AND MATERIAL CULTURE

We return now to methodology. Very little ancient material is capable of speaking unadulterated truth to the modern scholar, however remarkably complete and *in situ* a text, image, or material assemblage may be. Because of this, each class of evidence requires its own particular type of analysis and consideration. Though it may seem unrelated in what generally amounts to a discussion of *Archaeologia Homerica*, biblical archaeology is relevant to the present discussion because the study of the Sea Peoples has for so long fallen under this field, due to the prominence of the Philistines (whom we first encounter in the records of Ramesses III) in both the Hebrew Bible and the archaeology of the Levant. Homeric and biblical studies are also similar cases because of the judiciousness with which the textual evidence must be weighed against the material evidence, and they can inform each other in this process: for example, though archaeology has shifted away from the use of stylized ancient texts as "guidebooks" (as famously done by Heinrich Schliemann at Troy and by the 20th century "Bible and spade" archaeologists whose excavations dotted the landscape of Palestine), there has at times been a tendency to take other texts at face value—particularly day books, annals, and various royal declarations—despite the knowledge that such writings were composed for propagandistic purposes far more than to serve our modern definition of "history."

The walls of Ramesses III's "mansion of a million years" at Medinet Habu, also referred to as his "mortuary temple," are an excellent example of this type of evidence, adorned as they are with grandiose recountings of his deeds and accomplishments. Some of these were likely plagiarized from his namesake, Ramesses the Great, and perhaps from Ramesses' successor Merneptah, while others—including battles in Nubia and against the Hittites, and perhaps one of his multiple Libyan campaigns—are unlikely to have taken place at all.[7] It is from several of these inscriptions and reliefs that we derive much of our knowledge of the Sea Peoples. This is a problematic situation, to be sure, when their purpose and dubious veracity are taken into account. Confronting this issue requires judiciousness, but there is, in the words of one scholar, "room for the baby and the bathwater, in selective use, in reconstructing the Bronze and Iron Age prehistories of the Levant. In the Aegean, a similar solution allows archaeologists and historians to apply Homeric testimony critically."[8] Similarly, in Egypt, the written evidence left by pharaohs whose primary goal was self glorification (which could tend toward, in the words of Egyptologist Donald Redford, "jingoist doggerel, worthy of a 19th century music hall"), must be critically considered and carefully applied.[9]

Iconography is another category of evidence that must be approached and interpreted with the greatest of care, always keeping in mind that that which is seen is not the thing itself, but at best only a *representation* of the original. While we should not expect artistic representations to be exact replicas of their subjects, we should also remember to avoid the temptation to judge the artist's skill based on what we believe we know about how that subject should appear. This is particularly true when it comes to seafaring: as has been noted in the past, "there has been a strong and persistent tendency in dealing with the iconography of ancient ships to start with an idea of what things ought to look like and then to treat the ancient pictures as evidence on which to assess the skill of ancient artists."[10] Nautical archaeologist Shelley Wachsmann, an authority on seafaring and ship iconography from the Bronze Age Mediterranean, has pointed out the relevance of a work by Belgian painter René Magritte to the mind-set one must bring to the study and interpretation of iconography, writing that:

> It is worth reflecting on the meaning behind the iconic image of a smoker's pipe under which the phrase '*Ceci n'est une pipe*.' . . . Of course, Magritte is correct. We do not see an actual smoker's pipe but rather an image of one. To put it another way, *a representation of an object is not the object itself.* . . . we must keep this concept firmly in mind.[11]

Countless factors can influence visual representations: the artist's intended audience or audiences, the media utilized for the representation, the shared visual language of artist and beholder, and countless other points along a virtually unlimited spectrum. For example, it might not be necessary for a vase painter or graffiti artist's ship or sail to be perfect (or even plausibly functional) if the audience for which the image is intended can translate the artist's visual shorthand into the object it is meant to represent. However, an artist's potential knowledge of their subject is important to consider when seeking to extract fine details about ship construction from a pictorial representation. As archaeologist Caroline Sauvage has noted:

> Les représentations iconographiques soulèvent la question de leur exactitude et de la possibilité de restituer un type d'objet à partir d'un dessin. À priori, un graffito doit pouvoir nous livrer plus d'informations et être plus proche de la réalité qu'une representation artistique, les artistes n'étant pas toujours complètement familiers avec le milieu marin. D'un autre côté, les marins qui ont dû graver ces navires n'étaient pas forcement dotés d'un immense talent artistique et certaines « œuvres » sont donc fort difficiles à comprendre et a interpréter du fait de leur caractère schématique et épuré.[12]

Further, as we shall see below in representations of peoples and ships alike, the artistic styles of differing cultures and the limitations of different media must be taken into account when interpreting an image or drawing connections between images of similar appearance. For these reasons and more, it is important to avoid the temptation to take images at face value. This also holds true for linguistic interpretations, as I shall touch on more briefly below with regard to the Sea Peoples and longstanding assumptions about their relationships and points of origin.

## Material Culture and the Sea Peoples

The third category of evidence considered here is material culture, which is both the bailiwick of the archaeologist and fodder for intense disagreements, given how dependent interpretations are on what is axiomatically a partial and highly fragmentary picture. The search for, and study of, the Sea Peoples can serve as an instructive example about the double-edged sword that material remains can be, even when they seem to appear in relatively complete form. At the same time, it can also provide the basis for a discussion early in this study about the relevance to Homer's *Odyssey* and the Aegean world of this phenomenon and its heterogeneous, shifting coalitions, which may appear on the surface to be largely Near Eastern in orientation.

### *The 'Philistine Paradigm'*

The best known of the Sea Peoples are the *Pršt* 'Pelešet,' better known in modern translation as the *Philistines*. However, this group's prominence is not the result of a sustained presence in Egyptian or other Near Eastern records from the Late Bronze Age. In fact, aside from the texts, inscriptions, and reliefs of a single pharaoh, Ramesses III (1183–1152 BCE), they are almost entirely unknown to written history prior to the first millennium BCE, appearing only in the Onomasticon of Amenope, an Egyptian catalog of toponyms and *ethnika* in Palestine which dates to around 1100 BCE.[13] Instead, the Philistines' notoriety is the result of two key factors. The first is their identification with one of the most frequently mentioned—and, as the chief antagonist of the early Israelites, most vilified—peoples of the Hebrew Bible, while the second is the bright light that archaeology has been able to shine on their material culture, particularly in the southern Levant. Thanks to the extensive excavations that have been carried out at Ashkelon, Ashdod, Tel Miqne/Ekron, and Tel es-Safi/Gath, four of the five cities that made up the Philistine "pentapolis" on the southern coastal plain of Canaan, scholars have been able to identify key aspects of the Philistines' mixed material culture, and to trace both their arrival and their interactions and negotiations with the indigenous Canaanites and others in the region.

The latter is a great leap forward of sorts in the study of the Philistines in particular and the Sea Peoples in general. These groups had long been viewed as the very embodiment of Homer's "sackers of cities" (the epithet πτολιπόρθιος is specifically attached to Odysseus at *Odyssey* ix, 504), razing empires to the ground all around the Eastern Mediterranean and building anew on their ashes.[14] In the words of Ramesses III, "No land could stand before their arms, from Hatti, Kode, Carcemish, Arzawa, and Alashiya on. . . ."[15] Over the last few years, though, a more nuanced approach to migration studies, transculturalism, and ethnic negotiation has developed, which has helped to demonstrate the inaccuracy of this view—as has an increased willingness to recognize the significant quantities of Canaanite material culture that continue to be found at pentapolis sites following the Philistines' arrival.[16]

Study of the pentapolis sites in the southern coastal plain of Canaan has allowed scholars to reconstruct a general set of traits that can be identified as "Philistine," although recent field work at Gath in particular has demonstrated that the former understanding of these traits as a relatively easily identifiable "package" or "template," a view that stemmed from a culture-historical approach to Levantine archaeology, was—like the idea of the Sea Peoples as unstoppable marauders—an oversimplification.[17] Despite this evidence, though, the idea of the Philistines and other Sea Peoples as immigrants has had its detractors, with some arguing that these bearers of mixed material culture were natives of the Levant who have simply been misunderstood by modern scholars. Robert Drews, for example, declared the Philistines to be "one of the Iron Age names for people who in the Late Bronze Age would most often have been called 'Canaanites,'" and argued that "no Canaanite nation vanished, and no Philistine nation suddenly appeared. It was only the names that changed."[18] This extreme view was met with an equally forceful response by Kitchen, who wrote that:

> [T]he suggestion, occasionally made, that [the Sea Peoples, Philistines in particular] had been native to Canaan from old is nonsense, contradicting both the clear statement of . . . firsthand texts and the evidence of these peoples' material culture . . . Such a suggestion owes everything to the sociological/anthropological idiot dogma that nobody in antiquity ever migrated anywhere (especially in any quantity), in the teeth of abundant evidence to the contrary at all periods in recorded human history. It owes nothing to the facts of the case.[19]

Just how the "facts of the case" can prove (or at least support) a general population shift, and the presence of 'Sea Peoples' in particular, has been the subject of increasing study in recent years, with Philistine material culture continuing to play a key role.[20] One of the key markers of an intrusive presence is "deep change," or the appearance in a material assemblage of objects associated with individuals' or groups' private identity, as opposed to their public one(s).[21] This means domestic aspects of material culture, such as evidence for foodways, can serve as a key identifier of ethnic intrusion. Philistine material culture features several transcultural components, both public and private, which indicate Aegean, Cypriot, and Anatolian affinities. These include architectural modifications; the appearance in domestic contexts of rolled, unbaked clay loomweights ("spool weights") and round and keyhole hearths; and changes in foodways, including table and cooking wares like Aegean-style one-handled cooking jugs, and an increase in consumption of beef and especially pork, which was a far greater share of the Mycenaean diet than that of Late Bronze Age inhabitants of the Levant. While the presence of any of these items at a site does not automatically make that site Philistine, when taken in aggregate they serve to generally highlight that which sets Philistia apart from its neighbors in the region. Furthermore, many of these traits seem representative of the "deep change" we would expect to see if witnessing immigration or a migration, rather than, for example, a relatively static population which is turning out imitative ceramics in an effort to replace a lost source of valuable imports.[22]

## On the Issue of 'Pots and People'

Unfortunately, the clarity that archaeology has brought to many aspects of Philistine culture does not currently extend to *any* other Sea Peoples. The so-called "Philistine template" has not been found in nearly so complete a fashion anywhere outside the relatively contained area of the southern coastal plain of Canaan. Further, no set of material traits has been found to date that can be inarguably associated with any non-Philistine Sea Peoples group. This has unfortunately led to strong assumptions being made—in the absence of convincing evidence—about the origin, nature, and ethnicity of the Philistines' fellow-travelers among the Sea Peoples coalitions. This can perhaps be seen most clearly in the interpretation of so-called "Mycenaean (Myc) IIIC" pottery, an object class that has been associated more than any other single trait with the Philistines through the years—and, by extension, with the entire Sea Peoples phenomenon. This ceramic style has been referred to by many names over the years: Myc. IIIC:1b, Myc. IIIC:1, Myc. IIIC, Sea Peoples Monochrome, Philistine 1, White Painted Wheelmade III ware, etc. All of these terms refer to a ware which was manufactured locally (in the Levant and on Cyprus) in the tradition of Late Helladic IIIC pottery from the early 12th century Aegean.

### Aegean-Style Pottery: Imports and Imitations

In order to place this ware in its proper context, it is important to briefly review the role of Late Helladic pottery in the Eastern Mediterranean at the end of the Bronze Age, as well as the nature of the ceramic repertoire in the Late Bronze Age Levant. Mycenaean society reached its high point during the 14th and first part of the 13th centuries BC (LH IIIA:2 and IIIB:1), both domestically and in terms of international trade and influence. During this period, the Greek mainland was the destination of more Near Eastern goods, including royal objects from Egypt and Mesopotamia, than it had been previously.[23] However, the most visible marker of Mycenaean Greece's foreign influence was its exported pottery, which expanded to such a degree that Late Helladic ceramics figuratively blanketed the eastern and central Mediterranean in late 14th and 13th centuries BCE. Late Helladic IIIA and IIIB wares have been found at more than 350 sites, from Sardinia and Malta in the central Mediterranean, to Kilise Tepe in Anatolia, to Pyla-*Kokkinokremos* on Cyprus, to Qidš and Karkemiš in Syria, to el-Amarna in Egypt.[24] Petrographic studies conducted on ceramics from the Levant have found that almost the entire corpus of Mycenaean exports came from the northern Argolid, particularly the Berbati Valley.[25]

Aegean-style pottery had been produced as early as the 13th century (Late Helladic IIIB) on Cyprus and elsewhere in the Eastern Mediterranean, perhaps as a form of import substitution conducted by enterprising potters and traders who sought to profit from the demand for Mycenaean vessels or their contents.[26] However, at the end of the 13th century, after a slow ebb several decades in length, imports from the Greek mainland stopped altogether and Myc IIIC replaced imported Aegean pottery almost wholesale across the region, from Syria and southern Anatolia southward.[27] From the Middle Bronze Age to the end of the Late Bronze Age chronologically, and from the northern Levant to the south geographically, the pottery of this region is striking in its homogeneity and continuity—a fact that makes the advent of local pottery production in the Aegean style especially noteworthy.[28] This change is particularly marked in the initial layers of Philistine occupation in the southern Levant, where the material record shows both the appearance of these ceramics at the beginning of the 12th century alongside the many other attributes of Philistine material culture discussed above, and the development of this pottery type from a Monochrome phase into the Philistine Bichrome style that became the hallmark of this culture's golden age in the Iron Age Ib (late 12th through 11th centuries).[29] It was the identification of this pottery with Mycenaean styles in the first half of the 20th century CE that was largely for the initial association of the Philistines with the ancient Greeks, an association which has stuck—for better and worse—ever since.[30]

## Forcing the Sea Peoples into a Ceramic Mold

Unfortunately, the clear association of Myc IIIC pottery and other Cypro-Aegean attributes with the Philistines ultimately led to the assumption that these ceramics, and to a lesser degree other Cypro-Aegean traits, would serve as an "X marking the spot" where other Sea Peoples groups lived, encamped, or settled. This point of view is perhaps best summarized in archaeologist Ayelet Gilboa's description of the first Iron I excavations at Dor, a city in central Israel that has traditionally been associated with a group of Sea Peoples known as the *Sikil* or *Tjekker* because of a reference in the early 11th century Egyptian text *The Tale of Wen-Amon* ("I reached Dor, a town of the Sikils, and Beder, its prince, had fifty loaves of bread, one jug of wine, and one leg of beef brought to me"):[31]

> My uneasiness with this model started to develop following the excavations at Dor, the Šikila town according to Wenamun. In the mid-1980s, when [excavation director] Ephraim Stern first reached the Early Iron Age levels there, bets were laid. What would the Šikila material culture look like? Jokingly someone said that Šikila pottery would be something akin to that of Philistia—but painted in purple and yellow. This was the sort of expectation, to find something analogous to Philistia, but slightly different, as befits another Sea People. It seems that this is still what some scholars expect to be uncovered along the southern Levantine coast north of Philistia, something similar, but with a different ethnic tinge.
>
> The finds at Dor, however, have not lived up to expectations, and the 'western association' of the Šikila has turned out to be elusive. Though a few artifacts do find corollaries in Philistia, like a lion headed cup, incised scapulae and bimetallic knives, the broader picture is different. At Dor, in the earliest Iron Age phases, there are no 'western' architectural traits.[32]

This helps illustrate a downside of the detailed picture that literature and archaeology alike have painted of the Philistines. It can also serve as a representative example of the tendency, at the extreme, to project the greater evidence for one "culture" or group onto others for whom no such evidence exists. In the case of the present example, because we lack a remotely comparable level of information about their fellow Sea Peoples, the template of Myc IIIC pottery and other attributes of Philistine material culture has necessarily been extended to those who appear alongside them in the Egyptian sources, despite there not always being a clear reason to associate these traits with other Sea Peoples.

While ceramic evidence is a major factor in archaeology, we must be vigilant when it comes to remembering and applying the axiom that *pots do not equal people*. To this end, it is important to bear two points in mind:

1. The identification of one group's material culture does not itself necessitate an association between that culture and every other group with which they have come into contact or been otherwise connected.
2. The presence of pottery at a site does not prove the presence of traders or settlers from that pottery's point of origin—nor does it prove the presence

of traders or settlers from the point of origin of the *style* in which it is formed and decorated.

Portable objects in particular, like pottery, can be relocated with relative ease. This means that any single pot's find site may be many times removed from its point of origin or from its original owner. Likewise, as we have just noted, wares can be (and frequently were) produced in imitation of originals. This can be seen in particular with the Mycenaean-style ceramics from Cyprus and in the Levant, which were manufactured in increasing numbers as the Bronze Age transitioned into the Age of Iron. Because of this, it has been rightly argued that pottery could be seen as one of the least diagnostic markers of these outsiders if they were engaged in anything other than ceramic production or wholesale resettlement: "pottery can all but be excluded from the assessment . . . because there is no good reason why Sea Peoples serving with the Egyptians in Canaan should have included potters; certainly if their role was primarily military . . . [They] would surely have adopted whatever pots came to hand—Egyptian in Egypt, or Canaanite in Canaan."[33]

## Chasing the 'Sea Peoples' with Incomplete Evidence

Ultimately, we must face a difficult truth: no effective material culture template has been established for any non-Philistine Sea People because in large part *we do not know with any real degree of accuracy where they settled*, particularly outside of Egypt, and because *we would not know what to look for if we did*. As nature abhors a vacuum, so scholarship abhors an absence of both evidence and answers. Thus, the Cypro-Aegean Philistine Paradigm, with its emphasis on Mycenaean derivative pottery, has largely—and naturally—filled this void to date. The geographic discussion, on the other hand, has been driven by a juxtaposition of the aforementioned *Onomasticon of Amenope* and the aforementioned *Tale of Wen-Amon*, Egyptian texts that date near to the turn of the first millennium BCE. The latter, a literary work whose historicity should be taken with a grain of salt, recounts the misfortunes experienced by an Egyptian priest on his way to Byblos, on the Phoenician coast, to purchase wood for the sacred bark of Amun.[34] As we saw above, this text refers to Dor, on the central coast of Israel, as a city of the *Sikil*. The *Onomasticon of Amenope*, on the other hand, is not a literary text, but a catalog of places and peoples, a portion of which is presented in Table 2.1.

As we can see, the *Onomasticon of Amenope* names three Sea Peoples—the Sherden (268), Sikils (269), and Peleset (270)—as well as Ashkelon (262),

**Table 2.1.   Partial List of Names and Toponyms from the Onomasticon of Amenope[1]**

| | |
|---|---|
| 259. *N'ryn* (Unknown) | 270. Prst (Peleset/Philistines) |
| 260. Nhryn (Nahrin) | 271. Ḥrm (Khurma?) |
| 261. [Lost] | 272. [Lost] |
| 262. 'Isḳrûn (Ashkelon) | 273. [Lost] |
| 263. 'Isdd (Ashdod) | 274. Mki (Meki) |
| 264. Gdt (Gaza) | 275. Dwí (Djui) |
| 265. 'Isr (Assyria or Asher?) | 276. Ḥ3(í)w-nbw(t) ('Mediterranean Islanders' or 'Islands') |
| 266. Sbry (Shubaru or Sbír?) | 277. Iḳd (Iḳed) |
| 267. [Lost] | 278. Nḥ . . . (Neḥ . . . ) |
| 268. Šrdn (Sherden) | 279. [Lost] |
| 269. Tkr (Tjekker/Sikil) | 280. Srk (Serek or Seriqqa?) |

1. Gardiner 1947 171*–209*

Ashdod (263), and Gaza (264), three cities on the southern coastal plain of Canaan that have long been identified with the Sea Peoples in general, and the Philistines in particular. North-to-south directionality has been read into this portion of the *Onomasticon*, despite clear issues, the most glaring of which may be the fact that the three Philistine cities in the document—from the north, Ashdod, Ashkelon, and Gaza—are not listed in proper geographic order. When read in conjunction with *Wen-Amon*'s identification of Dor with the Sikils, the *Onomasticon* has been—and, unfortunately, still continues to be—used to place the Philistines in southern Canaan, the Sikils at Dor, and the Sherden at a site (or sites) to the north of these. The latter are most commonly associated with Akko and Tell Keisan on the Carmel coast, though other suggestions have been made, including the site of el-Ahwat on the Naḥal Iron in central Israel, where the excavator suggested there is architectural evidence for a settlement of *nuraghe*-building Sardinians who were stationed in Canaan as pharaonic mercenaries.[35]

As we have seen, though, the *Onomasticon* is both filled with lacunae and lacking a single, clearly directional reading, and thus it could just as easily be assigning the Sherden to Ashkelon, the Sikils to Ashdod, and the Philistines to Gaza as anything else. In fact, given the absence of Akko and Dor from Amenope's list of toponyms, such a reading may even be more likely than the traditional interpretation of this text. Either way, it is clear that any attempt to use this text as more than a *terminus ante quem* for the presence of these groups in Canaan—let alone as a map of Sea Peoples settlements—is a risky endeavor at best. Assumptions of foreign origin can also be tenuous at best. For example, after several years of field work and analysis at Dor, excavators Ayelet Gilboa and Ilan Sharon have concluded that this site was not home to any influx of foreigners at the end of the Bronze Age, but instead that the Sikils should actually be seen as having been synonymous with the Phoenicians and their coast.[36]

However, as will be demonstrated in more detail later, there may be good reasons to associate certain non-Philistine Sea Peoples with at least some aspects of Aegean culture, chief among which are their ships. This includes one of the main objects of this study, the *Š3rd3n3* (the Egyptian terms *Š3rd3n3*, *Šrdn*, and *Š3rdyn3* are also glossed 'Shardana' and 'Sherdanu,' though the more common 'Sherden' is followed here). However, subtler clues about these non-Philistine groups have all too often fallen victim to what may be called, without too much exaggeration, the Tyranny of the Philistine Paradigm. In light of this fact, it bears repeating that the only secure evidence we currently possess for Sherden inhabitation from the 12th century BCE onward places them not in the Levant, the Aegean, or the Central Mediterranean—all areas with which they have been associated—but *in Egypt*. While we know very little about their origins or other aspects of their culture, both texts and iconography paint a clear picture of their martial affinities, and of involvement by at least some in the battles of Ramesses II and III. These "Sherden of the Strongholds" or "Sherden of the Great Fortresses," as those in the Pharaoh's service are frequently referred to, appear in Ramesses II's depictions of the battle of Qidš (and perhaps of the storming of Dapur in Syro-Palestine, as well), and they appear throughout the campaigns recorded at Medinet Habu.[37]

Before we move on, it is important to offer one more methodological note. Even speaking of these "groups" as such carries with it its own inherent, culture-historical baggage: namely, the connotation that the Sherden or any other "Sea People" was a *monolithic group* of *uniform origin and ethnicity*, which participated *in its entirety* in the events with which they are associated, and that its members moved and settled *as a single unit*, in a single location or area. I wish to make abundantly clear that, while frequent references are made to "the Sherden" and to other "groups" in this study, uniformity in composition, geography, or movement is neither assumed nor implied. Where possible, ethnicity is treated in the mode of social anthropologist Fredrik Barth, who defined it in part as self-identification in relation to others.[38] However, among the evidence at hand, self-identification is a very rare occurrence. Because of this, group references are largely governed by, and directed at, elements of these "groups" which are, in turn, so defined and identified by the Egyptian, Hittite, and Ugaritic sources on which we are dependent. As we shall see, some of these terms may be derived from toponymic associations, some may accurately represent the ethnicity of those to whom they refer, and some may be designations assigned to truly heterogeneous coalitions out of simple expedience by our primary sources.[39]

## Chapter Three

# Raiders, Traders, and Sea Peoples in the Late Bronze Age and Beyond

πρὶν μὲν γὰρ Τροίης ἐπιβήμεναι υἷας Ἀχαιῶν
εἰνάκις ἀνδράσιν ἦρξα καὶ ὠκυπόροισι νέεσσιν
ἄνδρας ἐς ἀλλοδαπούς, καί μοι μάλα τύγχανε πολλά.
τῶν ἐξαιρεύμην μενοεικέα, πολλὰ δ' ὀπίσσω
λάγχανον

For before the sons of the Achaeans set foot on the land of Troy, I had nine times led warriors and swift-faring ships against foreign folk, and great spoil had ever fallen to my hands. Of this I would choose what pleased my mind, and much I afterwards obtained by lot.

*Odyssey* xiv, 229–233

## INTERCONNECTIVITY ON LAND AND SEA

The Late Bronze Age in the Eastern Mediterranean was a time of unprecedented communication and connectivity. It was characterized by palace-based economies, royal gift exchange, and cuneiform correspondence between polities great and small, and was anchored by the great empires of the time—Egypt, Hatti, Babylon, Mittani, and Assyria, as well as Aḫḫiyawa, which will be discussed in the next chapter. Despite the varied nature of our records, the widespread use of writing in the Late Bronze Age Eastern Mediterranean puts this period and place squarely within the realm of "history," and provides the most complete look at domestic politics and international systems to that point in human existence.

## 'Cuneiform Culture' and the Amarna Archive

Although scribes in various states around the Aegean and the Eastern Mediterranean maintained records and inscribed monuments in their own, localized systems of writing, such as Egyptian hieratic and hieroglyphic, Ugaritic alphabetic cuneiform, and Mycenaean Linear B, international relations and diplomacy were characterized by a "cuneiform culture."[1] As its name suggests, this culture was based on a common diplomatic language and script, rather than on ethnic homogeneity or civil structure or an allegiance to a common state or ruler. Our most complete evidence for this international correspondence comes from el-Amarna in Egypt, a site briefly mentioned above. When Pharaoh Amenhotep IV ascended to the throne in 1351 BCE, he instigated a revolution in Egyptian religion. He left behind the time-honored worship of Amun and the rest of the diverse Egyptian pantheon, replacing them instead with the worship of the solar disc, Aten. He shifted the capital of Egypt from Thebes, home to the temples at Karnak and Luxor, to a new city that he called "Akhetaten," or the "horizon of Aten," and changed his name from Amenhotep 'Amun is satisfied' to Akhenaten 'of great use to Aten.'

This upheaval of the Egyptian state was short-lived: with Akhenaten's death 27 years later, around 1334 BCE, the old order was restored.[2] However, the brief occupation and subsequent abandonment of Akhetaten, modern el-Amarna, has proved a boon to modern scholars, as a treasure trove of more than 300 letters from around the Near East has shined a bright light on international relations during the portion of the 14th century BCE now known as the "Amarna period." These letters, part of the royal archive, contain the Egyptian court's voluminous correspondence with peers and subordinates, including the 'Great Kings' of the age (Babylonian, Assyrian, Mitannian, and Hittite), *Hazannu* 'mayors' of Egypt's vassal polities in the Levant, and royal officials and family members. Almost all were written in Akkadian, or Babylonian cuneiform, which appears to have been the *lingua franca* of the age—the basis of the *cuneiform culture* mentioned above. The contents of the Amarna archive are both illuminating and, at times, humorous. For example, amidst a large quantity of letters requesting Egyptian gold (or complaining that the gold received was of poor quality),[3] an Assyrian ruler complains that the pharaoh's latest shipment was not even sufficient to pay the cost of the messengers who brought it,[4] while in another, the pharaoh responds angrily to the king of Babylon's refusal to give his daughter in marriage without first having proof that his sister—already one of the pharaoh's many wives—is still alive and well.[5]

This written communication complements the material evidence for the interconnectivity of the Eastern Mediterranean world during the Late Bronze Age. Vast terrestrial lines of communication penetrated deep into Anatolia and western Asia during this period, while the Mediterranean made the coasts of Anatolia, the Levant, the Aegean, and North Africa into what has been called a "single organic sphere connected by sea," allowing goods, ideas, and people to travel throughout the region.[6] This enabled the movement not just of valuable raw and finished materials, but also of people whose expertise would have been in high demand. As Homer notes in the *Odyssey*, skilled workers, including seers, healers, carpenters, and bards, were welcome nearly anywhere:

τίς γὰρ δὴ ξεῖνον καλεῖ ἄλλοθεν αὐτὸς ἐπελθὼν
ἄλλον γ᾽, εἰ μὴ τῶν οἳ δημιοεργοὶ ἔασι,
μάντιν ἢ ἰητῆρα κακῶν ἢ τέκτονα δούρων,
ἢ καὶ θέσπιν ἀοιδόν, ὅ κεν τέρπῃσιν ἀείδων;
οὗτοι γὰρ κλητοί γε βροτῶν ἐπ᾽ ἀπείρονα γαῖαν·
πτωχὸν δ᾽ οὐκ ἄν τις καλέοι τρύξοντα ἓ αὐτόν.

Who pray, of himself ever seeks out and bids a stranger from abroad, unless it be one of those that are masters of some public craft, a prophet, or a healer of ills, or a builder, aye, or a divine minstrel, who gives delight with his song? For these men are bidden all over the boundless earth.

*Odyssey* xvii, 382–386

Archaeological evidence like "Minoan-style" frescoes found at Alalaḫ and Kabri in the Levant, and at Tell el-Dab'a in Egypt, suggest that artists and artisans traveled extensively, while textual evidence supports at least some of this travel being conducted while on loan to various royal courts.[7] This is an example of the "international style" of art and luxury goods that developed at this time, driven by palatial elites and made up of, in the words of art historian Marian Feldman, "hybridized elements that cannot be associated with any one culture," which helped to create and foster a "hybridity of imagined community" among elites in the Late Bronze Age Eastern Mediterranean.[8]

Naturally, people with the means to transport such goods and people would also have been critical in such an environment. As we shall see, those who possessed both ships and knowledge of Mediterranean navigation—including private individuals, who may have served as merchants or intermediaries—were not only in high demand, but over time became integral to the entire system.

## Trade and Status: The Evidence from Ulu Burun

The wealth being transported by sea at this time is hinted at by the remains of a ship that sank around 1300 BCE off the coast of Ulu Burun, near Kaş in southern Turkey. Excavated between 1984 and 1994, the Ulu Burun vessel, which has been reconstructed as being roughly fifty feet long (fifteen meters), contained an extremely cosmopolitan cargo. Its wreckage contained Canaanite, Mycenaean, Cypriot, Egyptian, Nubian, Baltic, Northern Balkan, Old and Kassite Babylonian, Assyrian, and possibly even Sicilian items, as well as possible evidence for individuals of several nationalities on board.[9] The staple of the vessel's fifteen-ton cargo was metal ingots: ten tons of copper, likely of Cypriot origin, and one ton of tin, perhaps from northeastern Afghanistan.[10] These would have combined to create enough bronze to manufacture over 3,000 swords and spears and over a million arrowheads, or to fully outfit an army of 300 with everything from swords and shields to armor.[11] The second-largest cargo item by volume was terebinth resin, 1.5 tons of which was aboard the Ulu Burun ship in at least 149 Canaanite jars. This resin was used as incense in Egypt, and it may have been added as a preservative to jars whose primary contents were wine.[12]

Further examples of the ship's opulent cargo include glass ingots of Mesopotamian and Egyptian origin, musical instruments, elephant tusks and hippopotamus teeth, ostrich eggs, ebony logs, gold and silver jewelry of Syro-Canaanite design, faience, and other valuable items, as well as a solid gold Egyptian scarab of Nefertiti, wife of the pharaoh Akhenaten.[13] Personal items found in the wreckage, including weights in Syro-Canaanite standard, cylinder seals, and armament (including a sword, two daggers, and a single scale of armor), have led the excavators to suggest that as many as four Canaanite or Cypriot merchants were on board during the vessel's final voyage. Two Mycenaean short swords and seals, along with a drinking set composed of Late Helladic jugs, dipper juglet, and kylix, are similarly suggestive of two high-ranking Mycenaeans having been aboard the ship, performing what may have been the common role of escorting a precious shipment westward to the Aegean.[14]

A mace and Italian-type sword further compound the mix. The apparently multicultural nature of those on board the Ulu Burun ship contradicts visual evidence from Egypt in particular, where ships' crews are depicted as ethnically and visually uniform; however, it should not surprise us that those who traveled upon the sea were a diverse lot. This diversity would have intensified the ability of these vessels to serve, in effect, as floating "agents of transference," providing goods and ideas from far more cultures than the one responsible for the physical ship itself. As we shall see, though, it could also have lent itself to the development of a marauding "pirate culture" once opportunities for legitimate business became scarcer.[15]

One further discovery in the Ulu Burun wreckage that deserves mention is a wooden writing tablet, found inside a pithos. The tablet was in the form of a diptych, or a tablet that folds in similar fashion to a codex, and it was made up of two pieces of boxwood connected by an ivory hinge.[16] The tablet's presence suggests that at least one person at the ship's ports of call was literate, and may also be evidence for a scribe or literate individual aboard the vessel itself. The diptych is strikingly reminiscent of the "folded tablet" mentioned by Glaukos to Diomedes in his description of his grand-father Bellerophon's mission to carry a letter ordering his own death to his father-in-law in Lycia:

πέμπε δέ μιν Λυκίην δέ, πόρεν δ᾽ ὅ γε σήματα λυγρὰ
γράψας ἐν πίνακι πτυκτῷ θυμοφθόρα πολλά

So into Lycia
he sent him, charged to bear a deadly cipher,
magical marks Proitos engraved and hid
in folded tablets.

*Iliad* VI, 168–169[17]

This royal tablet has been connected to those found in an 8th century Neo-Assyrian context at Nimrud, near Mosul in modern Iraq.[18] However, such objects were not new inventions at that time; at the court of the Hittites, for example, there existed the title "Scribe of the Wooden Tablets."[19] The presence of a similar tablet on this vessel, which had both Near Eastern and Aegean connections, further demonstrates that Homer's diptych may not have been an anachronism at all—such objects were indeed in use in the region in the Late Bronze Age. Bronze objects found at Knossos and Tiryns have also been identified as possible hinges from wooden writing tablets, thereby giving the famed tablet of *Iliad* VI a potential home not just in the Mycenaean period, but in Greece itself.[20]

The Ulu Burun ship may have been one of many large merchantmen that plied the waters of the Eastern Mediterranean at this time on voyages of directional trade, stopping at regular ports of call to pick up or deliver royal exchange goods as well as commercial items. Its size and payload suggest that it foundered while sailing westward on a voyage of directional trade, perhaps palatially-sponsored commerce or royal gift exchange of the type found in the Amarna Letters. Meanwhile, the presence on board of large *pithoi* filled with Cypriot pottery, almost certainly destined for non-elite recipients, suggests there may also have been a private interest at play in this voyage, and may shed light on the role in the larger network of "sailor's trade," or transfer of materials for personal, rather than state, benefit.[21]

## Seaborne Raids and Coastal Defenses

The weaponry on board the Ulu Burun ship, and the likely presence of at least one armed individual from outside the Eastern Mediterranean region, may suggest that piracy either at sea or in port was a concern to the crew and to the expedition's sponsor. This is also supported by documentary evidence from the prosperous 14th and 13th centuries BCE, which clearly demonstrates the significant seaborne threat posed to coastal polities at this time. Egyptian inscriptions, letters from the Amarna archive, and Hittite documents refer to maritime marauders carrying out coastal raids, conducting blockades, and intercepting ships at sea (for the latter in Homer, see, for example, *Odyssey* iv 660–674). Like most sailing in the ancient Mediterranean, piracy was a seasonal pursuit, and in many cases the same groups seem to have partaken in it on an annual basis, with Cyprus, Egypt, and perhaps Troy, among others, serving as common targets, both historically and in the Homeric tradition. In the case of Troy, the repetitive nature of these raids (for example, *Iliad* V, 638–642 mentions Herakles sacking Troy a generation prior to the epic) makes identifying Homer's war exceedingly difficult, if not impossible, and may very well support the theory that the mythical war itself was an epic agglutination of many minor battles.

Of many contemporary attestations, three 14th century texts are particularly reflective of this reality. The first is an inscription by Amenhotep son of Hapu, an Egyptian official under the 18th dynasty pharaoh Amenhotep III (ca. 1388–1351 BCE), which refers to the need to secure "the river-mouths" (the Nile delta) against a maritime threat:

> I placed troops at the heads of the way(s) to turn back the foreigners in their places. The two regions were surrounded with a watch scouting for the Sand-rangers. I did likewise at the heads of the river-mouths, which were closed under my troops except to the troops of royal marines.[22]

The second text, a letter from the Amarna archive, is a record of correspondence from the king of Alašiya to Akhenaten. In this letter, the king of Alašiya responds to an accusation by the pharaoh that he was complicit in a raid on Egypt that was evidently staged from his island. The Alašiyan king replies by protesting that his territory, too, has fallen victim to maritime attack by a group referred to as the "Lukki."

> Why, my brother, do you say such a thing to me, "Does my brother not know this?" As far as I am concerned, I have done nothing of the sort. Indeed, men of Lukki, year by year, seize villages in my own country.
>
> el-Amarna (EA) 38[23]

The third text discussing seaborne threats is a slightly earlier Hittite document, dating to the early 14th century BCE, which is commonly referred to as the "Indictment of Madduwatta." It tells of a petty ruler in western Anatolia named Madduwatta, whose attempts at territorial expansion, both in Anatolia and on Alašiya, frequently raised the ire of his Hittite suzerain:

> His Majesty said thus [. . .]: "Because [the land] of Alašiya belongs to My Majesty, [and the people of Alašiya] pay [me tribute—why have you continually raided it?"' But] Madduwatta said thus: '[When Attarissiya and] the ruler [of Piggaya] were raiding the land of Alašiya, I often raided it too. But the father of His Majesty [had never informed] me, [nor] had His Majesty ever informed [me] (thus): 'The land of Alašiya is mine—recognize it as such!' If His Majesty is indeed now demanding back the civilian captives of Alašiya, I will give them back to him. And given that Attarissiya and the ruler of Piggaya are rulers independent of My Majesty, while (you), Madduwatta, are a servant of My Majesty—why have you joined up with [them]?
>
> Aḫḫiyawa Text (AhT) 3, §36[24]

If Madduwatta was carrying out seaborne raids against Cyprus, then it stands to reason that he had ships at his disposal, even if they were not permanently under his control. Given his western Anatolian orientation, it is possible that ships and seamen were the same *Lukki* as those mentioned in EA 38 above. Also known as the *Lukka*, this group, which will be discussed further below, may have hailed—or, at very least, staged piratical operations—from the region of Lycia in southwestern Anatolia. They may also have staged at least some of their raids from Cyprus, which seems to have served both as a target and as a refuge for sea raiders during the years surrounding the end of the Bronze Age.

AhT 3 is also noteworthy because it contains the earliest known reference to an entity called "Aḫḫiya." This land, which most scholars associate with Mycenaean Greece, will be discussed in greater detail a bit later, primarily in the form *Aḫḫiyawa*. As can be seen above, according to the text, Aḫḫiya was ruled by a man called "Attarissya":

> But [later] Attarissiya, the ruler of Aḫḫiya, came and was plotting to kill you, Madduwatta. But when the father of My Majesty heard, he dispatched Kisnapili, infantry, and chariotry in battle against Attarissiya. And you, Madduwatta, again did not resist Attarissiya, but yielded before him. Then Kisnapili proceeded to rush [. . .] to you from Ḫatti. Kisnapili went in battle against Attarissiya. 100 [chariots and . . . thousand infantry] of Attarissiya [drew up for battle]. And they fought. One officer of Attarissiya was killed, and one officer of ours, Zidanza, was killed. Then Attarissiya turned [away(?)] from Madduwatta, and he went off to his own land. And they installed Madduwatta in his place once more.
>
> AhT 3, §12[25]

The name Attarissiya has a familiar ring to those acquainted with the lineage of Agamemnon and Menelaus, whose father was the Mycenaean king Atreus (*Iliad* I, 16). While we cannot, of course, be certain that the Atreus of Greek epic ever personally existed—let alone that Attarissya and Atreus were the same historical figure—but a linguistic relationship between the two is certainly possible.[26] As we shall see, this is one of several very interesting linguistic similarities between individuals and polities known from the Late Bronze and Early Iron Age, and those known from later sources, including Homer.

## TRADE AND PIRACY

Given the unprecedentedly affluent and internationalist nature of the Late Bronze Age, it is to be expected that a robust underworld of pirates and brigands would have thrived just beneath the surface. After all, piracy is naturally most successful when coastal settlements and trade routes are present, regular, and prosperous:

> Raiders need traders upon whom to prey. . . . But those raiders are also, in a stronger sense, part of the world of trade; they are not just parasites. Like the transfer of goods between aristocratic estates or like government requisitions, piracy is simply another form of redistribution in an economic environment where markets are often scarce . . . piracy is not an exclusive calling: one season's predator is another season's entrepreneur. Piracy can be a means of capital accumulation, a prelude to more legitimate ventures.[27]

The Sea Peoples group perhaps most identified with piracy, the Sherden, is securely named for the first time in the Tanis II rhetorical stele from the early years of Ramesses II.[28] This inscription refers to the *Sherden* as "those whom none could withstand" and "whom none could ever fight against"—a reference which suggests that they, like Odysseus, Attarissiya, and the *Lukki* in the texts quoted above, had also been raiding coastal settlements for many years prior to that point:

> Son of Re, Ramesses II . . .
>     Whose might has crossed the Great Green (Sea),
>         (so that) the Isles-in-the-Mist are in fear of him,
>     They come to him, bearing the tribute of their chiefs,
>         [his renown has seized] their minds.
>     (As for) the Sherden of rebellious mind,
>         whom none could ever fight against,
>             who came bold-[hearted,
>     they sailed in], in warships from the midst of the Sea,

those whom none could withstand;
[(but) he plundered them by the victories of his valiant arm,
   they being carried off to Egypt]—(even by)
King of S & N Egypt, Usimare Setepenre,
   Son of Re, Ramesses II, given life like Re.

Tanis II Rhetorical Stele[29]

The seasonality of piracy and the references in Tanis II and EA 38 suggest that the same groups carried out these acts over lengthy periods of time. Read against this background, Odysseus' claim to having "nine times led warriors and swift-faring ships against foreign folk," and to having gathered great wealth through his efforts, could signal similar long-term activities.

## Identifying and Defining 'Piracy' in the Late Bronze Age

Before proceeding further on the topic of piracy, it is important to explore just what the term means and how it should be applied. This discussion has at least two threads: defining piracy itself (especially vis-à-vis warfare), and engaging in anthropological application of pirate studies to what we know of the Sea Peoples. The latter has been exhaustively carried out in recent years by archaeologists Louise Hitchcock and Aren Maeir, excavators of the Philistine site of Gath.[30] Leveraging historical pirate studies, they suggest that a range of objects associated with the Sea Peoples, such as Aegean-style drinking sets, feathered and horned helmets, and bird-head devices on ships, served as a shared material culture and visual language around which a "collective identity" coalesced. In at least some cases, this new collective identity could have substituted for that which was lost with the collapse of the Late Bronze Age order, both in the Aegean and around the Eastern Mediterranean. While still theoretical in nature, such a situation would certainly help to explain the seemingly mixed nature of the Sea Peoples in general, and the Philistines in particular.

### Piracy or Warfare?

Differentiating warfare and piracy in the Late Bronze Age, on the other hand, is a difficult undertaking, dependent as it is on clear definition of terms that did not necessarily exist at the time of which we are speaking. The concept is simple enough: in war, armies meet each other in a series of battles (on land or sea) for the purpose of serving a larger strategic goal, while piracy is simply the nautical version of banditry, carried out by criminals with ships. Unfortunately, a closer look causes this dichotomy to break down very quickly: nonstate actors, irregular troops, declared and undeclared conflicts, and a wide variation in the size and complexity of combatants and the organizations they represent all serve to compound the issue. Add also the geopolitical and military realities of the world as it was before the Westphalian state, before the Geneva conventions and law of armed conflict, and before the advent of professional standing armies—all of which, in the context of ancient studies, are extremely recent developments—and we may begin to appreciate the intricacy of the question, and the multiplicity of possible answers.

In modern scholarship, the term "piracy" is consistently used to describe sea attacks of almost any kind, from state-sponsored to private. Further, scholars have frequently argued that, in the Bronze Age, there was no distinction at all to be made between this and warfare.[31] In the "War and Piracy at Sea" chapter of his seminal work *Seagoing Ships and Seamanship in the Bronze Age Levant*, Shelley Wachsmann cast the difference between the two as depending on the involvement or absence of a state (in the form of troops or vessels), even if that involvement is one-sided. For example, he classifies the Egyptian defeat of Sherden "in the midst of the sea" that is recounted in Tanis II as warfare, along with three sea battles against the "enemies from Alašiya" recounted in the Hittite text KBo XII 38 (this text will be discussed further below).[32] Raids, on the other hand—perhaps conducted by these same enemies—are classified as piracy.[33]

While acts of war and of piracy can be placed into these categories, the distinction between them can be difficult to negotiate. If, for example, a fleet of nonstate actors—Lukka, Sherden, or crews of raiders led by Odysseus—were to conduct a successful raid on the Egyptian coast, striking quickly, gathering plunder, and escaping to open water, then that would, under this system, be classified as piracy. However, if something went awry on that raid, and the aggressors were unfortunate enough to come into contact with Egyptian troops, either while ashore (as we see in *Odyssey* xiv, 258–268), while afloat but still in sight of land (as we see in the Medinet Habu relief), or even in the open water (as Tanis II seems to suggest), this would transform the undertaking from *piracy* to *war*. In other words, it is not the involvement of the *nonstate* actor that dictates the terminology employed to describe this type of action or conflict, but that of the *state* actor.

Historian Philip de Souza, in his important study *Piracy in the Graeco-Roman World*, declined to split hairs on the issue, instead arguing that the lack of a term for "pirate" or "piracy" meant that no such undertaking was recognized in the Bronze Age. "It cannot be said that there is evidence of piracy in the historical records," he wrote, "without some distinctive terminology. People using ships to plunder coastal settlements are not called pirates, so they cannot really be said to be practicing piracy . . . [instead] it seems to me that there is no other possible label for this activity than warfare."[34] Replacing one umbrella classification (piracy) with another (warfare) is, of course, an over-simplification. On the other hand, de Souza wrote elsewhere that, "if piracy is defined in general terms as any form of armed robbery involving the use of ships, then it seems to have been commonplace in the ancient Mediterranean world by the Late Bronze Age"—still a generalization, but one which seems more supported by the evidence.[35] The difference between the two statements is purely conceptual: piratical acts were being carried out in the Late Bronze Age (and certainly before), but a specific vocabulary surrounding the under-taking had not fully formed.[36]

As we noted briefly above, piracy typically involves nonstate actors. As Augustine wrote, in a retelling of a Ciceronian anecdote, "It was an elegant and true reply that was made to Alexander the Great by a certain pirate whom he had captured. When the king asked him what he was thinking of, that he should molest the sea, he said with defiant independence: 'The same as you when you molest the world! Since I do this with a little ship I am called a pirate. You do it with a great fleet and are called an emperor'" (Aug. *de Civ. Dei* IV.4.25).[37]

This point of view rings true across the millennia. In the late 19th century CE, attorney William Edward Hall noted that, "Piracy includes acts differ-ing much from each other in kind and in moral value; but one thing they all have in common; they are done under conditions which render it impossible or unfair to hold any state responsible for their commission."[38] An important corollary to this is that, if the perpetrators do belong to a state or organized community, their actions are a violation against their own state as well as that of their victims, and their own community can be responsible for disciplin-ing the offenders. This scenario is hinted at in EA 38, as the King of Alašiya declares, "My brother, you say to me, 'Men from your country were with them.' . . . If men from my country were (with them), send (them back) and I will act as I see fit."[39]

### Acts of Piracy in the Context of War

While *acts of a piratical nature* can be perpetrated by one state or politi-cal unit against another, *piracy* itself is not carried out between states. This position was perhaps most explicitly defended by Hall, who unequivocally declared that "acts which are allowed in war, when authorized by a politi-cally organized society, are not [themselves] piratical."[40] This is in keeping with the aforementioned definition of "piracy" that includes the requirement that no state be able to be held liable for its perpetrators. At its most extreme, then, acts between states that are piratical in nature would be classified as privateering, which, while considered "but one remove from pira[cy]," is

itself, to quote Fernand Braudel, "legitimate war."[41] This "might serve public
as well as private interests; at once a business opportunity, a tool of war and
a factor in the diplomacy between nations," writes historian David Starkey,
who continues:

> [T]hat privateering was, and still is, confused with piracy is hardly surprising
> given the similarities in the aims and methods of the two activities. Both pri-
> vateersman and pirate were intent on enriching themselves at the expense of
> other maritime travelers, an end which was often achieved by violent means, the
> forced appropriation of ships and merchandise. However, there had always been
> a theoretical distinction between the two forms of predation.[42]

The difference between a Privateer, or what we might call a "Legitimate
Pirate," and an "Illegitimate Pirate," then, is no more and no less than a gov-
ernment or ruler's investment in each. It is unlikely, of course, that freebooting sailors at the end of the Late Bronze Age were carrying physical letters
of marque while plundering foreign ships; such documentation, at least in
the form we think of it, is an invention of the early second millennium CE.
However, state sanction of piratical acts obviously predates the conflicts of
late medieval and early modern history, and we should recognize that nonstate actors committing piratical acts on behalf of a supportive state are very
much the ancient equivalent of the privateer, both medieval and modern.[43]
This is not to say that states involved in a conflict with each other cannot
(or do not) consider their adversary to be engaging in piracy through certain
seaborne acts of violence. The use of privateers, both in war proper and to
harass adversaries, is also well documented in later Greek history, from the
Classical to the Hellenistic periods.[44]

Piratical operations can also be seen as a form of guerrilla warfare on the
sea. Long looked down upon by states that boasted effective armies, irregular
fighters have been described as "cruel to the weak and cowardly in the face
of the brave"—a statement that is likely only half true, with the latter portion
being a response borne of frustration.[45] Likewise, counter-piracy operations
could be classified as asymmetric warfare, or "nontraditional warfare waged
between a militarily superior power and one or more inferior powers."[46] Documentary evidence suggests that in the Late Bronze Age, civilized people were
expected to communicate both the date and location of a battle, and to wait
until their adversary had arrived and completed preparations before engaging.
Only barbarians utilized the element of surprise, exploiting their opponents'
weaknesses by attacking under cover of darkness and avoiding pitched battle
with regular troops. In one scholar's words, "This is not war . . . it is just guerrilla activity—small-scale warfare, by small people, of small moral stature."[47]
However, for those without a professionally trained and equipped military

force at their disposal, such tactics offered the best chance not only of success, but of survival. Because of this, for the barbarian—or for any nonstate actor—war was, by its nature, an irregular or guerrilla affair. Piracy was similarly hit-and-run, at least in part for the same reason, thus making true warfare and guerrilla activity on land, and piracy at sea, indistinguishable only for the non-state actor.

In the ancient records, rather than being unable to differentiate between warfare and piracy, we can safely say that we are seeing elements of both. Hit-and-run raids conducted from the sea, such as those carried out year after year by the "men of Lukki," should in fact be classified as piracy, as are the unnamed threats that armed escorts, such as those that may have been aboard the Ulu Burun ship, seem to have been employed to protect against. However, once confederations like those described by Ramesses III become involved, it is likely that we have shifted from banditry on the sea to *warfare*—even if the nature of the actions taken by either side can be described as piratical.

## Trade and Piracy, Once Again

As we have seen, the line between a raider and a trader can vary depending on the circumstances. Odysseus provides us with a case study in the liminality of the seafarer at this time, demonstrating for us how a single individual can shift almost seamlessly between legitimate seafarer and pirate (and back again). As we shall see, he claims to have gathered great wealth while carrying out raids in the service of the pharaoh. The difference between his success in this endeavor, and the great wealth he gathered while previously leading his ships on coastal raids, is the legitimacy conferred on the former by a ruler (and, by extension, a state or polity). Homer openly acknowledges this dual nature of the seafarer, with foreigners being met with a standard greeting of sorts:

> ὦ ξεῖνοι, τίνες ἐστέ; πόθεν πλεῖθ᾽ ὑγρὰ κέλευθα;
> ἤ τι κατὰ πρῆξιν ἦ μαψιδίως ἀλάλησθε,
> οἷά τε ληιστῆρες, ὑπεὶρ ἅλα, τοί τ᾽ ἀλόωνται
> ψυχὰς παρθέμενοι κακὸν ἀλλοδαποῖσι φέροντες;

> Strangers, who are ye? Whence do ye sail over the watery ways? Is it on some business, or do ye wander at random over the sea, even as pirates, who wander, hazarding their lives and bringing evil to men of other lands?

*Odyssey* ix, 252–255[48]

The complexity of the relationship and tension between these pursuits is further reflected by the fact that, in Homer's epics, a successful pirate seems to have held more prestige and higher status than a merchant, whose gain was attributed to "greed":

τὸν δ᾽ αὖτ᾽ Εὐρύαλος ἀπαμείβετο νείκεσέ τ᾽ ἄντην:
'οὐ γάρ σ᾽ οὐδέ, ξεῖνε, δαήμονι φωτὶ ἐΐσκω
ἄθλων, οἶά τε πολλὰ μετ᾽ ἀνθρώποισι πέλονται,
ἀλλὰ τῷ, ὅς θ᾽ ἅμα νηὶ πολυκλήϊδι θαμίζων,
ἀρχὸς ναυτάων οἵ τε πρηκτῆρες ἔασιν,
φόρτου τε μνήμων καὶ ἐπίσκοπος ᾖσιν ὁδαίων
κερδέων θ᾽ ἁρπαλέων

Then again Euryalus made answer and taunted him to his face: 'Nay verily, stranger, for I do not liken thee to a man that is skilled in contests, such as abound among men, but to one who, faring to and fro with his benched ship, is a captain of sailors who are merchantmen, one who is mindful of his freight, and has charge of a home-borne cargo, and the gains of his greed.'

*Odyssey* viii, 158–164

On a large scale, polities simultaneously supported both participation in the international exchange system, and the raids that seem designed to undermine that system. One scholar notes this dichotomy with regard to the Mycenaeans:

It seems, therefore, that on the one hand the populations of the south-eastern Aegean including Mycenaeans were maintaining relations of exchange with the areas of the eastern Mediterranean, exporting pottery and perhaps the know-how of innovative weapon technology. On the other hand they undertook raids and joined military coalitions fighting against the Egyptians and perhaps the Hittites.[49]

On a smaller scale, the use of private intermediaries, itinerant sailors, traders, and in some cases mercenaries may have begun as an effort by states to expand their economic influence and regional prowess, and to gain an edge on their partners and rivals. Over time, the symbiotic relationship between employer and employee matured and mutated to such a degree that these middle-men became integral parts both of international communication and of national economic activity. In other words, they became "an essential part of a trade network, a position obtained because of their peculiar expertise: capital in the form of a boat and knowledge of navigation, the requirement for successful maritime commerce."[50]

This can be illustrated by the maritime "small worlds" framework of inter-connecting *cabotage* circuits, whereby the long haul portions of international trade routes—between, for example, Ugarit or Cyprus and Kommos or the Peloponnese—were supplemented by local transshippers, who distributed goods from their initial points of entry to their final destinations in the relatively close vicinity, while also participating in regional trade.[51] These mariners would have carried with them not just goods, but information and potentially innovation (in approaches, technologies, or otherwise) that would have been transferred to willing partners in the zones of exchange into which they sailed, including ports, waystations, and more.[52] The ramifications of such a practice may have been far-reaching indeed, as long-distance maritime trade routes in the Eastern Mediterranean may themselves have been a direct result of these *cabotage* circuits.[53]

On the other hand, incidents of freebooting would naturally tend to increase in number and severity when markets and resources were scarce, and when strong polities who could provide security, by means of arms if necessary, were lacking.[54] This upset a delicate equilibrium on the seas, further deteriorating both communication and the transport of goods. Such a situation seems to have developed toward the end of the Bronze Age, when too great a dependence on foreign sources of raw materials and prestige goods by the palatial authorities in the Aegean and Eastern Mediterranean may have contributed to a disproportionately severe response to tremors in the international structure of communication and trade.[55] Thus, as the Late Bronze Age wore on and the economic situation became less favorable from the point of view of some of these "fringe" merchants and mariners, a number may have "reverted to marauding practices," with a result being that "the image of 'Sea Peoples' familiar to us from the Egyptian sources emerged."[56]

The end of the Bronze Age was a time of accelerated innovation in, and widespread adoption of, maritime tactics and technology—a fact that may have resulted, at least in part, from that increase in freebooting and marauding. The "island and coastal populations of the Aegean, the pirates, the raiders and the traders," wrote one scholar, have been credited in the past with being "the most innovative and experimental boat designers"—a statement that is likely accurate, if unnecessarily restrictive vis-à-vis geography.[57] As we shall see, the piratical element of these "nomads of the sea" may have driven the development of superior warships, raiding craft, and tactics whose technological needs were often at odds with the merchant vessels upon which they may have preyed.[58]

## Chapter Four

# Mycenae, Aḫḫiyawa, and the Collapse of the Late Bronze Age Order

ἐκ πόλιος δ᾽ ἀλόχους καὶ κτήματα πολλὰ λαβόντες
δασσάμεθ᾽, ὡς μή τίς μοι ἀτεμβόμενος κίοι ἴσης.

There I sacked the city and slew the men; and from the city
we took their wives and great store of treasure. . .

*Odyssey* ix, 41–42

In order to better understand the place of Mycenaean Greece in the Late Bronze Age Eastern Mediterranean, it is important to address the evidence for, and debate surrounding, a polity we have met in passing a few times thus far: Aḫḫiyawa (*URUa-ah-hi-ya-a*). Mentioned in twenty-eight texts between the 15th and 13th centuries BCE, or approximately 0.1 percent of the 25,000 currently known Hittite documents, Aḫḫiyawa has been placed everywhere from the Greek mainland, including Mycenae and Boeotian Thebes (or a confederation of mainland polities), to Miletos, Cilicia (or *Adana*), Crete, Cyprus, and Thrace.[1] Within the Interface alone, locations from Troy in the far north to Rhodes in the far south have been suggested. It is both noteworthy and characteristic of the conflicting opinions stemming from the cryptic and incomplete evidence on this topic that, scarcely two decades ago, an Egyptologist declared Aḫḫiyawa to have been equivalent to Mycenae itself, the Great King of Aḫḫiyawa to have been the *wanax* of Mycenae, and the Mycenaean and Egyptian courts to have been in written contact (in Akkadian), while a Classical scholar urged caution, calling Aḫḫiyawa's connection to the Mycenaean world "an unproved (and . . . unlikely) theory."[2]

Ultimately, this term has most commonly been accepted as referring to a polity or confederation of polities within the sphere of Mycenaean Greece, perhaps constituted along the lines of the Trojan expedition in Homer's *Iliad*—led

41

not by a ruler of all Greeks, but by a *primus inter pares*.[3] Certainly the claim in AhT 3 (the "Indictment of Madduwatta," quoted earlier) that Attarissiya of Aḫḫiyawa was capable of mustering one hundred chariots and one thousand infantry suggests a pooling of resources by a coalition of contributors that could be (re)constituted at times of need, as no single Late Helladic palace seems to have been in command of such resources.[4] We must also assume, given the location of the battle described in this text, that a similar pooling of resources was behind the mustering of ships necessary to transport at least a portion of these forces across the Aegean to Anatolia.

## AḪḪIYAWA, ACHAEA, AND MYCENAEA(NS)

The "Indictment of Madduwatta," which also references regular coastal raiding, is the earliest known Aḫḫiyawa text. The last known mentions of Aḫḫiyawa in Late Bronze Age texts come from the important coastal *emporion* of Ugarit (Tel Ras Shamra in modern Syria), where they were found in the house of Urtenu, a merchant with close ties to the royal family. Parallel documents sent from the Hittite court to the local king 'Ammurapi around 1200 BCE, these texts refer to LU *Hi-ya-a-ú* and LU *Hi-ya-ú-wi-i* 'the (Aḫ)ḫiyawan,' and LU.MEŠ *Hi-a-ú-wi-i* 'the (Aḫ)ḫiyawans,' who are evidently waiting in Lycia for a shipment of metal ingots (PAD.MEŠ):

> Concerning those owing a service obligation about whom you have appealed to My Majesty—on this occasion have I not sent Satalli to you? Now I have been told that the (Aḫ)ḫiyawan is tarrying in [the land] of Lukka, but that there are no (copper) ingots for him. In this matter don't tell me that there is no appropriate action. Give ships to Satalli, so that he may take the ingots to the (Aḫ)ḫiyawans. On a second occasion My Majesty will not again send to you persons owing a service obligation.
>
> AhT 27A (=RS 94.2530), §7[5]

> In respect to those owing a service obligation about whom you have been appealing—on the first occasion you . . . Satalli. Let him take (copper) ingots to the (Aḫ)ḫiyawan; he shall take (them) to the land of Lukka. His Majesty will [not] again send you [persons] owing a service obligation. Regarding the treaty [tablet] that His Majesty made for you—no one will alter this treaty of yours.
>
> AhT 27B (=RS 94.2523), §6[6]

The same aphaeresized formulation "(Aḫ)ḫiyawa" is found much later in a late 8th century Luwian-Phoenician bilingual from Çineköy, thirty kilometers south of Adana in Cilicia:

I am Warika, son of [. . .], descendant of Mukasa, (Aḫ)ḫiyawan king, [servant of] the Storm-God, [man of the Storm-God].
[I], Warika, extended [(the territory of) the city of (Aḫ)ḫiyawa],
[and made prosper] the (Aḫ)ḫiyawan plain through the help of the Storm-God and my paternal gods.
I added horse to horse;
I added army to army.
and (Aḫ)ḫiyawa and Assyria became a single house.

Çineköy Inscription of Warika[7]

This inscription equates Luwian *hat-ta-wa* 'Hiya(wa)' with Phoenician *DN-NYM* 'Danunim.' In a related bilingual, ascribed to one of Warika's subordinate rulers from Karatepe, the term "Adanawa" is used in place of Luwian *Ḫiyawa*, and the Phoenician term used to refer to the people living in this kingdom is "Danunian" (in Assyrian annals, the term "Que" is used to refer to this territory, which may result from *Ḫiyawa* > *\*Qawe* > *Que*).[8] As can be seen from the Çineköy translation above, the inscriptions' dedicators claim to be of the House of Mopsos (Luwian *Mukasa* = Phoenician *MPŠ*), the legendary Greek seer and founder of cities whose documented travels span from Asia Minor to the city of Ashkelon on the southern coastal plain of Canaan, a location that is highly relevant here for its connection to the Philistines:

φησὶ δ᾽ Ἡρόδοτος τοὺς Παμφύλους τῶν μετὰ Ἀμφιλόχου καὶ Κάλχαντος εἶναι λαῶν μιγάδων τινῶν ἐκ Τροίας συνακολουθησάντων: τοὺς μὲν δὴ πολλοὺς ἐνθάδε καταμεῖναι, τινὰς δὲ σκεδασθῆναι πολλαχοῦ τῆς γῆς. Καλλῖνος δὲ τὸν μὲν Κάλχαντα ἐν Κλάρῳ τελευτῆσαι τὸν βίον φησί, τοὺς δὲ λαοὺς μετὰ Μόψου τὸν Ταῦρον ὑπερθέντας τοὺς μὲν ἐν Παμφυλίᾳ μεῖναι τοὺς δ᾽ ἐν Κιλικίᾳ μερισθῆναι καὶ Συρίᾳ μέχρι καὶ Φοινίκης.

Herodotus says that the Pamphylians are the descendants of the peoples led by Amphilochus and Calchas, a miscellaneous throng who accompanied them from Troy; and that most of them remained here, but that some of them were scattered to numerous places on earth. Callinus says that Calchas died in Clarus, but that the peoples led by Mopsus passed over the Taurus, and that, though some remained in Pamphylia, the others were dispersed in Cilicia, and also in Syria as far even as Phoenicia.

Strabo 14.4.3[9]

καὶ μικρὸν προελθὼν πάλιν φησίν ‘ ἡ δέ γε Ἀταργάτις, ὥσπερ Ξάνθος λέγει ὁ Λυδός, ὑπὸ Μόψου τοῦ Λυδοῦ ἁλοῦσα κατεποντίσθη μετὰ Ἰχθύος τοῦ υἱοῦ ἐν τῇ περὶ Ἀσκάλωνα λίμνῃ διὰ τὴν ὕβριν καὶ ὑπὸ τῶν ἰχθύων κατεβρώθη.

And a little further on, he says again—'But Atergatis (as Xanthus the Lydian says), being taken prisoner by Mopsus, king of Lydia, was drowned with her son in the lake near [Ashkelon], because of her insolence, and was eaten up by fishes.'

Athenaeus 8.37[10]

"The land Hiyawa" is also mentioned on a 10th century BCE stele dedicated to the Storm God from Arsuz (modern Uluçınar, just south of İskenderun on the Mediterranean coast). The inscription says in part:

I (am) Suppiluliuma, the Hero, Walastanean/Walastinean King, the son of King Manana
[. . .] The city/land Adana 'put me to the stick,'
and I overcame,
I routed? also the land Hiyawa, / or I turned? to the land Hiyawa also,
and I made my skill pass before the city. . .

ARSUZ 2 §§1, 11–14[11]

The toponym Ḫiyawa seems to have been transferred some time after the Hittite empire receded beyond Cilicia, perhaps as an *ethnikon* brought by Greek-speakers who also bore elements of Aegean material and linguistic culture with them.[12] Just when this may have taken place remains a matter of debate. Luwian philologist Rostislav Oreshko has posited that "the appearance of Ah-hiyawa in KARATEPE and ÇİNEKÖY as a designation of a local entity can be interpreted only as the result of a transfer of the term at some point following the fall of the Hittite Empire at the beginning of 12th century BC," while archaeologist Gunnar Lehmann suggests that it may not have been until the early first millennium BCE (roughly the date of the ARSUZ 2 inscription).[13] If the date hypothesized by Oreshko is correct, it does not seem to have taken very long for the toponymic form of this *ethnikon*, and the cultural memory of Mopsos, to become all that remained of the once-intrusive population that brought it to the southern coast of Asia Minor. The memory itself was enduring enough, though, that centuries later the Cilicians were still referred to as *Hyp-Akhaioi* 'Sub-Achaeans' (Herodotus *Hist.* 7.91).

## Tanaya and the Danaans

*Danunim* may also be related to *Tanaya*, a term thought to refer to some part of the Greek world, perhaps the mainland. This toponym is found in 18th dynasty records, including in those of Thutmosis III (ca. 1479–1425 BCE) and Amenhotep III (ca. 1388–1351). An account of tribute received by Thutmosis III following his seventeenth and final Asiatic campaign, in his forty-second regnal year, contains the following:

[. . . Benevolence of the chief] of Tanaya:
Silver: a jug of Keftiu workmanship along with vessels of iron
. . . with silver handle(s) 4, making 56 dbn, 3 kdt

Year 42 Inscription, Annals of Thutmose III at Karnak[14]

The records of Amenhotep III contain three references to Tanaya. Two are in topographic lists from the temples of Amun-Ra at Karnak and of Amun at Soleb (the latter was in Nubia, now northern Sudan).[15] The third mention of this toponym, on a statue base at the pharaoh's mortuary temple at Kom el-Hetan near Luxor, is of particular interest. Famous for the so-called "Colossi of Memnon" standing at its entrance, the rear of this temple also contains five statue bases (remnants of what had been, in antiquity, ten larger-than-life-sized statues of the pharaoh). Each base features a list of toponyms on its front and sides, written onto the lower bodies of bound, kneeling individuals in a form referred to as "captive ovals."[16] The names featured on the base containing the term Tanaya make up what is commonly known as the "Aegean List" of Amenhotep III. At least fourteen of the seventeen inscribed terms have been identified with locations in the Aegean, including Knossos, Amnisos, Phaistos, and Kydonia on Crete, the island of Kythera, and Mycenae, Nauplion, Messenia, and the Thebaid on the Greek mainland.[17]

Only two of the terms on the statue base appear anywhere else in the known Egyptian corpus: *Keftiu*, which is identified with Crete, and *Tanaya*. These are inscribed on the front of the base, set apart from and oriented opposite to the rest of the list. This arrangement may denote the categories into which the remainder of the terms are to be classified, with some associated with Keftiu and the rest Tanaya.[18] This toponymic list has been seen as reflecting the itinerary of a diplomatic mission to the Aegean by the court of Amenhotep III, a view which may be supported by the presence on Crete, Rhodes, and mainland Greece of objects—faience plaques, scarabs, and a vase—inscribed with the royal cartouches of the pharaoh and his wife, Queen Tiye.

Amenhotep III's reign began in the Late Minoan IIIA:1 period, and the timing of the possible embassy's arrival, inferred from a scarab found in a tomb at Knossos, generally aligns with the Late Helladic and Late Minoan IIIA:1.[19] This period is marked by the end of the Third Palace Period on Crete and the beginning of Mycenaean ascendancy over the Aegean region, and the fact that the majority of these objects (including the vase, two scarabs of Queen Tiye, and all of the faience plaques) were found at Mycenae itself, suggests that this Helladic center may have been the specific target of an Egyptian embassy. Oxford archaeologist Jorrit Kelder has suggested "that *Tanaju* [=Tanaya] is the last entry in the list (despite the fact that there is sufficient space on the base for additional names) suggests that *Tanaju* constituted the very edge of the world known to the Egyptians."[20] If the target of the embassy was Mycenae itself, the other toponyms on the itinerary may denote stops made on the route there and back.[21]

It seems on linguistic evidence alone that *Danunim* can also be associated in some way with the *D3iniwn3* 'Denyen' or 'Danuna' known from Ramesses III's accounts of Sea Peoples invasions that are inscribed on the walls of Medinet Habu. This is not, however, is not a new term in the Near Eastern corpus, as *Da-nu-na* is also found in EA 151, a 14th century letter from the Amarna archive:

> The king, my lord, has written to me: 'That which you have heard from within Canaan, send to me; the king of the land of Danuna is dead and his brother became king afterwards and his land is at peace; fire destroyed the palace of the king of Ugarit; it destroyed half of it and half of it not; but the Hittite army is not there; Etakkama, the ruler of Kedesh and Aziru are at war—it is with Biryawaza that they are at war; I have experienced the brutalities of Zimredda when he assembled the ships (and) troops from the cities of Aziru against me.'

EA 151:49–67[22]

## The Status of Aḫḫiyawa

The rulers of Aḫḫiyawa are clearly identified in some Hittite texts as being similar in rank and importance to the other so-called Great Kings of the age. However, a closer look suggests that such status was far from secure. In a late 13th century suzerain treaty between King Tudḫaliya IV of Ḫatti and King Šaušgamuwa of Amurru (AhT 2 = CTH 105), the Hittite king declares:

> And the kings who (are) of equal rank with me, the King of Egypt, the King of Karadunia (=Kassite Babylonia), the King of Assyria, ~~the King of Aḫḫiyawa~~, if the king of Egypt is a friend of My Sun, let him also be a friend to you, if he is an enemy of My Sun, let him be your enemy also.[23]

As noted by the strikethrough in the quote above, the name Aḫḫiyawa was erased shortly after the document's writing, perhaps even by the original scribe. It has been suggested that the haphazard nature of the inscription marks the existing copy as a rough draft, and that the scribe may simply have been following the standard formula for the listing of great kings when he realized his mistake.[24]

Prior to the Šaušgamuwa treaty, in a mid-13th century document frequently referred to as the "Tawagalawa letter" (AhT 4), Tudḫaliya IV's predecessor Ḫattušili III had directly addressed the ruler of Aḫḫiyawa as "My Brother, the Great King, my equal" at least thirty-seven times.[25] The Tawagalawa letter focuses on a freebooter named Piyamaradu (${}^m$*Pí-ya-ma-ra-du-uš*) who seems to have found safe haven in Aḫḫiyawan territory between regular incursions into western Anatolia. Piyamaradu seems to have been quite the thorn in Ḫattušili's side, as he appears in five separate Aḫḫiyawa-related texts (AhT 4, 5, 7, 15, and 26). The Tawagalawa letter, though, is also significant for its reference to a prior conflict between Aḫḫiyawa and Ḫatti that seems to have centered on Troy (also known as *(W)Ilios*), saying, "about the matter of the land of Wiluša [${}^{URU}$*Wi${}_s$-lu-ša*] concerning which he and I were hostile to one another . . . we have made peace."[26]

The erasure of Aḫḫiyawa from the list of Great Kings in the Šaušgamuwa treaty reinforces the fluid nature of Late Bronze Age geopolitics, particularly on the periphery of the great empires of the age (Egypt, Babylonia, Ḫatti, and Assyria, the latter of which had supplanted Mittani as a Near Eastern power by the mid-13th century). This case also points to the changes that were beginning to take place in the region as the end of the Bronze Age approached. As has been noted, the world of Homer's epics is reflective of this period in many ways, with the *Iliad*'s tension between a major polity on the eastern side of the Aegean and the Helladic coalition to the west, and with *Odyssey*'s haunting portrayal of the rending apart of the social and political fabric of the Eastern Mediterranean world. This is highlighted by the above-quoted reference to Troy as an object of contention between Ḫatti and Aḫḫiyawa in AhT 4—not to mention the early or mid-13th century mention in CTH 76 of *Alaksandu* as king of Wiluša, with whom the Hittite king Muwatalli II had engaged in a treaty.[27]

Aegean culture had a clear foothold in western Anatolia during the Late Bronze Age. The site of Miletos (Hittite *mi-la-wa-ta* 'Millawanda') displays Minoan material culture dating to the period before the fall of the Cretan palaces. Following this, Miletos became a Mycenaean center, and remained so from the beginning of the 14th to the mid-13th century BCE, with a brief hiatus around 1400 when the site was destroyed by the Hittite king Muršili II. The final loss of Miletos, which came under Hittite control in the late 13th century (as seen in AhT 5, the "Milawata Letter" of Tudḫaliya IV), may have served as the ultimate death knell of Mycenaean influence in western Anatolia, and it is possible that this was connected to the removal of the Aḫḫiyawan king from the list of "Great Kings" of the age.[28]

## Sea Raids and Foreign Entanglements

Both texts and material finds provide evidence for military action by Aegeans in western Anatolia from the 15th century BCE onward. Weapons in the Mycenaean tradition have been found at Izmir and Ḫattuša, while a bowl dating to the 15th or 14th century BCE found at the Hittite capital of Boğazköi featured a carving of what may be a Mycenaean warrior (Figure 7.8; more on this below).[29] Textual examples include references to a late 15th or early 14th century rebellion against the Hittite empire in western Anatolia by a confederation of twenty-two polities known as the "Aššuwan league," and perhaps the aforementioned Šaušgamuwa treaty, from the late 13th century, which prohibits "any ship [of] Aḫḫiyawa" from being allowed to go to the king of Assyria.[30] While the latter has typically been read as an embargo on the transport of Mycenaean goods to Assyria, the combination of the inability of ships to reach Assyria, the overall lack of evidence for Mycenaeans as shippers of their own goods to Eastern Mediterranean destinations, and the location of this demand within the text—in a section dealing with military rather than economic matters—may make an alternate explanation more likely.

To this end, it has been suggested that the demand Tudḫaliya makes in this treaty is not that Aḫḫiyawan *goods* be prevented from reaching Assyria via Amurru, but Aḫḫiyawan *mercenaries*—as Hittitologist Trevor Bryce termed it, "shiploads of freebooting Mycenaeans trawling the Mediterranean in search of either plunder or military service in the hire of a foreign king."[31] This proposal seems to be supported by evidence for Aegean involvement in the martial affairs of the Eastern Mediterranean from the middle of the second millennium BCE to the end of the Bronze Age, either in an official capacity or as mercenaries in foreign armies. Particularly noteworthy examples from outside Anatolia include a 14th century Egyptian papyrus from el-Amarna (EA 74100), which shows at least two warriors in boar's tusk helmets running toward a fallen Egyptian soldier, and a bronze scale of armor from the Greek island of Salamis stamped with the royal cartouche of Ramesses II, which may have belonged to a Mycenaean serving in an official capacity in the pharaonic military.[32] This also fits with the scenario presented in the macronarrative of the *Odyssey*, and in the micronarrative of the Second Cretan Lie, wherein groups of sailors banded together or joined with foreign armies in search of plunder, on their own or on behalf of others after the fall of the Mycenaean palatial system had begun (this will be addressed further below).

## Slaves and Plunder from Anatolia

Hittite texts referencing Aḫḫiyawa frequently mention both raids and captives (NAM.RA^meš), and thus may serve as evidence for Aegean seafarers obtaining slaves and other plunder through such means, and spiriting them back to territory under the control of Aḫḫiiyawa (for a Homeric parallel to this, see *Odyssey* xiv, 229–232, cited above). Later legend may preserve a kernel of memory about the remnants of the NAM.RA^meš being removed from western

Anatolia and transported to Aḫḫiyawan territory. For example, the "cyclopean" walls of Tiryns were built, according to myth, by Cyclopes who "came by invitation from Lycia":

τῇ μὲν οὖν Τίρυνθι ὁρμητηρίῳ χρήσασθαι δοκεῖ Προῖτος καὶ τειχίσαι διὰ Κυκλώπων, οὓς ἑπτὰ μὲν εἶναι καλεῖσθαι δὲ γαστερόχειρας τρεφομένους ἐκ τῆς τέχνης, ἥκειν δὲ μεταπέμπτους ἐκ Λυκίας

Now it seems that Tiryns was used as a base of operations by Proetus, and was walled by him through the aid of the Cyclopes, who were seven in number, and were called 'Bellyhands' because they got their food from their handicraft, and they came by invitation from Lycia.

Strabo *Geographica* VIII 6.11[33]

This could be interpreted as a reference to the appropriation of Lukka NAM. RA^MEŠ in the 13th century BCE to act as manual laborers on the Greek mainland.[34] Certainly the Cyclopean masonry and corbeling techniques at the citadels of Athens, Gla, Mycenae, Midea, Pylos, Thebes, and Tiryns, as well as the Lion Gate at Mycenae itself, have much in common with Hittite architecture, with the late 13th century BCE (Late Helladic IIIB:2) fortification wall of the Unterburg at Tiryns being perhaps the best example given the aforementioned mythological explanation of this site's construction.[35] The connection between Mycenaeans and Lycians has been seen in participation by both *Ekwesh*, whom some scholars have identified with *Achaeans*, or Mycenaean Greeks, and *Lukka* in the assault on the Nile delta by a coalition of Libyans and Sea Peoples around 1207 BCE in the fifth regnal year of the Pharaoh Merneptah (although, as we shall see further below, this identification of the Ekwesh is highly unlikely). Additionally, another mythological account that references the Cyclopean masonry at Tiryns also tells of an "army of Lycians" accompanying Proitos back to Greece from Asia Minor, where he had been exiled by his twin brother Akrisios, and helping him to retake a portion of his kingdom:

Λυγκεὺς δὲ μετὰ Δαναὸν Ἄργους δυναστεύων ἐξ Ὑπερμνήστρας τεκνοῖ παῖδα Ἄβαντα. τούτου δὲ καὶ Ἀγλαΐας τῆς Μαντινέως δίδυμοι παῖδες ἐγένοντο Ἀκρίσιος καὶ Προῖτος. οὗτοι καὶ κατὰ γαστρὸς μὲν ἔτι ὄντες ἐστασίαζον πρὸς ἀλλήλους, ὡς δὲ ἀνετράφησαν, περὶ τῆς βασιλείας ἐπολέμουν, καὶ πολεμοῦντες εὗρον ἀσπίδας πρῶτοι. καὶ κρατήσας Ἀκρίσιος Προῖτον Ἄργους ἐξελαύνει. ὁ δ' ἧκεν εἰς Λυκίαν πρὸς Ἰοβάτην, ὡς δέ τινές φασι, πρὸς Ἀμφιάνακτα· καὶ γαμεῖ τὴν τούτου θυγατέρα, ὡς μὲν Ὅμηρος, Ἄντειαν, ὡς δὲ οἱ τραγικοί, Σθενέβοιαν. κατάγει δὲ αὐτὸν ὁ κηδεστὴς μετὰ στρατοῦ Λυκίων, καὶ καταλαμβάνει Τίρυνθα, ταύτην αὐτῷ Κυκλώπων τειχισάντων. μερισάμενοι δὲ τὴν Ἀργείαν ἅπασαν κατῴκουν, καὶ Ἀκρίσιος μὲν Ἄργους βασιλεύει, Προῖτος δὲ Τίρυνθος.

Lynceus reigned over Argos after Danaus and begat a son Abas by Hypermnes-
tra; and Abas had twin sons Acrisius and Proetus by Aglaia, daughter of Mantin-
eus. These two quarreled with each other while they were still in the womb, and
when they were grown up they waged war for the kingdom, and in the course
of the war they were the first to invent shields. And Acrisius gained the mastery
and drove Proetus from Argos; and Proetus went to Lycia to the court of Iobates
or, as some say, of Amphianax, and married his daughter, whom Homer calls
Antia, but the tragic poets call her Stheneboea. His in-law restored him to his
own land with an army of Lycians, and he occupied Tiryns, which the Cyclopes
had fortified for him. They divided the whole of the Argive territory between
them and settled in it, Acrisius reigning over Argos and Proetus over Tiryns.

Ps-Apollodorus Bibliotheca II 2.1[36]

## WRITTEN RECORDS FROM MYCENAEAN GREECE

Another glimpse of the results of these raids may be found in archives from
mainland Greece—in particular, those from Pylos. First, though, we should
address the nature of the written records during this period. Writing in the
Late Bronze Age Aegean world was very limited in comparison to the literatures, legends, international correspondence, and enumerated deeds of
kings known from Near Eastern texts. The logosyllabic Linear B script was
used on the Greek mainland and at Cretan sites like Knossos to keep palace
records pertaining to palace administration and economics. Though the dearth
of information they contain on topics like international commerce and private
enterprise suggests that these activities may have taken place outside the narrow purview of the palaces' administrations, it is important to note that none
of the records found to date were intended to be permanently kept: they were
inscribed on tablets of unbaked clay, and only inadvertently preserved.

The information on Greek affairs at this time that has been most completely published comes from the Pylian archives, and is made up of records
from a single year which were baked by the fire that destroyed the palace at
the end of the 13th or early in the 12th century BCE. Despite the limitations
of such a small temporal sample, though, these records have frequently been
extrapolated to Mycenae, Tiryns, Thebes, and other LH IIIB contemporaries
of Pylos about whose organization and affairs we have less detail.

### International Trade and Communication

The Linear B records are almost completely silent on any aspects of trade,
industry, or other economic activities that were conducted independently of
the palaces, or which may have been the purview of entrepreneurs or nongov-

ernmental intermediaries. This includes international relations and foreign trade, as well as the production of many types of goods (as opposed to the taxation of them, a matter in which the palace naturally had an interest). The local economy, on the other hand, within which the palace has been seen as "the focal point of the redistributive system, mobilizing both goods and services," is chronicled in some detail in the extant records, as are palatially-controlled industries such as bronze-working and the production of prestige goods, wherein craftsmen were apparently dependent on the palace for raw materials and, in at least some cases, for subsistence.[37] This does not mean that entrepreneurs and third-party actors were not present in the Mycenaean economy; on the contrary, in fact, it seems quite likely that they were.[38] Instead, it means that, if these elements of the economy did exist, they appear to have occupied a space outside that which was governed by the Mycenaean palaces and recorded in the Linear B tablets—though whether individuals had the means, and whether the Mycenaean economy was structured in such a way, to support this remains an open question.[39]

Evidence for at least some Mycenaean exposure to foreigners can be found in the use of foreign loan-words and ethnics. As might be logically expected, particularly if the majority of maritime trade was conducted by those from outside the Aegean, the number of foreign ethnyms and toponyms employed by the writers of the Linear B archives appears to increase as the people and places to which those terms refer grow geographically nearer. Egypt, Cyprus, Phoenicia, and even the Ionian islands appear rarely if at all in the 14th and 13th centuries BCE, while Ugarit, the Syrian port that served as the chief *entrepôt* for Late Helladic pottery in the Levant, is equally conspicuous by its absence (a situation that notably went both ways until the discovery of AhT 27A and B, which mention "(Aḥ)ḥiyawans").[40]

## *The Myth of the Mycenaean 'Thalassocracy'*

This fits with a form of the aforementioned "small worlds" framework, whereby international trade routes were supplemented by local networks, which shepherded goods from their initial points of entry (for example, Kommos on Crete) to their final destinations in the relatively close vicinity, while also participating in regional trade.[41] It does not, however, fit with the long-held view of Mycenae as a "thalassocracy" whose people and influence were as far-flung around the Eastern Mediterranean as their pottery. Until the late 20th century of the common era, the major driving force of maritime commerce in the Eastern Mediterranean was thought to have resided in the Aegean, with the countless imported Late Helladic ceramics assumed to have been delivered by Mycenaean sailors in Mycenaean ships, and *emporia* and trading hubs farther east being seen as evidence for Mycenaean outposts and colonies, particularly on Cyprus and in the Dodecanese, where they have been seen as "rivaling in some respects those of the Greek mainland itself."[42]

Not only were elements of Aegean art and culture that appear in the Near East assumed to have been brought there by Mycenaeans, but innovations brought back to the Aegean from the Near East were also thought to have traveled with Mycenaean seafarers, rather than having been carried by Canaanites or Cypriots. However, this long-standing view of the role of Mycenae in the Eastern Mediterranean world always rested on precious little evidence. Egyptian reliefs, for example, show Syro-Canaanite ships offloading cargo at ports of entry, not Mycenaean ships, while the only Aegeans depicted on the walls of the 18th and 19th dynasty tombs at Thebes are Minoans (*Keftiu*) who only appear in 15th century BCE contexts. There are also no Mycenaeans to be found in the Amarna Letters, with their detailed records of palatial communication and exchanges of gifts.[43] Even in Homer, while piratical endeavors seem to be assumed of most sailors, maritime trade clearly falls within the purview of the Phoenicians, who are described as ναυσίκλυτοι (idiomatically "great mariners" or "men famed for their ships"; *Odyssey* xv, 415).[44] Most of what remains is pottery, and the strength of evidence is significantly tempered when we recognize that, in the words of one scholar, "the occurrence of Mycenaean pottery outside areas settled by Mycenaeans proves no more than that the pottery got there"—not how it was transported, or by whom.[45]

Despite this lack of evidence for direct trade, the paradigm of the Mycenaean thalassocracy only began to shift in the second half of the 20th century, with the discovery and excavation off the coast of Cape Gelidonya in modern Turkey of a shipwreck dating to roughly 1200 BCE.[46] This 10-meter-long vessel's cargo was primarily Cypriot copper, along with smaller amounts of Attic copper, bars of tin, and broken bronze tools which had likely been collected as scrap metal to be used as payment for goods or services, or to melted and recast by a traveling bronzesmith or by the metals' end purchaser.[47] The transport of massive amounts of copper is attested in the Amarna Letters (for example, EA 34 mentions 100 talents, or over 3,000 kg, and EA 35 mentions 500, or 16,000 kg), while physical remains like those of the Gelidonya wreck also combine with textual evidence to paint a clearer picture of a much smaller, yet likely more robust, export trade in Cypriot copper. In RS 94.2475, for example, a text dating to the late 13th century, King Kušmešuša of Alašiya (the only Alašiyan king for whom we have a name) writes to King Niqmaddu III of Ugarit, whom he addresses as his "son"—diplomatic parlance for a ruler of lower rank—about 33 ingots of copper (roughly 900 kg) that he intends to send him.[48]

While the metals found in the Gelidonya wreck shed further light on the nature of exchange at the end of the Bronze Age, other items found at the site were valuable for their impact in turning the Mycenaean-centric vision of maritime trade on its head. The sixty stone pan-balance weights found in the wreckage were based on Near Eastern, not Aegean, standards, while personal items owned by members of the crew—scarabs, a scarab-plaque, an oil lamp, stone mortars, an Egyptian razor, and a Levantine cylinder seal—further demonstrated their Near Eastern identities.[49] The Gelidonya wreck also served to reinforce the role private entrepreneurs probably played in the Late Bronze Age metals trade and other international communications, including, it seems likely, the distribution of Mycenaean and Mycenaean-style pottery.

## Captive Women: The *ra-wi-ja-ja*

As noted above, the Mycenaean Linear B texts carefully recorded matters which were directly associated with palatial administration, including as well people and *materiel* under palatial control. This includes female workers, many of whom may have been slaves, although they have also been seen as refugees both from within the Greek mainland itself, and from Mycenaean territories in western Anatolia.[50] Women from Lemnos (*ra-mi-ni-ja* = *Lâmniai*), Chios (*ki-si-wi-ja* = *Kswiai*), Miletos (*mi-ra-ti-ja* = *Milatiai*), Knidos (*ki-ni-di-ja* = *Knidiai*), Halikarnassos (*ze-pu$_2$-ra$_3$* = *Dzephurrai*), and Asia (*a-\*64-ja* = *Aswiai*, perhaps the aforementioned Hittite *a-aS-Su-wa 'Aššuwa,'* and possibly *A-SU-JA* in Linear A) are all represented in the Pylian archives, where they appear among those listed as dependents of the palace, receiving rations from the state.[51] *Do-e-ra* (= δοῦλος), perhaps privately-owned slaves, appear in tablets from Knossos, though not Pylos, while people referred to as *ra-wi-ja-ja* (= *\*lâwiaiai*) 'women taken as plunder' or 'captives' also appear in multiple Pylian tablets (PY Aa 807, Ab 596, and Ad 686), though unfortunately no mention is made of their homelands and they do not seem to appear in contemporary iconography.[52] Prehistorian Barbara Olsen has suggested that the lack of ethnic information and of association with specific tasks may mean that the *ra-wi-ja-ja* were more recently captured than their counterparts who do have such associations, and that the term therefore may have been used to designate new captives who were awaiting assignment, so to speak.[53]

The 2nd millennium BCE has been referred to as "a period when a veritable epidemic of run-away wives plagued the various civilizations [and when p]owerful, sea-oriented kingdoms relied on their navies to retrieve the errant spouses."[54] While this would fit well with the Homeric picture of Helen eloping with Paris and being pursued by a seaborne coalition of Achaeans, the evidence for such a situation is far less certain than it is for the taking as plunder of women, some of whom had probably previously been married, as well as for both the exile and the repatriation of royal wives. For example, while RS 18.06, the Ugaritic text cited as evidence for the "runaway wives" claim, does in fact mention the preparing of ships by King Ammiṭṭamru II to "capture and punish his sinful wife," the text actually seems to describe a mission to repatriate the woman in question, who had been exiled to Amurru for an unnamed crime.[55]

As might be expected, the theme of captured women appears repeatedly in Homer (for a representative sampling, see *Iliad* I, 32, 184, II, 226, VI, 456, IX, 125–140, 270–285, 477, XVI, 830–833, XIX, 295–302, XX, 193, XXIII, 259–261, and *Odyssey* iv, 259–264, vii, 103–106, ix, 41–42, xi, 400–403). It seems, then, as Classicist Sarah Morris put it, that "rather than the romantic recovery of native women like Helen, the enslavement of fresh laborers (as Cassandra and other Trojan women became the prize of Greek warriors in the epic tradition) was a serious objective." Raids would typically have resulted in the killing of men and the capturing of women and children, perhaps, according to one theory, to "bolster up a declining labour force" on the mainland.[56]

Consider also *Odyssey* xiv, 202–203, in which Odysseus claims to be himself the son of a woman who was purchased as a slave:

ἐμὲ δ᾽ ὠνητὴ τέκε μήτηρ
παλλακίς

a bought woman, a concubine,
was my mother.

*Odyssey* xiv, 202–203

How the hero's fictional mother was originally acquired, prior to her sale to Odysseus' father, is not mentioned. However, the precedent in Hittite and Linear B texts for Aḫḫiyawans taking female captives certainly raises the possibility that she came to Crete via a similar seaborne raid. Further, one Hittite inscription seems to recount the exile to Aḫḫiyawa of a Hittite Queen:

And while my father [was] (still) alive, [so-and-so . . .], and because (s)he [became hostile] to my mother, [ . . . ] he dispatched him/her to the Land of Aḫḫiyawa, beside [the sea].

AhT 12 (= CTH 214.12.A = KUB 14.2), §2[57]

The text is too fragmentary to be sure which Hittite king and queen it should be assigned to. The most likely candidate seems to be Muwatalli II, who ruled from 1295–1272 BC, and his wife Tanuḫepa. However, it could also fit as a reference to Suppiluliuma I (1350–1322 BCE) and his first wife Henti, or to Muršili II (1321–1295 BCE) and his Babylonian wife Tawananna.[58] Whomever the queen in question was, the fact that she was banished to Aḥḥiyawa suggests complicity on the part of the receiving polity, thereby adding an even greater layer of complexity to the relations between these entities, particularly with regard to the role and transfer of women between them.[59]

## EXISTENTIAL THREATS, PALATIAL DESTRUCTIONS, AND SEA PEOPLES

The regional collapses and sea changes that struck the Eastern Mediterranean in the years before and after 1200 BCE were every bit as remarkable as the internationalism that had marked the period before. Palaces, cities, and empires from the Aegean to Anatolia and the Levant were destroyed; migratory peoples and refugees were on the move by land and sea; Egypt's New Kingdom was set on an inexorable path toward decline; the ethnic composition of localities and territories was altered; and the socio-political and core-periphery economic systems which had fueled the opulent palatial world of the Late Bronze Age came to a relatively abrupt end around the turn of the 12th century. Ugarit has long been seen as a "type site" for the destructions of this time. This prosperous trading kingdom suffered a seemingly sudden devastation *circa* 1200 BCE, with pots left in kilns, arrowheads littering the streets, and the last correspondence of the king left unbaked and unsent. After its destruction, the site was permanently abandoned and ultimately forgotten by history until its rediscovery and subsequent excavation three thousand years later, in the 20th century CE.[60]

### A Complex Collapse

Dramatic as this seems, we now know that the events of this time were far more complex than the few lines of prose offered by Ramesses III (*"No land could stand before their arms, from Ḫatti, Kode, Karkemiš, Arzawa, and Alašiya on . . ."*),[61] which were long thought to accurately describe the events of these "Crisis Years" and the role of the Sea Peoples in them. As archaeologist Eric Cline wrote in his recent book *1177 BC: The Year Civilization Collapsed*:

> . . . the Sea Peoples may well have been responsible for some of the destruction that occurred at the end of the Late Bronze Age, but it is much more likely that a concatenation of events, both human and natural—including climate change and drought, seismic disasters known as earthquake storms, internal rebellions, and "systems collapse"—coalesced to create a "perfect storm" that brought this age to an end.[62]

The series of events that took place over a significant temporal period and across a wide geographic area, which have been referred to as a "watershed" event by one scholar and labeled with the catch-all of "the catastrophe" by another, did in fact leave in its wake an Aegean and Eastern Mediterranean world that bore little resemblance to that which had preceded it.[63] However, Ugarit only occupies one point along a broad spectrum of events and outcomes. Rather than facing total destruction and upheaval, some regions and polities, like the Phoenician coast in modern Lebanon and northern Israel, seem to have continued largely as before, albeit with a veneer of bureaucracy having been removed, which resulted in increased self-determination actualized though growth in international contacts.[64] In many areas, there were new cultures and new populations to be interacted with, and a complex process of identity and cultural negotiation to be engaged in by an indigenous people that was still very much present.

Though newcomers are visible in the material record at some sites (but hardly all), the engagement with material influences and the negotiation of status and identity that took place across this massive area in this period were incredibly diverse in nature. Some areas seem to have gained access to new elements of foreign material culture, either via trade or the movement of peoples. Others coexisted with newcomers, some of whom bore with them Aegean-style material culture which has been variously connected to the Greek mainland, the Interface, and/or Cyprus. An example of this is Kazanli Höyük in Cilicia, where, in the late 13th or early 12th century BCE, there appears locally-manufactured pottery which is in the Aegean style, but whose closest stylistic correlates are found on Cyprus and in the East Aegean.[65]

At Tell Afis in Syria, indigenous occupation is clearly continuous Iron I despite a 12th century destruction, albeit with a more agro-pastoral focus and temporarily debased architecture and organization. Here, Aegean-style table wares and cylindrical loomweights appear alongside indigenous cooking and storage methods.[66] This may suggest cohabitation with elements of an intrusive population, but if not, it certainly suggests—at very least—communication and exchange.[67] In the 'Amuq Plain, which will be discussed in greater detail below, the previously uninhabited site of Tell Ta'yinat shows an intrusive presence at the beginning of the Iron Age, complete with rolled loomweights and Aegean-style pottery that shares characteristics with Cypriot ceramics of the Late Cypriot (LC) IIIB Late-LC IIIC transition.[68] Still other sites, like Kinet Höyük and Kilise Tepe in Cilicia, incorporated newcomers who displayed different orientations altogether, while the appearance and spread on the Syrian coast of the Cypriot "cooking pot à la *stéatite*," or band-handled cooking pot, demonstrates further interaction with foreign material culture in the region.[69]

At the other end of the spectrum, some of these Aegean-affiliated groups settled in relatively large numbers and created new polities, such as those on the southern coastal plain of Canaan that came to make up *Philistia*. Even within and across these, though, significant variance can be seen in the nature of both the intrusive material culture and the relationships with the indigenous population.[70] This is partly due to differences in social negotiation and between new and old populations and to the increasingly-recognized complexity of their migration. It is also due to the diverse nature of the Sea Peoples themselves, as reflected in the material culture of sites in Cilicia, the 'Amuq, Philistia, and in areas of the coastal Levant between them.[71]

## Collapse of the Mycenaean Order

Already around 1230 BCE (the transition from Late Helladic IIIB:1 to IIIB:2), signs can be seen of growing unease within the Mycenaean palaces, perhaps in response to looming external threats. At Mycenae and Tiryns, for example, walls were extended, and additional domestic buildings were built within the settlements' citadels.[72] The famed Lions Gate of Mycenae, the fortifications that surround the Upper and Lower Citadels at Tiryns, and the walls around Midea were constructed at this time, amid what has been called a program of "retrenchment and accelerating regression" in the Mycenaean world.[73] At both of these sites, and at Athens, this retrenchment apparently included making structural alterations to defenses in order to ensure access to potable water from safely within the city walls, while in Boeotia, the citadel of Gla was destroyed and abandoned.[74] At Pylos and Mycenae, storage facilities in close proximity to the palace were expanded in the 13th century, perhaps to bring them under closer control of the palatial authorities in response to a growing menace or anticipated attack.

In keeping with the modern uncertainty about the cause and effect of this growing menace and final collapse, however, it has also been suggested that another purpose of these fortifications—or a result of them—was to insulate the ruler from the masses, possibly in response to unrest driven by growing inequality in status and lifestyle.[75] Whatever the driving force behind these increased fortifications, Mycenaean society as a whole seems to have been reaching its tipping point as the end of the LH IIIB approached. This was exacerbated by the economic fragility of the palatial system itself, as historian Sigrid Deger-Jalkotzy has noted:

> [T]oo specialized and too centralizing, the Mycenaean palace economies apparently did not react adequately to disruptive factors. . . . Some scholars hold that the palaces reacted to economic pressure and unstable conditions by tightening

political control over their territories and by further centralizing the economy. If so, a rigid centralization must have added to the vulnerability of the system and prepared the ground for a collapse as soon as the center was hit.[76]

The primary victims of the collapse at the end of the LH IIIB seem to have been the palaces and the ruling structure that had marked the Aegean Bronze Age, neither of which would be seen again.[77] Several sites were at least partially destroyed by fire, including Mycenae, Tiryns, and Midea in the Argolid; Dimini in Thessaly; Thebes and Orchomenos in Boeotia; and Pylos in Messenia.[78] Settlement patterns also changed, with the number of inhabited sites on mainland Greece shrinking significantly and long-occupied areas like Laconia, Thessaly, and Messenia being abandoned. Other sites were repurposed, as can be seen in the partial reoccupation of the citadels at Mycenae, Tiryns, and Midea, in the nucleated settlements that arose in the Argolid and on Crete, and in the increased post-palatial prosperity of sites like Lefkandi on Euboea.[79] Extensive theories have been put forward about the ultimate cause of the collapse, including invasion, economics, seismic events, revolt, climate change, systems collapse, or a combination of these and other factors; however, much like the crises at the end of the Bronze Age in the wider Eastern Mediterranean, the ultimate cause remains, and will continue to remain, a matter of debate.[80]

Linear B tablets from the last days of Pylos may serve as evidence for these events and the attempted response to them. This key palatial center in the Peloponnese was destroyed in the late 13th or early 12th century (Transitional LH IIIB:2–IIIC Early). As noted above, it was subsequently abandoned along with much of the Messenian hinterland.[81] Three well-known sets of tablets, commonly grouped together, have been seen by some scholars as communicating an effort to coordinate a large-scale defensive action or evacuation in response to an existential threat from the coast. Given the fragmentary state of inscriptional evidence from the last days of Mycenaean Greece, though, we cannot be certain whether the activities described here represent a state of emergency or simply business as usual.[82] The first group, known as the *o-ka* tablets, lists the disposition of military personnel, perhaps in the city's waning days. They document 770 watchers being assigned to the task of guarding 10 coastal sites, with each detachment led by a high-ranking individual known as an *e-qe-ta*.[83] The second, a single tablet (PY Jn 829, or text 829 of the Jn series from Pylos), records the collection of bronze from Pylian temples for the purpose of forging "points for spears and javelins"—another martial reference, and a further suggestion of increased military readiness in response to an increasing threat.

## The Pylian 'Rower Tablets'

The third relevant record from Pylos is comprised of three texts (PY An 610, An 1, and An 724) commonly grouped together and referred to as "rower tablets" for their references to *e-re-ta* (= ἐρέται) 'rowers,' or in the case of An 724 *ki-ti-ta o-pe-ro-ta e-re-e* 'landowner who owes service as a rower,' being called up to man what was most likely a fleet of oared galleys.[84] As we have seen, consensus about the nature (and even the existence) of the "crisis" reflected by the Pylian tablets is elusive. An attempt at middle ground on this issue has been made with the suggestion that these texts be viewed as reflecting a "general climate of wariness in the weeks immediately preceding the destruction," which came about as a result of "a very human threat."[85] The apparent lack of fortifications surrounding Pylos in the Late Bronze Age has been a lingering question, particularly in light of the city having been in what may be seen as a state of emergency in the time just before its demise.[86] Though it remains possible that Pylos was unwalled at this time, a 2.5 meter wide, 60 meter long topographic anomaly was identified during geophysical exploration in the late 1990s, which "runs roughly parallel to the contours on the steep northwestern side of [a] ridge and . . . continues beyond a modern two-meter-high terrace . . . may well indicate the remains of a massive fortification."[87] The date of this potential structure, however, remains unclear.

The type of ships referenced in the Rower Tablets will be discussed further below. If indeed they do reflect a palatial response to a coastal threat, it seems likely that they signify one of three courses of action. The first is a *general evacuation*: though the depopulation of Messenia in the wake of the palatial destruction is suggestive of some organized movement of peoples from the area at this time, an evacuation by flotilla was unlikely to have been logistically feasible.[88] Likewise, should the impetus for such an evacuation have come from the coast, rather than overland, it does not seem logical that Pylians would have chosen to sail ships laden with people, belongings, and livestock directly into the teeth of an existential *seaborne* threat.

The second option is an *elite evacuation*—an evacuation organized by, and limited to, palatial elites who sought to escape as their situation became precarious late in the 13th century BCE. There is little doubt that the highest level of Mycenaean Greece's stratified society suffered most from the collapse of the palatial system; after all, "the key elements lost in the disasters were the trappings of those in power: the *megaron* proper, the enriching contact with other cultures, the elaborate administrative system, and, with nothing to record, the art of writing."[89] Others have suggested that Mycenaean elites may have fled to the Cyclades either in advance or in the wake of the destructions in the late 13th and early 12th centuries (Late Helladic IIIB:2 and IIIB-IIIC transition): "The Cycladic islands, not very far from the main Mycenaean palaces of the Peloponnese, were the obvious places of refuge for the refugee *wanaktes* after the collapse of the Mycenaean empire. They could find refuge quickly in small ships and, if need be, in successive waves. There were no major urban centres in these islands and they would not, therefore, feel threatened by the local population."[90]

The site of Koukounaries on the northwestern coast of Paros, founded around 1200 BCE (in the transitional LH IIIB:2-IIIC Early), may be an example of such a site.[91] Its acropolis boasts a "mansion" or palatial structure, complete with storerooms and prestige items (bronze, worked ivory, a bit for horses, weapons, and more) that support both prosperity and trading activity.[92] The site was destroyed by fire in the mid-12th century (LH IIIC Developed), but remained inhabited until around 1100 BCE. The acropolis seems to have been fortified, though it has also been suggested that these "fortifications" were actually terraces put in place for structural support. It has been suggested that the arrival on Paros of high-status immigrants from the Greek mainland resulted in the transference of a smaller form of the palatial system from the mainland to the islands. Whether the Pylian tablets are accepted as referencing just such an event is dependent, of course, on many factors, including whether time would have been found amidst such frantic preparations to commemorate them in writing.[93] The lack of written records attesting their presence at Paros and other possible island refuge sites also seems to contradict the theory that the deposed *wanaktes* and their retinues relocated and re-established their rulerships, as it was these elites who controlled the art of writing in the Mycenaean world.[94]

A third possible purpose of the Rower Tablets is a *coordinated naval action.* These tablets may document a calling-up of crew members in preparation for a direct, and ultimately unsuccessful, naval action against a seaborne threat, either from within or from without. We shall address this topic in more depth shortly.

## Chapter Five

# The Sea Peoples and the Egyptian Records

An increase in anxiety about maritime threats is seen elsewhere in the Eastern Mediterranean, as well, including in Egyptian inscriptions and reliefs and in texts from the last years of Ḫatti and Ugarit. The Bronze Age was never free from such threats, as we have already seen; however, it seems that an increase in "the scale of [seaborne] movement" as this period drew to a close was accompanied by a decline in "the ability of the established powers to cope with the problem."[1] Evidence from several sources, many of which have been cited above, suggests that seaborne threats increased in number and severity as the age of Bronze gave way to that of Iron, perhaps playing a central role in the widespread destructions and overall collapse of the palatial system that marked this watershed period in Mediterranean history.

## THE SEA PEOPLES AND RAMESSES III

Just where the so-called 'Sea Peoples' fit into these events has long been a matter of shifting perspective and fierce debate. Were they the primary instigators of the collapse that marked the end of the Bronze Age in the Eastern Mediterranean, as Ramesses III seems to suggest? Were they simply fellow victims? Were they displaced people(s), who migrated eastward amidst the collapse of the known world? Or were they simply local opportunists who used the sudden removal of the top stratum of their society to their own advantage? As the study of this period and its people has become more nuanced, it has become increasingly recognized that each is partly true, but none is sufficient to explain the situation on its own.

## Sea Peoples at Medinet Habu

The majority of documentary evidence for the Sea Peoples comes from the Ramesside period in Egypt, or the 13th and early 12th centuries BCE. As noted earlier, the most famous representations of these warriors come from Ramesses III's "mansion of a million years" at Medinet Habu, among whose many monumental reliefs are two massive battles with the Sea Peoples—one on land and one at sea (Figs. 5.1 and 5.2). These reliefs, carved on the exterior north wall of the temple, are part of a seven-part sequence that depicts:

1. The equipping of troops for the campaign against the Sea Peoples;
2. The march to "Djahi," where the land battle is said to have taken place;
3. The land battle;
4. A lion hunt;
5. The sea battle;
6. Ramesses III receiving Sea Peoples prisoners; and
7. Ramesses III presenting prisoners (both Sea Peoples and Libyans) to the Theban Triad of Amun, Mut, and Khonsu.

While the lion hunt initially appears to be a *non sequitur* within this series, Egyptologist David O'Connor has suggested that this highly stylized scene

**Figure 5.1.   Ramesses III's land battle against the Sea Peoples, from the north exterior wall at Medinet Habu**
Epigraphic Survey. 1930. *Medinet Habu I: Earlier Historical Records of Ramses III.* Plate 34. Courtesy of the Oriental Institute of the University of Chicago.

**Figure 5.2. Ramesses III's sea battle against the Sea Peoples, from the north exterior wall at Medinet Habu**
Epigraphic Survey. 1930. *Earlier Historical Records of Ramses III*. Plate 39. Courtesy of the Oriental Institute of the University of Chicago.

was actually the most important of these images because of its symbolic value: the Sea Peoples are equated metaphorically with lions, thus "suggest[ing] the Egyptians found the Sea Peoples especially challenging opponents, as compared to their more traditional enemies." He continues:

> This symbolic representation of order overcoming chaos emphasizes the degree to which the historical events involved were equated with generalized cosmological processes. . . . Next in importance come the two great battle scenes, immediately flanking the lion-hunt; this placement, as much as the complex compositional structure of both, reinforces the equation between these real events, and the imagined cosmic ones represented by the lion hunt.[2]

The depictions of land and sea combat against the Sea Peoples are significant both for the information that they provide and for their clear importance to Ramesses III himself: at over 400 square meters, they account for nearly 40 percent of the surface area covered by all battle reliefs at Medinet Habu.[3] The land battle depicts ox-carts along with women and children of what seem to be multiple ethnicities amidst the Sea Peoples warriors, suggesting that the "invasion" may have been part of a migratory movement from the Aegean and western Anatolia.[4]

There also seem to be unarmed youths wearing the same feathered headdresses as the adult males—perhaps adolescents in the process of initiation into adulthood.[5] Horn-helmed warriors, likely Sherden, also appear in this scene, as well as in the march to Djahi and the lion hunt, but they are shown in their more common setting—as members of the Egyptian army. Only feathered headdresses are found among the prisoners presented to Ramesses III, and then by Ramesses III to the Theban Triad; however, in the naval battle, horn-helmed warriors are depicted only among the enemy, where they man two of the five Sea Peoples ships, with feathered headdresses accounting for the other three. The visual detail of the naval battle, considered the first ever depicted, will be discussed further below.

Each relief in the sequence is accompanied by an inscription, relevant portions of which are presented below:

Words spoken by the officials, the companions, and the leaders of the infantry and chariotry: "Thou art Re, as thou risest over Egypt, for when [thou] appearest the Two Lands live. Great is thy strength in the heat of the Nine [Bows], and thy battle cry (reaches) to the circuit of the sun. The shadow of thy arm is over thy troops, so that they walk confident in thy strength. Thy heart is stout; thy plans are excellent; so that no land can stand firm when [thou] art seen. Glad is the heart of Egypt forever, for she has a heroic protector. The heart of the land of Temeh is removed; the Peleset are in suspense, hidden in their towns, by the strength of thy father Amon, who assigned to thee every [land] as a gift.

Inscription Accompanying the Equipping of Troops[6]

. . . His majesty sets out in valor and strength to destroy the rebellious countries. [. . .]
His majesty sets out for [Djahi] like unto Montu, to crush every country that violates his frontier. His troops are like bulls ready on the field of battle; his horses are like falcons in the midst of small birds [before] the Nine Bows, bearing victory. Amon, is august father, is a shield for him; King of Upper and Lower Egypt, Ruler of the Nine Bows, Lord of the Two Lands. . .

Inscription Accompanying the March to Djahi[7]

. . . awe at the sight of him, as when Set rages, overthrowing the enemy in front of the sun bark, trampling down the plains and hill-countries, (which are) prostrate, beaten from tail to head before his horses. His heat burns up their bodies like a flame. Hacked up is their flesh to the duration [of eternity].

Inscription Accompanying the Land Battle[8]

The lions are in travail and flee to their land. The lion, the lord of victory, concealed, going forward, and making a conquest—his heart is full of his might; stout of heart, relying upon his (strong) arm, able to enter straight ahead against the one who assails him when he attacks; the lion, destroying in — —. His arrow has penetrated into their bodies. They [gather] themselves together in front of [him, (as) wretch]ed as jackals, while they howl like a cat. The strength of his majesty is like a flame in their limbs, so that their hearts have burned up because of his heat. A mighty ruler; there is not one like unto him, for his strong arm has protected Egypt. Montu is his [protection], repelling his enemies and averting all evil (from) before [him]. The soldiers are glad; the officials rejoice;

the guardsmen exult to the sky, for [their] lord is mighty like Montu, and his battle cry and his fame are like (those of) Baal. All lands are under his feet like Re forever; King of Upper and Lower Egypt: Usermare-Meriamon; Son of Re: Ramesses III given life.

### Inscription Accompanying the Lion Hunt[9]

. . . Now then, the northern countries which were in their islands were quivering in their bodies. They penetrated the channels of the river-mouths. Their nostrils have ceased (to function, so) their desire is to breathe the breath. His majesty has gone forth like a whirlwind against them, fighting on the battlefield like a runner. The dread of him and the terror of him have entered into their bodies. They are capsized and overwhelmed where they are. Their heart is taken away, their soul is flown away. Their weapons are scattered upon the sea. His arrow pierces whom of them he may have wished, and the fugitive is become one fallen into the water. His majesty is like an enraged lion, attacking his assailant with his paws; plundering on his right hand and powerful on his left hand, like Set destroying the serpent "Evil of Character." It is Amon-Re who has overthrown for him the lands and has crushed for him every land under his feet; King of Upper and Lower Egypt, Lord of the Two Lands: Usermare-Meriamon.

### Inscription Accompanying the Naval Battle[10]

. . . As for the countries who came from their land in their isles in the midst of the sea, as they were (coming) forward toward Egypt, their hearts relying upon their hands, a net was prepared for them, to ensnare them. They that entered into the Nile mouths were caught, fallen into the midst of it, pinioned in their places, butchered, and their bodies hacked up. I have caused that you see my strength, which was in that which my arm has done, while I was alone. My arrow hit the mark without fail, while my arms and my hand were steadfast. I was like a falcon in the midst of small fowl, for my talon did not fail upon their heads. Amon-Re was on my right and on my left, and the awe of him and the terror of him were in my person. Rejoice ye, for that which I commanded is come to pass, and my counsels and my plans are perfected. Amon-Re repels my foe and gives to me every land into my grasp.

### Inscription Accompanying the Reception of Prisoners[11]

. . . I went forth that I might plunder the Nine Bows and slay all lands. Not a land stood firm before me, but I cut off their root. I have returned in valor, my arms (laden) with captives, the leaders of every land, through the decrees which issued from thy mouth. That which thou has promised has come to pass. Thy mighty sword is mine, a reinforcement that I may overthrow every one who assails me and the lands may behold me (only) to tremble, for I am like Montu before them. [. . .]

Words spoken by the great fallen ones of T[j]ekker, who are in the grasp of his majesty, in praise of this good god, the Lord of the Two Lands: User-mare-Meriamon: "Great is thy strength, O mighty king, great Sun of Egypt! Greater is thy sword than a mountain of metal, while the awe of thee is like (that of) Baal. Give to us the breath, that we may breathe it, the life, that which is in thy grasp forever!

Inscription Accompanying the Presentation of Captives[12]

These events are usually situated in Ramesses III's eighth regnal year (ca. 1175) because of their connection to an inscription from the temple's first court:

Year 8 under the majesty of (Ramesses III). . . The foreign countries made a conspiracy in their islands. All at once the lands were removed and scattered in the fray. No land could stand before their arms, from Ḫatti, Kode, Karkemiš, Arzawa, and Alašiya on, being cut off at [one time]. A camp [was set up] in one place in Amor [Amurru]. They desolated its people, and its land was like that which has never come into being. They were coming forward toward Egypt, while the flame was being prepared before them. Their confederation was the Philistines, Tjeker, Shekelesh, Denye(n), and Wesesh, lands united. They laid their hands upon the lands as far as the circuit of the earth, their hearts confident and trusting: 'Our plans will succeed!'

Now the heart of this god, the Lord of the Gods, was prepared and ready to ensnare them like birds . . . I organized my frontier in Djahi, prepared before them:—princes, commanders of garrisons, and maryanu. I have the river-mouths prepared like a strong wall, with warships, galleys, and coasters, (fully) equipped, for they were manned completely from bow to stern with valiant warriors carrying their weapons. The troops consisted of every picked man of Egypt. They were like lions roaring upon the mountaintops. The chariotry con-sisted of runners of picked men, of every good and capable chariot-warrior. The horses were quivering in every part of their bodies, prepared to crush the foreign countries under their hoofs. I was the valiant Montu, standing fast at their head, so that they might gaze upon the capturing of their hands. . .

Those who reached my frontier, their seed is not, their heart and their soul are finished forever and ever. Those who came forward together on the sea, the full flame was in front of them at the river-mouths, while a stockade of lances surrounded them on the shore. They were dragged in, enclosed, and prostrated on the beach, killed, and made into heaps from tail to head. Their ships and their goods were as if fallen into the water. . .

Great Inscription of Year 8[13]

These land and sea battles are also mentioned in several other inscriptions, spanning years five to twelve of the pharaoh's reign—two-thirds of the time covered by the temple's records overall, as it was constructed in Ramesses III's twelfth year. This scattering of Sea Peoples appearances across both time and space at Medinet Habu could be seen either as reinforcing their importance, or suggesting that—much like the raids for which we have already seen evidence—encounters with these groups were a repeated affair. If the latter, then the sequence of reliefs dedicated to the land and sea battles may be representative of several much smaller conflicts, although it could also denote a pair of major engagements toward which the previous skirmishes had been building.

Ramesses III's fifth year is most commonly associated with the first of his two (alleged) campaigns against the Libyans. In the reliefs associated with this campaign, as in those depicting the second Libyan campaign (situated in regnal year 11), feather-hatted and horn-helmed warriors are shown fighting on the side of the pharaoh, rather than as members of a Libyan coalition.[14] However, the Great Inscription of Year 5 does also mention the Peleset and Sikils/Tjekker by name and refers to a combined land and sea invasion, and the determinatives used in the text feature the characteristic feathered headdresses of the (non-Sherden) Sea Peoples:

> The northern countries shivered in their bodies, namely the Philistines and the [Sikils]. They [were] cut off [from] their land, coming, their soul finished. They were tuhir-warriors on land, and another (group) on the Great Green (sea). Those who came by [land] were overthrown and slain [. . . .]; Amen-Re was after them, destroying them.
>
> Those who entered the Nile mouths were like birds snared in the net, made into a mash (?) [. . . .], their arms; and their hearts removed, taken away, no longer in their bodies. Their leaders were brought away and slain; they were prostrate and made into pinioned [captives . . . .]. They [cried out] saying, 'There's a charging lion, wild, powerful, seizing with his claw. A Unique Lord has arisen in Egypt, un[equaled], a warrior precise (with the) arrow, who cannot miss. [. . . .] the ends of the outer ocean.
>
> They tremble with one accord, (saying): 'Where can we (go)?' They sue for peace, coming humbly through for fear of him, knowing (that) their strength is no (more), and that their bodies are enfeebled, (for) the renown of His Majesty is before them daily.

Great Inscription of Year 5[15]

At the front of the temple is a poorly preserved stele that recounts, among other topics, the defeat of foreign invaders, which includes further mention of the Sea Peoples:

> . . . I overthrew the Tjek[er], the land of Pele[set], the Danuna, the [W]eshesh, and the Shekelesh; I destroyed the breath of the Mesh[wesh], —, Sebet, —, devastated in their (own) land. I am fine of plan and excellent of—. . .

South Rhetorical Stele of Year 12[16]

Another inscription accompanies a relief showing Ramesses III at the head of three lines of Sea Peoples prisoners, all in feathered headdresses, whom he is preparing to present to the gods Amon and Mut. The text says in part:

> . . . The sword is mine as a shield, that I may slap the plains and hill-countries which violate my frontier. Thou causest the awe of me to be great in the hearts of their chiefs, the terror of me and the fear of me before them. I have carried away their runners, pinioned in my grasp, to present them to thy ka, O my august father! My strong arm has overthrown [those] who came to exalt themselves: the Peleset, the Denyen, and the Shekelesh. Thy strong arm is that which is before me, overthrowing their seed. . .
> [. . .]
> Words spoken by the fallen ones of the Denyen: "Breath, breath, thou good ruler, great of strength like Montu in the midst of Thebes!"
> [. . .]
> Words spoken by the fallen ones of Peleset: "Give us the breath for our nostrils, thou King, son of Amon!"
>
> Presentation of Sea Peoples Captives to Amon and Mut[17]

Finally, the temple's Eastern High Gate features two rows of bound captives, each of which serves as the determinative for his description. The text on and above the northern relief reads:

> Words spoken by the chiefs of northern foreign countries whom His Majesty brought away captive: "Breath, breath, O mighty King, Horus, powerful of falchion! Give us the breath which you give that we may live [and relate your prowess].
> The vile chief of Khatti as captive.
> The vile chief of Amor.
> The leader of the enemy of Tjeker.
> The Sherden of the Sea.
> The leader of the Sha[su-Bedouin].
> The leader of the enemy of Pe[leset].
>
> Inscription on the Eastern High Gate[18]

As these inscriptions show, five different groups of Sea Peoples are named at Medinet Habu: the *Pršt* 'Peleset' (= Philistines), *T3k3r* (also *T3kk3r*) 'Tjekker' or 'Sikils,' *Š3krwš3* 'Shekelesh,' *W3š3š3* 'Weshesh,' and *D3iniwn3* 'Denyen' or 'Danuna' (who have at times been linked to the Δαναοι). A later inscription of Ramesses III, on a rhetorical stele in Chapel C at Deir el-Medineh, also mentions the Peleset and the *Twrš* 'Teresh'—among up to 24 groups, all but two of which have been lost—as defeated enemies who had "sailed in the midst of t[he s]ea."[19] The contradiction between the Medinet

Habu inscription and the Deir el-Medineh stele—namely, the appearance of the Teresh on the latter, and their absence from the former—is similar to the changes seen in another, later document, the Great Harris Papyrus (Papyrus Harris I; British Museum 10053). This posthumous *res gestae* of Ramesses III omits the Shekelesh from the narrative of the pharaoh's encounters with the Sea Peoples, replacing them instead with the Sherden:

> . . . I extended all the frontiers of Egypt and overthrew those who had attacked them from their lands. I slew all the Denyen in their islands, while the Tjeker and the Philistines were made ashes. The Sherden and the Weshesh of the Sea were made nonexistent, captured all together and brought in captivity to Egypt like the sands of the shore. I settled them in strongholds, bound in my name. Their military classes were as numerous as hundred-thousands. I assigned portions for them all with clothing and provisions from the treasuries and granaries every year.

> Great Harris Papyrus[20]

For many decades, the Great Harris Papyrus text was held to support the belief that Ramesses III settled the Sea Peoples in general—and Philistines in particular—in Canaan following their defeat in the land and sea battles memorialized at Medinet Habu.[21] However, much like the aforementioned assumptions that have long underpinned scholarly readings of the *Onomasticon of Amenope*, this interpretation is not supported by the text itself. Instead, the Great Harris Papyrus states unequivocally that those who were captured (in the most literal reading, only the *šrdn wšš n p3 ym* 'Sherden and Weshesh of the Sea') were brought *to Egypt* (*kmt*), where they were "settled . . . in strongholds" (*nḥtw*). Such a situation was also described by Odysseus following his failed Egyptian raid, which will be discussed in more detail below:

> αὐτίκ' ἀπὸ κρατὸς κυνέην εὕτυκτον ἔθηκα
> καὶ σάκος ὤμοιϊν, δόρυ δ' ἔκβαλον ἔκτοσε χειρός:
> αὐτὰρ ἐγὼ βασιλῆος ἐναντίον ἤλυθον ἵππων
> καὶ κύσα γούναθ' ἑλών: ὁδ' ἐρύσατο καί μ' ἐλέησεν,
> ἐς δίφρον δέ μ' ἕσας ἄγεν οἴκαδε δάκρυ χέοντα.

> Straightway I put off from my head my well-wrought helmet, and the shield from off my shoulders, and let the spear fall from my hand, and went toward the chariot horses of the king. I clasped, and kissed his knees, and he delivered me, and took pity on me, and, setting me in his chariot, took me weeping to his home.

> *Odyssey* xiv, 276–280

As we shall see, this is also supported by further documentary evidence for Sherden in particular having been incorporated into the Pharaoh's army and stationed in strongholds—once again, in Egypt.[22]

## THE SEA PEOPLES AND RAMESSES THE GREAT

Though he boasts the best-known of our available inscriptions and images, as we have seen, Ramesses III was not the first pharaoh to encounter groups associated with the Sea Peoples. A century prior, in the formulaic Aswan stele of his second year (ca. 1277 BCE), Ramesses II claimed among other conquests to have "destroyed" [*fḫ*; also 'captured'] the warriors of the Great Green (Sea)," so that Lower Egypt can "spend the night sleeping peacefully."[23] The Tanis II rhetorical stele, which, as we saw above, mentions the defeat and impressment of seaborne Sherden warriors, is frequently assumed to be connected to the same battle as that referenced in the Aswan stele. There is no clear evidence that this is the case, however: the aggressor is not named in the Aswan inscription, and as noted above, various groups seem to have raided the coasts of the Eastern Mediterranean with relative frequency during this period.

### Defending the Egyptian Coast

Shortly after their defeat at the hands of Ramesses the Great, Sherden soldiers appear in relief as members of the Egyptian army, perhaps having been pressed into service. Judging from written records, this coincides with a dissipation of the threat to Egypt from this and other Sea Peoples groups, which seems to have lasted for the remainder of Ramesses II's reign. The defeat and capture of Sherden and other raiders may have contributed to this, as may a series of forts established by Ramesses II in the western delta and along the North African coastal road. This line of forts stretched from Memphis to the Mediterranean coast and as far west as Zawiyet Umm el-Rakham, some 300 km from Alexandria, likely serving multiple purposes, such as protecting water sources and serving as depots or processing centers into Egypt from beyond her borders.[24]

However, whatever their additional activities, it seems likely that one of the main purposes of these forts was to defend the desert coast and the fertile Nile delta from restless, eastward-looking Libyans, marauding Sea Peoples, or a combination of both.[25] The threat of seaborne raiders has been noted, and will be further discussed shortly; however, we should note that there was a growing hostility between Egypt and its Libyan neighbors at this time, as well. Both the 19th and 20th Egyptian dynasties dedicated significant time and resources to limiting the eastward push of Libyan tribes (Tjemeh, Tjehenu, Kehek, Meshwesh, Libu, and others), as can especially be seen in the records of Merneptah and Ramesses III. This effort ultimately failed, as Libyans eventually settled in the western delta in force, and the 22nd dynasty (10th–8th centuries BCE) began a period in which Egypt was ruled by Libyan pharaohs, beginning with a Meshwesh, Shoshenq I.

## *The Fortress of Zawiyet Umm el-Rakham*

The defensive role of these forts seems particularly relevant for Zawiyet Umm el-Rakham, a fort established at the western edge of the Egyptian frontier that has been grimly described as an "isolated military outpost reared against a backdrop of near total emptiness."[26] As noted above, Zawiyet sat on the Marmarican coast nearly 300 km from Alexandria, but it was a scant 20 km west of the small, lagooned site of Marsa Matruh, thought to have been the southwesternmost known point on the Late Bronze Age maritime trading circuit.[27] The relationship between Zawiyet and Marsa Matruh remains an open and interesting question. Matruh's heyday appears to have been the 14th century BCE, or the last third of the 18th Egyptian dynasty. Its decline, in turn, corresponds chronologically with Zawiyet Umm el-Rakham's establishment in the 13th century (the Late Bronze Age maritime trade network will be discussed in more detail below).

A massive site nearly 20,000 m² in size, with a plastered glacis and heavily fortified gate, the fort's imposing nature against the largely barren landscape is contradicted by evidence for its residents' peaceful interactions with the native population surrounding it. Based on the scale of the fortress, which incorporated between 1.3 and 1.8 million bricks, the excavator has argued that the time and effort required for construction, and the necessary cultivation of land around it referred to in inscriptions, would have required a docile indigenous population in the surrounding area at the very least, if not the active participation of that population as a labor force.[28] A significant number of foreign imports have been found at Zawiyet, including Canaanite amphorae, Cypriot base-ring juglets, and Minoan and Mycenaean coarseware stirrup jars.[29] These facts, in combination with the aforementioned evidence for increased piratical activity in the Eastern Mediterranean around this time, may suggest that Zawiyet Umm el-Rakham was constructed both to defend Egypt's westernmost flank against invasion, and to provide a fortified replacement for the maritime trade network's most remote node.

While inscriptional evidence demonstrates how devastating seaborne raids on unprotected coastal outposts could be, the Tanis II stele and some of Odysseus' own tales, which we shall discuss below, show the flip side of that coin: the danger to raiding parties that could come from contact with regular troops, or from loitering long enough that a crowd could be raised to fight them. Thus, Zawiyet may have stood as a deterrent against raids, providing a heavily fortified and highly defensible site for direct importation of the goods being traded on the Eastern Mediterranean circuit. However, it is worth taking a closer look at just how much a part of the network Matruh might have been, particularly given the non-native character of Bates's Island, the settlement excavated there, which rests on a small island in the easternmost of the site's lagoons.

What was there to be gained, one might ask, from setting up a trading outpost in such a remote location? The site was far from natural resources or valuable commodities, and it seems unlikely that an indigenous population largely made up of nomadic pastoralists would have been major trading partners. In light of this, it has recently been suggested that Marsa Matruh was not a trading outpost *per se* at all, but that its naturally protected harbor and system of lagoons was used as a base for sea raiders like the Sherden and others. As we shall discuss further below, in his Second Cretan Lie, Odysseus follows a direct, or "blue water," route from Crete to Egypt to conduct his raid on the Nile delta, rather than traveling south from Crete and east via the Marmarican coast. However, the value of a protected harbor or inlet which could provide shelter and concealment, and which could support the staging of maritime operations, would have been valuable to any seafarers, including (and perhaps especially) pirates. Other coastal sites around the Eastern Mediterranean and Aegean seem to have been used in such fashion, as we shall see below with regard to Crete and Cyprus. The chronology of inhabitation on Bates's Island fits with letters like EA 38 and inscriptions like that of Amenhotep son of Hapu, which describe similar activity and precautions taken against it. Further, as we have seen, the site's abandonment seems to coincide directly with the establishment of Zawiyet Umm el-Rakham and the rest of Ramesses II's coastal outposts.[30]

## THE SEA PEOPLES RISE AGAIN: THE REIGN OF MERNEPTAH

Effective as they may have been for the duration of his lengthy reign, Ramesses II's line of fortresses does not appear to have survived long past his death in 1213 BCE (Zawiyet, for example, seems to have been abandoned by Merneptah's fifth year).[31] As if on cue, as these defenses went out of use, Sea Peoples—Sherden included—arose once again in Pharaonic records, this time in the accounts of Ramesses' son and successor Merneptah (1213–1203

BCE). An example of this can be seen in a fragmentary passage from Papyrus Anastasi II:

> . . . Sherden of the Great Green [Sea] that are captives of His Majesty, they are equipped with all their weapons in the court, and bring a tribute of gallons of barley and provender for their chariotry, as well as chopped straw.

P. Anastasi II, Verso, Frag. Text 5[32]

The threat to Egypt became much more immediate in Merneptah's fifth regnal year (ca. 1207 BCE), when a migratory coalition tens of thousands strong of Libyans and Sea Peoples invaded from the west, managing to occupy a portion of the western delta for one month before being routed by the pharaoh's army in the six-hour Battle of Perire. The battle is recounted in two inscriptions, the Athribis Stele and the monumental Great Karnak Inscription:

> Year 5, third month of third season, third day, under the majesty of King [Merneptah] . . . Re himself has cursed the people since they crossed into [Egypt] with one accord . . . They are delivered to the sword in the hand of Merneptahd-Hotephirma. . . [Pharaoh's] fame against the land of Temeh . . . and how they speak of his victories in the land of Me[shwesh] . . . making their camps into wastes of the Red Land, taking—every herb that came forth from their fields. No field grew, to keep alive . . . The families of Libya are scattered upon the dykes like mice—. There is found among them no place of [refuge] . . . every survivor among them [is carried off as a living captive]. They live on herbs like [wild] cattle—. . .

| | |
|---|---|
| . . . Ekwesh [of] the countries of the sea, whom had brought the wretched [fallen chief of Libya, whose] hands [were carried off] | 2,201 [+x] men |
| Shekelesh | 200 men |
| Teresh | 722 [+ x] men |
| —Libya, and Sherden, slain | —men |

Athribis Stela[33]

> [Beginning of the Victory which His Majesty achieved in the land of Libya, . . .whom Mariyu son of Di]di [brought together]: Ekwesh, Teresh, Luk(k)a, Sherden, Shekelesh, Norther[ners, wander]ers of all lands, [. . . who slays] with his sword, by the power of his father Amun—(even) the King of South and North Egypt, Baienre Meriamun, Son of Re, Merenptah, given life.
> . . . Then(?) [. . . spies were sent out?. . ., then one came to inform His Majesty, In Year 5, 2nd Month of] Shomu, day <1?>, as follows:

'The despicable, fallen ruler of Libya (Libu), Mariyu son of Didi, has descended upon the land of Tejenu (in Libya), along with his troops, [. . . and also the . . .] Sherden, the Shekelesh, the Ekwesh, the Lukka and Teresh, and calling up ("taking") every single warrior and every able-bodied man of his country. He has brought (also) his wife and his children [. . .] chief [men] of the camp. He has reached the Western frontier in the terrain of Pi-Ir[u].'

"Then His majesty was angry with them (=Libyans) like a lion. . ."

"List of prisoners who were carried off from this land of Libya (Libu), together with the foreign countries that he had brought with him. . .

[Tursha], Sherden, Shekelesh, Ekwesh, of the foreign countries of the sea (ya(a)m), who had no fore[skin, slain, whose hands were carried off, because they had no] foreskins:

[. . .]

| | | |
|---|---|---|
| Shekelesh | 222 men | Making 250 hands |
| Teresh | 742 men | Making 790 hands |
| Sherden | — | [Making]— |

[Ek]wesh who had no foreskins, slain, whose hands were carried off, (for) they had no [foreskins]—

. . . Shekelesh and Teresh who came as enemies of Libya—

—Kehek, and Libyans, carried off as living prisoners 218 men

Great Karnak Inscription[34]

It is from the Great Karnak Inscription's reference to those who were *n n3 ḫas.wt n p3 ym* 'of the foreign countries of the sea' that we derive the modern term "Sea Peoples." As seen above, five of these groups are named in Merneptah's records, the Sherden (*Šrdn*), *Ikwš* 'Ekwesh,' *Škrš* 'Shekelesh,' *Twrš* 'Teresh,' and *Rkw* 'Lukka,' with all but the latter being referred to as *n p3 ym* 'of the sea.' The lack of such a designation for the Lukka is interesting because, as we saw in EA 38, they had been associated with seaborne raiding since at least the reign of Akhenaten over a century earlier. Perhaps this is connected to the fact that the most recent mention of this group in Egyptian records prior to Merneptah comes from Ramesses II's account of the Battle of Qidš, where they are listed among the land-based troops of the Hittite king Muwatalli II.

All five groups are also referred to in line one as *mḥ.t[yw] iw.w n t3.w nb.w* 'northerners coming from all lands.'[35] As mentioned earlier, identification of the Ekwesh with Achaeans (and Aḫḫiyawa) is both linguistically and geographically tempting, and has been accepted by some scholars. Perhaps the most important argument against the identification of Ekwesh as Achaeans is the apparent practice of circumcision by the former, who, according to the Great Karnak Inscription, "had no foreskins." While it may seem strange for pharaonic records to have made note of whether or not their enemies were circumcised, the Egyptian method of calculating enemy war dead consisted of collecting the phalli of the uncircumcised slain, and the hands of those who, like the Ekwesh, "had no foreskin," which were then sorted and counted by scribes. This process is shown in a relief at Medinet Habu showing the aftermath of the Libyan war of Ramesses III's fifth year, with the caption: "Total, hands: 22,659; Total, hands: 22,532; Total, phalli: 22,860; Total, hands: 22,535; Total, phalli: 22,535."[36]

The Ekwesh practice of circumcision stands in contrast to what is known of the cultural norms of Bronze Age Aegeans,[37] as well as of the *Peleset*, the later Sea Peoples group identified with the biblical Philistines whose lack of circumcision is well documented in the Hebrew Bible as a major point of differentiation with the Israelites (for example, in 1 Sam. 17:26, David asks, "Who is this uncircumcised Philistine, that he should defy the armies of the living God?").[38] Their engagement in this practice prompted John Hooker, a scholar of Mycenaean Greece, to declare that "it would be agreeable to have heard the last of the ludicrous equation of the circumcised Ekwesh with [Achaeans]."[39]

Unlike the Great Karnak inscription, the Athribis Stele applies the epithet "of the sea" only to the Ekwesh. The other two inscriptional references to this battle, on the Cairo Column and Heliopolis Victory Column, contain between them the mention of only one Sea Peoples group, the Shekelesh, followed by "and every foreign country."[40] Three of the Sea Peoples named by Merneptah are also found in the records of Ramesses III, though each appears in a different source: the *Shekelesh* at Medinet Habu, the *Sherden* in the Great Harris Papyrus, and the *Teresh* in the Deir el-Medineh stele (Table 5.1).

It is interesting to note the participation of the Sherden in another attack on Egypt so shortly after the end of Ramesses II's reign. While a nautical role for this group in Egyptian society will be explored further below, both Ramesses II's inscriptions commemorating his "victory" over the Hittite armies of Muwatalli II at the Battle of Qidš (ca. 1275 BCE), and the Papyrus Anastasi II fragment quoted above, refer to Sherden prisoners of war serving in Egypt's expeditionary forces. A reference in Papyrus Anastasi II to "Sherden thou didst carry off through thy strong arm" having "plundered the tribes of the desert" may also suggest that some number of the Sherden captured by Ramesses II were dispatched to, or stationed in, the western deserts of Libya— perhaps at an outpost along the pharaoh's aforementioned line of fortresses:

> The victorious army is come after he has triumphed, in victory and power. It has set fire to Isderektiu and burnt the Meryna. The Sherden thou didst carry off through thy strong arm have plundered the tribes of foreign lands [or "the tribes of the desert"]. How delightful is thy going to Thebes, thy war-chariot bowed down with hands and chiefs pinioned before thee!

P. Anastasi II, R4.7–5.3[41]

**Table 1.** 'Sea Peoples' Groups Listed in the Key Inscriptions of Merneptah and Ramesses III

| Great Karnak Inscription, Athribis Stele | Medinet Habu | Papyrus Harris I | Deir el-Medineh |
|---|---|---|---|
| Sherden | Peleset | Peleset | Peleset |
| Teresh | Weshesh | Weshesh | Teresh |
| Shekelesh | Shekelesh | Sherden | |
| Ekwesh | Denyen | Denyen | |
| Lukka | Tjekker | Tjekker | |

This would fit with Ramesses II's claims to have settled captured foes in areas distant from those whence they came (easterners in the west, westerners in the east, northerners in the south, etc.). An example of such a claim can be found on the southern wall of the Great Hall in the temple at Abu Simbel, where a representation of the pharaoh smiting Libyans is accompanied by text claiming that the Shasu of Canaan (northeast of Egypt) were stationed in the west by the pharaoh, and the Libyan *ḥnw 'Tjehenu' sent east:[42]

> He has placed the Shasu in the Westland and has settled the Tjehenu on the ridges. Filled are the strongholds he has built, with the plunder of his puissant arm/sword.

A reference to the Canaanite god Horon at the fortress of el-Gharbaniyat, located 70 kilometers west of Alexandria, may also support this. While Horon was venerated in Egypt from the 18th dynasty due to a syncretistic relationship with Horus, it has been suggested that this reference signals such a stationing of troops from the eastern delta or Palestine in this western fort.[43] When considered in this context, the "Sherden whom thou hast taken in thy might" being sent against "the tribes of the desert" in Papyrus Anastasi II can be seen as reporting that these warriors have been stationed in one of Ramesses II's western fortresses, particularly if they originated from an Aegean, Anatolian, or Levantine location. Given this context, Zawiyet Umm el-Rakham is even more of an interesting case.

As noted above, evidence from the site demonstrates a level of cooperation and interaction between the personnel stationed there and the indigenous Libyans.[44] This, combined with the fact that these western fortresses did not survive beyond the end of Ramesses II's reign, may suggest that some occupants of this outpost—perhaps some of the Sherden who had been dispatched against "the tribes of the desert"—either used this opportunity to throw off the mantle of Egyptian hegemony, or were swept up in the Libyan movement that culminated in the famous battle of Merneptah's fifth year. If this was the case, they may have fallen back on that which had proven beneficial to them so many times in the past, putting their martial prowess to work for whomever was the prevailing power in the area at a given time, as well as whomever could promise the greatest opportunity for plunder.

## Chapter Six

# The Changing Face of
# War and Society

As we have already seen, pharaonic records are not the only documentary evidence of Eastern Mediterranean powers being threatened by maritime foes in the waning years of the Late Bronze Age. The Hittites in particular, who were not historically inclined toward maritime affairs, seem to have been forced to look to the sea with more interest at this time, perhaps as a result of the threat that an increase in coastal raiding posed to their Syrian and southern Anatolian interests.

### THE HITTITES AND THE SEA

Two texts from the early 12th century in particular seem to show increased Hittite concern with threats from the Mediterranean coast and beyond. In the first, a Hittite king, likely Šuppiluliuma II (the last Hittite king, who reigned *circa* 1207–1178 BCE), writes to the prefect of Ugarit about the *Šikala* (LÚ. MEŠ KUR.URU.*Ši-ka-la-iu-ú* and KUR.URU *Ši-ki-la)* "who live on ships," and requests that a Ugaritian who had been taken captive by them be sent to Ḫattuša so that the king can question him about this people and their homeland:

> . . . I, His Majesty, had issued him an order concerning Ibnadušu, whom the people from Šikala—who live on ships—had abducted.
> Herewith I send Nirgaaili, who is *kartappu* with me, to you. And you, send Ibnadušu, whom the people from Šikala had abducted, to me. I will question him about the land Šikala, and afterwards he may leave for Ugarit again.

> RS 34.129[1]

79

Among the revealing elements of this text is its demonstration that the Hittites were not previously familiar with the *Šikala* people, nor with their land. The *Šikala* have been connected to two groups of Sea Peoples from the aforementioned records of Merneptah and Ramesses III: the *Škrš = šá-ka-lú-ša* 'Shekelesh'[2] and the *Škl = ši-ka-ar* 'Sikil' or *Tkr* 'Tjekker.'[3] A microcosm of the disagreement over the latter is Semitic philologist Anson Rainey's argument for 'Sikil' on the basis of Assyrian dialectical features in RS 34.129, while Egyptologist Donald Redford has argued for 'Tjekker' on the grounds of Egyptian orthography.[4] Recent efforts have sought to downplay Aegean influence and the role of migration in the Sea Peoples phenomenon by suggesting that most, if not all, were refugees from formerly Hittite-controlled territories in western Anatolia; however, Šuppiluliuma's ignorance of the people and land *Šikala* provides a strong counterindication to this suggestion.[5]

## 'The Ships of Alašiya Met Me in the Sea'

The second text, also attributed to Šuppiluliuma II, mentions a series of three naval skirmishes against the "ships of Alašiya," followed by a land battle, presumably against the same people he had fought at sea:

> The ships of Alašiya met me in the sea three times for battle, and I smote them; and I seized the ships and set fire to them in the sea.
> But when I arrived on dry land(?), the enemies from Alašiya came in multitude against me for battle. I [fought] them, and [. . . . . .] me [. . . . . .]. . ."
>
> KBo XII 38[6]

This second text is reminiscent of Ramesses III's claims of having fought land and sea battles against migratory Sea Peoples, which would have taken place at generally the same time. The similarity in both chronology and narrative raises the possibility that Šuppiluliuma may also have been facing repeated waves of raiders or migrant warriors—perhaps the same ones mentioned in Egyptian records—while clearly reinforcing the threat felt from the previously distant Mediterranean coast during the last days of the Hittite Empire.

The term "ships of Alašiya" is interesting, given our previous encounters with Cyprus in the context of maritime threats. The island had long been a target of seaborne raids by pirates from southwestern Anatolia and the Aegean: AhT 3, for example, speaks of Aḫḫiyawans "often" raiding the land of Alašiya and taking captives, while in EA 38, which refers to raids on both Egypt and Cyprus by the Lukka, the king of Alašiya is quick to protest that those who struck the Egyptian coast did not sail from an area under his control. Thus, Cyprus also seems to have functioned much as

Crete did in Odysseus' tale to Eumaios, with a portion of the island being used as a base for launching raids against coastal polities around the Eastern Mediterranean. It is likely that the vessels against which Šuppiluliuma fought were called "ships of Alašiya" not because they were a Cypriot force dispatched by their ruler, then, but either because they had sailed eastward via Cyprus, or because they were using a portion of the island as a forward staging area.

## 'I Have Sent You a Boat'

A third text, also from Boğazköi, may provide still more evidence for Hittite interest in maritime developments during the Late Bronze Age. In this heavily reconstructed letter, dated to the mid-13th century BCE (a few decades prior to Šuppiluliuma's letter about the *Šikala*), Ramesses II evidently writes to the Hittite king Ḫattušili III that he is sending a pair of ships (one at that time and one the following year), so that his shipwrights can "draw a copy" of it for the purpose of building a replica:

[. . . . . .] her/it (or their/them)
[. . . . . . 'so'] said [the King of the land of Ḫatti] to him. [ _____ ]
[So (say) to my brother: As to this ship, so I have now told] you [the decision to bring it [to you]
[and I sent my messengers to the king of the land of Amurru], so they bring it
[and they said to him, as follows: 'Bring it to the king of the land of Ḫatti' -s]o they said to him.
[. . . . . . See, I have now sent you] a boat and a second
[ship I will send next year. Yo]ur [carpenters], intended to draw a copy
[according to these ships I'll bring you. . . .] and they should draw a copy
[and they shall rebuild the ships, and my brother will] let customize the frames (?)
[artfully]. With bitumen
[they are the ships shalt pitch outside and from the inside . . ., [prev]ent [water] from entering
[in these ships (and) to not allow it to go down in the mid]dle of the sea!
[The blueprint for this ship that let you bring the King—on a black]board he has written it.
[. . . . . . Bl]ue(print)
[. . . . . .] they made/like make/the they made
[. . . . . .] it/him (= the ship?)
[. . . . . . we]ak (?) [. . . . . .] [ _____ ]
[. . . . . . v]ery [. . .
[. . . . . .] . . . [. . . *terminated/interrupted*

KUB III 82[7]

Sizable gaps make this Akkadian text, and Hittitologist Elmar Edel's re-construction, both challenging and highly speculative. This is particularly the case with regard to the reference to building a ship from a blueprint—something for which there is no clear precedent until nearly a millennium later.[8] However, though the reference to building replicas is reconstructed, the instruction to caulk the ships with bitumen so they do not "go down in the middle of the sea" may suggest Ramesses II intended for the Hittite king to build seaworthy vessels, even if the copy to be drawn is unlikely to have been a true architectural design.[9] Whatever the intent behind the letter, it is remarkable that Ramesses II may have been sending not just a craftsman or shipwright, but *a physical ship* to the Hittites for replication.

It is further remarkable because of the Hittites' aforementioned lack of affinity for the sea. As a land empire, Ḫatti had long relied on its coastal vas-sals to move goods by sea and project naval power—primarily its northern Syrian territories like Ugarit, but probably those in Cilicia and Lycia to some degree, as well.[10] This is likely reflected in KBo XII 38 above, with mariners from one of Ḫatti's coastal dependencies probably being tasked with actually carrying out the three battles against the "enemies from Alašiya," under the orders of the Hittite king (although Bryce has offered the interesting sugges-tion that the *Ḫiyawa*-men in the land of Lukka, referenced in AhT 27A and B above, may have been the land and sea-fighting mercenaries in question).[11] Edel connected this sequence of battles to the letter from Ramesses II to Ḫattušili III, suggesting that the ship sent for copying may have been spe-cifically designed to fight against the Sea Peoples.[12] While this is possible, it seems unlikely. Ramesses II's defeat of the Sherden demonstrates that Egypt had discovered a successful method for dealing with these coastal marauders "whom none could [previously] withstand"; however, evidence is lacking for the independent Egyptian development of a new type of ship capable of dispatching this threat at sea. Instead, if the ship being sent to Ḫatti did have to do with the Sea Peoples, it seems more likely that it was one of the Sea Peoples' captured ships that was being sent, so that Ḫattušili could learn about this new threat and its associated technology, much like Šuppiluliuma later sought to do with the Šikala. Further, it stands to reason that the ship was not being sent to landlocked Ḫattuša at all, but to one of its coastal vassals, perhaps Ugarit, where the expertise needed to study and understand such a vessel would have been more likely to reside.

## REFUGEES AND REFUGE SETTLEMENTS

The settlement changes and destructions that marked the end of the Late Bronze Age affected polities around the Aegean and Eastern Mediterranean, including at Odysseus' fictive home port of Crete, which had been a key node in the Late Bronze Age maritime trade network.[13] Though not a universal phenomenon, many settlements across Crete appear to have been abandoned or destroyed at the end of the 13th century (Late Minoan IIIB), while inhabitants took advantage of the island's geography to found new sites with larger, more concentrated populations in defensible areas of the island, both inland and on coastal hilltops.[14]

Inland refuge settlements took advantage of precarious positioning, heavy natural fortifications, and distance from the coast to provide safety and defense, seemingly in response to a new (or, at least, more serious) threat from the sea. Coastal hilltop settlements, on the other hand, were primarily founded on rocky promontories overlooking the water. These not only provided for early warnings of approaching ships, but they may also have been used as bases for seaborne raiding of exactly the type claimed by Odysseus. One scholar has explained these and similar sites on the Cyclades and Cyprus, discussed below, as "phenomena [which] reflect the way of thinking of people who quite simply live by and work on the sea," saying that "it is probable that sailors always look for such points, in a way similar to shepherds who often look for the same places for the *mandras*, and their houses."[15]

Similar sites in the Cyclades, like Koukounaries on the island of Paros, may have been used as bases for piracy (though as we have seen, Koukounaries has also been interpreted as a refuge site for palatial officials fleeing the mainland), while the promontory site of Maa-*Paleokastro* on western Cyprus provides a relevant example of one or both from outside the Aegean world.[16] This site, which offered both a clear view of, and easy access to, the sea, was home to a short-lived but highly-defensible settlement of mixed Aegean and Anatolian nature in the years surrounding and immediately following 1200 BCE.[17] The lack of potable water and arable land in the vicinity of Maa reinforces the primary emphasis its inhabitants placed on defensibility and sea access. The location of this site in a secluded area of the island, away from Cypriot settlements, appears to reflect a strategic separation from those already inhabiting the western part of Cyprus, although for military and mercantile reasons alike the site's establishment and construction may well have been sanctioned, and physical assistance may even have been provided, by those already present on Cyprus.[18] The material evidence from the site, which included Myc IIIC pottery, loomweights of both rolled and perforated styles, ashlar masonry, Aegean-style organization of domestic space, and the presence of hearths, led the excavator to suggest that its founders were a heterogeneous group of Anatolians, eastward-moving Aegeans, and some Cypriots—a makeup that led the site's excavator to identify the inhabitants of Maa-*Paleokastro* with the similarly heterogeneous Sea Peoples, as well as with Mycenaeans fleeing the palatial destructions in the Aegean.[19]

## NEW WARRIORS AND NEW WARFARE?

Along with the evidence for an increase in coastal threats and piracy, which we have discussed in depth above, this period is also marked by the sudden appearance of a new type of warrior in Eastern Mediterranean iconography, as well as the first known representations of naval battles. These new warriors, who are pictured wearing so-called "feathered headdresses," are found in martial scenes on land and at sea across the Aegean and Eastern Mediterranean beginning in the late 13th or early 12th century BCE (Transitional LH IIIB:2–IIIC Early). They have typically been associated with the Sea Peoples who are so well known from Ramesside Egyptian and other contemporary records.

Though commonly referred to as feathers in scholarship—and thus, for consistency, in the present study—these helmets or headdresses could represent many things, including leather, folded linen, rushes, straw, or even hair stiffened with lime.[20] As we saw in the previous chapter, the reliefs at Medinet Habu portray them, and the warriors on whom they appear, in great detail (Figs. 5.1 and 5.2). The plumed portions are largely identical, but individual groups of warriors seem to be differentiated from each other by the patterns on their headbands.[21] These include zigzag, circular, and crosshatched patterns, with some headdresses featuring two courses of the same pattern and one (perhaps two) featuring both circular decoration and cross-hatching.[22] A physical analog to these depictions may be found in an object from a wealthy chamber tomb (Tomb 3) at Portes, located in the western Peloponnese. Along with weapons, armor, pottery, and bronze objects, Tomb 3 contained the bronze-plated, cylindrical base of a helmet, adorned with horizontal rows of bronze strips and circular beads or rivets, one above the other, to a height of nearly 16 cm (over 6 inches)—a similar, if less compact, pattern to that seen at Medinet Habu and elsewhere. The interior of the Portes base was lined with a tightly woven straw hat or skullcap, and may have been topped with material of some sort to give the appearance that we see in contemporary iconography.[23]

In contrast to the crisp, clear illustrations of Egyptian relief, characters painted on Mycenaean vases are portrayed more schematically and stylistically, and in far less detail. In the case of the feathered headdresses depicted at Medinet Habu, the Aegean analog appears to be a much less detailed set of dark spikes or lines protruding from the head, sometimes set above a checkered or zigzag band. Most examples of the latter style take the form referred to as the "hedgehog helmet" for its similarity to Aegean portrayals of hedgehogs in similar media, though representations from the Dodecanesian island of Kos are more straw or rush-like in appearance. While Aegean pottery specialist Arne Furumark suggested that these helmets were fashioned from the skin of actual hedgehogs, it seems more likely that the resemblance, even if intentional, was more an artistic convention than it was the result of fashioning headwear out of hedgehogs, particularly in light of the Near Eastern and Dodecanesian analogues discussed here.[24]

The best-known example of the "hedgehog"-style headdress, and the most complete picture of warriors in full complementary combat gear, comes from the Warrior Vase, a krater found by Heinrich Schliemann in the now-eponymous "House of the Warrior Vase" at Mycenae (Fig. 1.2).[25] Each side of the vessel, which like almost all examples of the motif is dated to the Late Helladic IIIC Middle (roughly the mid-12th century to the early 11th century BCE), features a procession of warriors. On the obverse are six bearded soldiers marching in step to the right. They carry nearly-circular shields and leather "ration bags," and on each warrior's right shoulder rests a single spear with a leaf-shaped point. They wear corslets, kilts, greaves, and horned helmets with plumes flowing from the crest (see further below). The five soldiers on the reverse are identical except for the placement of their spears, which are cocked in each soldier's right arm in preparation for throwing; the absence of the ration bags; and the composition of their helmets, which are hedgehog-style instead of horned. This latter scene finds a nearly identical analogue in the painted limestone "Warrior Stele," also from Mycenae (Fig. 6.1).

**Figure 6.1. LH IIIC 'Warrior Stele' from Mycenae featuring armed men in hedgehog-style helmets in the upper course, and a hedgehog in the lower course**
Tsountas, Ch. 1886. "Graptē Stēlē ek Mykēneōn." *Ephēmeris Archaiologikē* 4: 1–22. Plate I.

Several further comparanda also come from Mycenae, all of which date to the LH IIIC Middle. This was a period in which the introduction of new features into ceramic decoration—and perhaps new people into mainland Greece—may have been at its peak.[26] These examples include a fragmentary larnax featuring up to three hedgehog-helmed warriors, as well as three more krater fragments, one of which may be the only example of a helmet simultaneously adorned with horns *and* hedgehog motif. The second may show two warriors with spears and round shields walking in front of a horse, while the last either shows two soldiers in hedgehog helmets or a soldier and an actual hedgehog.[27] Of particular interest in the present discussion are fragments of a larnax from Mycenae[28] and of a krater from Tiryns, each of which shows a warrior's head with a zigzag-patterned band around the bottom of the headdress that is conspicuously similar to some of the feathered hats from Medinet Habu (Fig. 6.2).

Examples of this motif have been found elsewhere on the Greek mainland, as well, including on a krater from Iolkos in Thessaly that shows three warriors wearing such headdresses, two of whom carry spears (one shield also remains) and the third of whom may be wearing a metal corslet.[29] A rhyton or stirrup

**Figure 6.2a.   Fragment of a LH IIIC Middle krater from Mycenae showing a bearded warrior wearing a hedgehog helmet or feathered hat with zigzag band**
Furtwängler, A. and Loeschcke, G. 1886. *Mykenische Vasen: Vorhellenische Thongefässe aus dem Gebiete des Mittelmeers.* Berlin. Figure 37.

**Figure 6.2b.** **Warriors wearing feathered headdresses with zigzag bands from the land battle relief at Medinet Habu**
Epigraphic Survey. 1930. *Medinet Habu I: Earlier Historical Records of Ramses III.* Chicago. After plate 34.
Courtesy of the Oriental Institute of the University of Chicago.

jar from Tiryns shows a soldier in full armor (wearing greaves, corslet, kilt, and hedgehog helmet, and armed with a short sword) who may be in the act of leaping, while krater fragments from the same site show what appear to be a hedgehog-helmed warrior leading a horse and another carrying a spear over his shoulder.[30] Further examples are found on kraters from Amarynthos on Euboea and from Thermon, which depict a man in a hedgehog headdress following what may be a chariot and driver, and a series of warriors in a fashion reminiscent of the Warrior Vase, respectively.[31] Finally, two LH IIIC Middle krater rim fragments of unknown geographic provenience show hedgehog headdresses, one of which is clearly a helmet, while a Late Minoan IIIC Middle figurine fragment from Faneromeni Cave in eastern Crete may also be an example of this motif.[32]

Representations of warriors with this style of headdress appeared on Cyprus and in the Levant around this time, as well, several decades after they had been carved on the walls at Medinet Habu. A seal from the mid-12th century Level IIIB at the major Cypriot site of Enkomi shows a bearded, shield-bearing warrior wearing a feathered hat with a beaded band.[33] A chariot-borne hunting scene on an ornate ivory game box from Tomb 58 at the same site, also dated to the 12th century BCE, includes two footmen who wear kilts and a bead-banded feather headdresses in the same style (Fig. 6.3).[34] Further transcultural components of this relief include the depiction of the animals in an Aegean style known as the "flying gallop," and the chariot wheels'

**Figure 6.3. Feather-hatted footman accompanying a chariot in a hunting scene on a 12th century game board from Enkomi**
Evans, A. J. 1900. "Mycenaean Cyprus as Illustrated in the British Museum Excavations." *Journal of the Royal Anthropological Institute 30*: 199–220. Figure 6.

six spokes, which follow in the Near Eastern tradition (Mycenaean chariots featured four spokes per wheel, while Near Eastern chariots had favored six spokes since the 15th century).[35]

In the Levant, a seal from Tomb 936 at Tell el-Far'ah (S), a 12th century chamber tomb, shows what has been interpreted as a "feather-hatted person" presenting an offering to the Egyptian god Amun (Fig. 6.4).[36] This image

**Figure 6.4a. Scarab from Tomb 936 at Tell el-Far'ah (S) showing what may be a feather-hatted individual making an offering to the Egyptian god Amun**
Uehlinger, C. 1988. "Der Amun-Tempel Ramses' III. in p'-Kn'n, seine Südpalästinischen Tempelgüter und der Übergang von der Ägypter- zur Philisterherrschaft: Ein Hinweis auf Einige Wenig Beachtete Skarabäen." *Zeitschrift des Deutschen Palästina-Vereins* 104: 6–25. Figure 4.

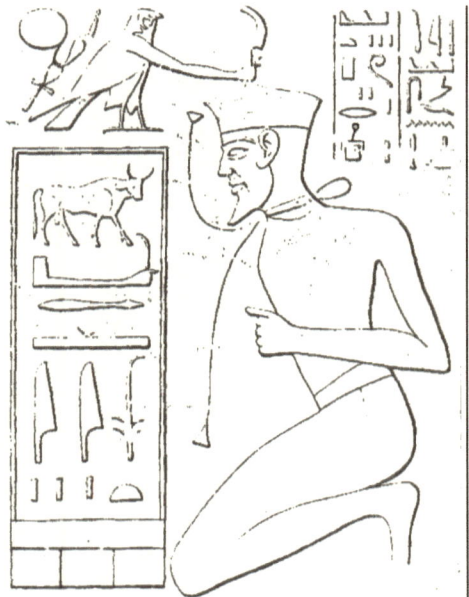

**Figure 6.4b. Captive Philistine 'prince' from Medinet Habu**
Epigraphic Survey. 1932. *Medinet Habu II: Later Historical Records of Ramses III*. Chicago. Plate 118c. Courtesy of the Oriental Institute of the University of Chicago.

compares favorably both to a "Philistine prince" pictured in the first court at Medinet Habu as one of many symbolic victims of Ramesses III (the image is captioned, "The countries of the Peleset, whom his majesty slew").[37] It is also similar in appearance to the determinatives applied to the names (*m-sh-k-n* and *m-r-y-w*) of the conquered Peleset and Tjekker chiefs in the Great Inscription of Year 5, which Redford has suggested may be connected to the aforementioned Mopsos tradition.[38] Additionally, a Philistine bichrome krater from Ashkelon (late 12th–early 11th century) shows two warriors with feathered headdresses in the "hedgehog" tradition. On one side, a warrior, perhaps holding a shield, is pictured face to face with a dolphin or sea monster. On the other side, a hedgehog-helmed figure, perhaps carrying a kylix, rides what may be a chariot (only one wheel of which is visible). In their initial publication of the krater, archaeologist Lawrence Stager, the excavator of Ashkelon, and Penelope Mountjoy, an authority on Aegean-style pottery, suggested that the chariot-borne figure was taking part in a funeral procession, perhaps in the wake of a shipwreck that claimed the life of the figure on the other side.[39]

Though surprisingly little in Philistine material culture suggests strong ties to the sea, such a representation would be far from surprising. The danger of being shipwrecked has haunted man since he first set out upon the sea, and Homer himself makes good use of the specter of storms and sinkings alike in metaphor and in narrative:

ἡ δ᾽ ἔθεεν Βορέῃ ἀνέμῳ ἀκραέϊ καλῷ,
μέσσον ὑπὲρ Κρήτης: Ζεὺς δέ σφισι μήδετ᾽ ὄλεθρον.
ἀλλ᾽ ὅτε δὴ Κρήτην μὲν ἐλείπομεν, οὐδέ τις ἄλλη
φαίνετο γαιάων, ἀλλ᾽ οὐρανὸς ἠδὲ θάλασσα,
δὴ τότε κυανέην νεφέλην ἔστησε Κρονίων
νηὸς ὕπερ γλαφυρῆς, ἤχλυσε δὲ πόντος ὑπ᾽ αὐτῆς.
Ζεὺς δ᾽ ἄμυδις βρόντησε καὶ ἔμβαλε νηῒ κεραυνόν:
ἡ δ᾽ ἐλελίχθη πᾶσα Διὸς πληγεῖσα κεραυνῷ,
ἐν δὲ θεείου πλῆτο: πέσον δ᾽ ἐκ νηὸς ἅπαντες.
οἱ δὲ κορώνῃσιν ἴκελοι περὶ νῆα μέλαιναν
κύμασιν ἐμφορέοντο: θεὸς δ᾽ ἀποαίνυτο νόστον.
αὐτὰρ ἐμοὶ Ζεὺς αὐτός, ἔχοντί περ ἄλγεα θυμῷ,
ἱστὸν ἀμαιμάκετον νηὸς κυανοπρῴροιο
ἐν χείρεσσιν ἔθηκεν, ὅπως ἔτι πῆμα φύγοιμι.
τῷ ῥα περιπλεχθεὶς φερόμην ὀλοοῖς ἀνέμοισιν.
ἐννῆμαρ φερόμην, δεκάτῃ δέ με νυκτὶ μελαίνῃ
γαίῃ Θεσπρωτῶν πέλασεν μέγα κῦμα κυλίνδον.

And she ran before the North Wind, blowing fresh and fair, on a mid-sea course to the windward of Crete, and Zeus devised destruction for the men. But when we had left Crete, and no other land appeared, but only sky and sea, then verily the son of Cronos set a black cloud above the hollow ship, and the sea grew dark beneath it. Therewith Zeus thundered, and hurled his bolt upon the ship, and she quivered from stem to stern, smitten by the bolt of Zeus, and was filled with sulphurous smoke, and all the crew fell from out the ship. Like sea-crows they were borne on the waves about the black ship, and the god took from them their returning. But as for me, Zeus himself when my heart was compassed with woe, put into my hands the tossing 1 mast of the dark-prowed ship, that I might again escape destruction. Around this I clung, and was borne by the direful winds. For nine days I was borne, but on the tenth black night the great rolling wave brought me to the land of the Thesprotians.

Odyssey xiv 289–315[40]

## Sea Peoples and Self-Representations: The Northern Philistines

Moving northward across the Levant to Tell Ta'yinat, archaeologist Brian Janeway recently published the first known sherd featuring a hedgehog-helmed individual to be found in Syria.[41] As can be seen in Figure 6.5, this fragment shows a figure in silhouette from mid-torso up, with nine spines protruding from the crown of his head. He appears to hold lines of some sort, which connect to the leftmost edge of a textured image that appears similar to the mane of a horse. Most of the latter representation is lost, but that which remains may suggest that this vessel once featured a chariot scene.[42]

**Figure 6.5.   Krater body sherd from Tell Ta'yinat featuring a hedgehog-helmed individual**
Janeway, B. 2017. *Sea Peoples of the Northern Levant? Aegean-Style Pottery from Early Iron Age Tell Tayinat*. Winona Lake. Plate 9.15.

This is only the second hedgehog helmet depiction to have been found within a purported Sea Peoples settlement, following the Ashkelon krater mentioned immediately above. It comes from Tell Ta'yinat, ancient *Kunulua*, a site located on the 'Amuq plain (later known as the plain of Antioch). Tell Ta'yinat was part of a polity known to scholars from hieroglyphic Luwian inscriptions as *Wadasatani* or *Walistin*. Based on epigraphic evidence from several sites, Walistin has been reconstructed as a sizable Iron Age kingdom extending from the Amuq plain north to the Bay of Iskanderun, inland to Aleppo, and south to Hama. Recently, Luwian philologist David Hawkins reinterpreted the pronunciation of toponym *Walistin*, arguing that it instead should be read as *Palistin*. The similarity of this toponym to the southern Canaanite ethnonym *Philistine* has combined with the Aegean-style pottery forms found at Tell Ta'yinat in early 12th century contexts to spark new interest in this site, perhaps as the location of a northern Philistine settlement.[43]

The earliest epigraphic evidence for *Palistin* comes from a Neo-Hittite context. In a relief called ALEPPO 6, which is associated with major architectural renovations at the Temple of the Storm God at Aleppo in Syria, an individual named Taita references himself as "Hero and King of Palistin."[44] Like the polity of Ḫiyawa discussed earlier, the toponym for the territory Taita oversaw seems to have been a lingering remnant of a materially and chronologically ephemeral agro-pastoral settlement with Cypro-Aegean affinities, which was present at Tell Ta'yinat and the surrounding area beginning in the middle or late 12th century BCE.[45] Unoccupied since the end of the Early Bronze Age, Ta'yinat in the Iron I (Field Phases 6 through 3) appears to have been a "rudimentary village settlement" with agro-pastoral focus, with architectural remains mainly consisting of silos, pits, and small houses built atop the site's previous inhabitation level.[46]

Unlike the preceding Late Bronze Age, when the neighboring mounded site of Alalaḫ was a major importer of Mycenaean ceramics (particularly those associated with the typical Aegean drinking set, such as amphoroid kraters and globular flasks), the Aegean-style pottery appearing in the 'Amuq in this period is of local manufacture and displays a wider variety of forms and less standardization of size and decoration.[47] Also appearing at this time are intrusive domestic elements like unperforated, cylindrical loomweights and a small number of Aegean-style cooking pots.[48] The intrusive population seems to have lived peacefully alongside the indigenous inhabitants of the 'Amuq, as evidenced in part by the continuation of local cooking traditions, ultimately leaving as their legacy to the region the toponym *Palistin*, which, like the possibly-related *Philistia* (= Roman *Palaestina* = modern *Palestine*) in southern Canaan, would far outlast their own relevance and archaeological visibility.[49]

## Sea Peoples and Self-Representations: Anthropoid Coffins from Beth Shean

The northern cemetery at Beth Shean, an Egyptian administrative center in Canaan from the late 18th or early 19th dynasty until the end of the mid-12th century BCE, may have produced examples of the feather-hatted phenomenon in an altogether different medium: five clay anthropoid coffins (of over fifty total) whose decoration bears a clear resemblance to the Sea Peoples warriors from Medinet Habu (Fig. 6.6).[50] Each coffin lid features decorative courses around its subject's forehead that find parallels in the aforementioned iconographic portrayals, while one (from Tomb 66) also features vertical fluting above the forehead decoration—a possible attempt to portray feathers.

The style of these coffins is referred to as *grotesque*, as a result of their facial attributes—eyes, eyebrows, nose, mouth, ears, and beard—being appliquéd, giving them a warped appearance. The other style of clay anthropoid coffin from Egypt, Canaan, and Nubia, known as *naturalistic*, features faces carved

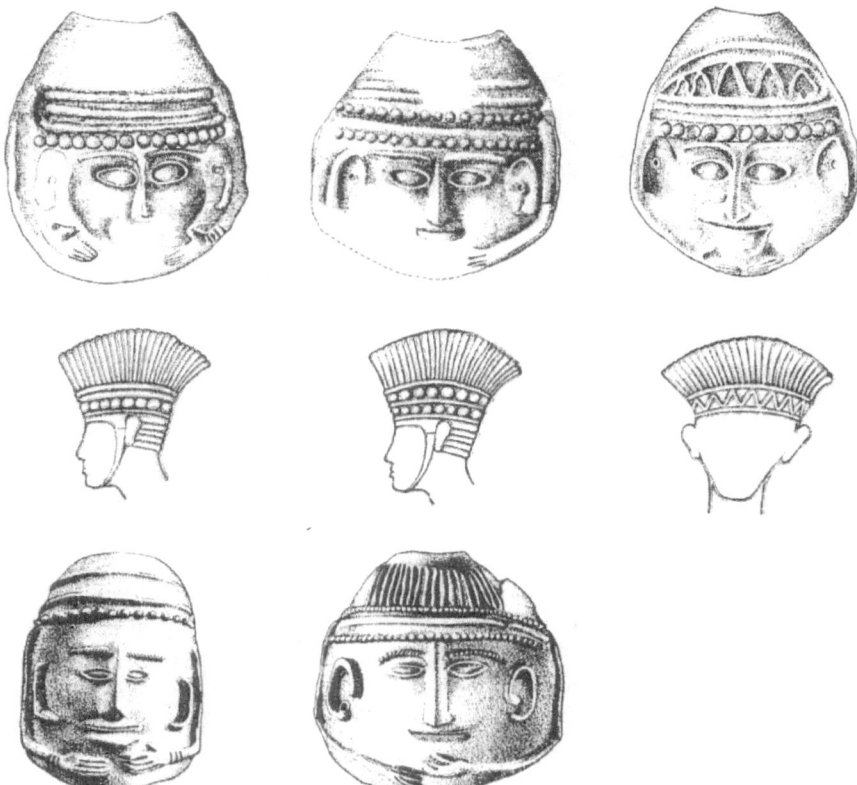

**Figure 6.6.** **Grotesque anthropoid coffin lids from Beth Shan compared with Sea Peoples profiles from Medinet Habu**
Oren, E. D. 1973. *The Northern Cemetery of Beth Shan*. Leiden. Page 136, Figures 1–10.

in relief that "mimic the basic appearance of an Egyptian wood or cartonnage coffin," sometimes with relief Osiris beard and painted decoration.[51] The terminology used to describe this dichotomy was coined in the early 20th century by archaeologist C. S. Fisher, who assigned the naturalistic coffins at Beth Shan to women and their grotesque counterparts to men.[52] However, an interesting chain of scholarly interpretations across the 20th century led these burial containers, steeped as they already were in Egyptian history by the turn of the 12th century BCE, not just to be associated with Sea Peoples, but to have credit for their presence both in the Levant and *in Egypt* given to the Philistines.[53]

Some scholars since at least the time of Flinders Petrie have associated grotesque-style anthropoid coffins with Aegean artistry. They have been referred to as "Aegean-style anthropoid coffins," explained as the Aegeanization of an Egyptian burial practice, and connected to the gold and electrum funerary masks from Grave Circles A and B at Mycenae.[54] Such suggestions encounter problems, of course, one of which is the four centuries of chrono-logical separation between the northern cemetery at Beth Shean and the 16th century BCE Mycenaean shaft graves, and another of which is the lack of evidence for this type of burial tradition in the Late Bronze or Early Iron Age Aegean world.[55] Partly because of this Aegean association, though, and partly because of Ramesses III's aforementioned claim to have "settled [Sea Peoples] in strongholds, bound in my name," anthropoid burial containers in the grotesque style began to be associated with Sea Peoples mercenaries of the Ramesside pharaohs. This, in turn, led to the suggestion that the custom of burial in clay anthropoid coffins as a whole was brought to Canaan by the best-known of these groups, the Philistines, despite this interment method's long history as an Egyptian practice. This misconception led to yet another: the association of the Philistines with clay anthropoid coffins in Egypt, where these burials were seen as evidence for, in the words of one scholar, "colo-nies of [Philistines] . . . in the Nile Delta and on Egypt's southern frontier in Nubia."[56]

More recently, there was a reflexive move to reassign all anthropoid coffins in Canaan and Egypt alike back to the Egyptians—including those found at Beth Shean.[57] The answer is likely to be found in the middle ground between these hypotheses: while anthropoid coffins are clearly an Egyptian interment method, the five from Beth Shean may represent Egyptianizing burials of a small number of Sea Peoples-related mercenaries, conscripts, or recruits serving in the pharaoh's garrison there in the 12th century.[58]

## Sea Peoples and Social Status

Together, the Ta'yinat sherd and the Ashkelon krater, and perhaps the Far'ah seal and Beth Shean coffin lids, serve as what may be the only self-representations of Sea Peoples in their identifying regalia. The greatest value provided by these examples is the fact that, as self-representations, they can signal to the modern observer—as they did to contemporaries at the time of their creation—just which aspects of their appearance were most critical to their self-identification as individuals and as members of the group(s) with which they most closely identified.

Some level of social status would have been necessary to engage in the act of commissioning such objects as the Beth Shean coffins and the Enkomi and Tell el-Far'ah (S) seals. Though they may have begun as mercenaries or rank-and-file soldiers, the occupants of the Beth Shan coffins had, by the time of their deaths, clearly attained the status required to commission such burial sculpture, while the designs implemented demonstrate a keen interest in preserving and presenting their ethnic identities for all eternity. Reading across the two objects from Enkomi may provide insight into the social growth and development that went into attaining such status—progression from companion on a hunt to commissioner of a seal shows an increase in station that may be reflected once again in the coffins from Beth Shan. Further, the scene on the game box shows individuals acting in service to nobility in general or to the crown in particular—a very similar role to that which the individuals interred in the Beth Shan coffins may have carried out in the service of the pharaoh.

Both the seals and coffins seem to follow a pattern of foreigners who had attained certain rank adopting a local motif or medium of expression, while choosing to clearly mark themselves as "others" through the self-representations they commissioned.[59] This attainment of status by a foreigner in Egypt—particularly one with a possibly martial bent—seems to parallel Odysseus' own claim, which we shall explore further below, that after suffering ignominious defeat and capture in his attempted raid on the Nile delta he became a man of "much wealth" while living in the land of the Pharaohs (*Odyssey* xiv, 276–277, 285–286).

# Chapter Seven

# Hedgehog Helmets, Sea Peoples, and Ship-to-Ship Combat

It may be no coincidence that some of the earliest representations of feather-hatted and hedgehog-helmed warriors are found in the earliest known scenes of ship-to-ship combat, and in conjunction with oared galleys (more on the latter below). Perhaps the earliest known representation of the feathered headdress from the Aegean and the Interface is on an unstratified locally made krater from Bademgediği Tepe (ancient Puranda) in southwestern Anatolia (Fig.7.1). This site appears to have been occupied at the end of the 13th century, after a settlement hiatus, by outsiders from the West Anatolian coast who produced, among other ceramics, pottery characteristic of the LH IIIC Early.[1] Mountjoy has dated the krater from Bademgediği to the Transitional LH IIIB2–IIIC Early or LH IIIC Early (late 13th or early 12th century) based on the appearance of rowers who appear belowdecks, though it has also been seen as a product of the mid-12th century Late Helladic IIIC Middle.[2]

The latter, if accurate, would make the vessel and its representation synchronous with three other key naval representations—those from Pyrgos Livanaton (Homeric Kynos, north of modern Livanates; *Iliad* II, 531), from Seraglio on Kos, and from Liman Tepe in western Anatolia—as well as with the vast majority of feathered headdress and "hedgehog" helmet representations known to date (Figs. 7.2 and 7.3).[3] However, Mountjoy has also noted that her dating of the Bademgediği krater may necessitate a backdating of the Koan sherds from LH IIIC Middle to at least LH IIIC Early, or from the mid-1100s to the beginning of the 12th century.[4]

The implications of such a shift would be significant, as it would place the earliest representations of "feather-hatted warriors" in southwestern Anatolia and the Dodecanese less than a quarter century prior to their appearance in Egyptian relief, and well before their proliferation (though perhaps not their initial appearance) on the Greek mainland in the late 12th and early 11th

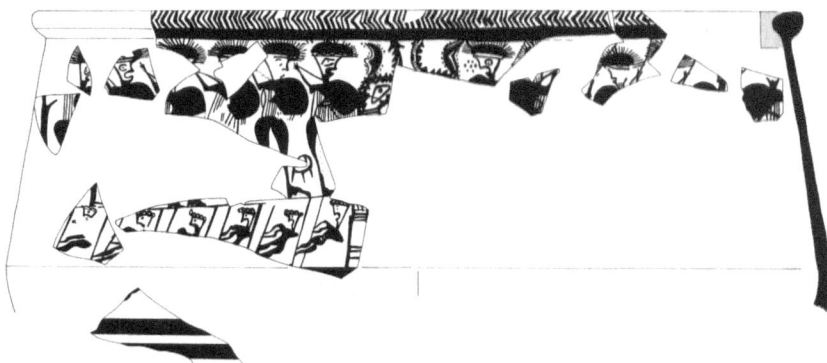

**Figure 7.1.   Fragments of Transitional LH IIIB:2–IIIC Early or LH IIIC Early krater from Bademgediği Tepe showing antithetic oared ships manned by hedgehog-helmed warriors**
Mountjoy, P. A. 2011. "A Bronze Age Ship from Ashkelon with Particular Reference to the Bronze Age Ship from Bademgediği Tepe." *American Journal of Archaeology* 115: 483–488. Figure 3.

**Figure 7.2.   Fragment of a LH IIIC Early or Middle krater from Liman Tepe depicting a possible rower wearing a hedgehog helmet**
Aykurt, A. and H. Erkanal. 2017. "A Late Bronze Ship from Liman Tepe with Reference to the Late Bronze Age Ships from İzmir/Bademgediği Tepesi and Kos/Seraglio." *Oxford Journal of Archaeology* 36: 61–70. Figure 5.

**Figure 7.3. LH IIIC Middle krater from Kynos featuring a scene of warfare between hedgehog-helmed warriors aboard antithetic oared galleys**
Mountjoy, P. A. 2011. "A Bronze Age Ship from Ashkelon with Particular Reference to the Bronze Age Ship from Bademgediği Tepe." *American Journal of Archaeology* 115: 483–488. Figure 2.

centuries. This, in turn, may suggest that at least some of these warriors originated in the area of southwestern Anatolia and the Dodecanese—perhaps the "isles in the midst of the sea" spoken of at Medinet Habu—and spread from there westward to the Aegean, and south- and eastward to Cyprus and the Levant. It also helps to reinforce the agglutinative nature of raiding parties, which are far less likely to have remained relatively intact from their initial points of origin than to have added to their size and diversity with each stop around the Aegean and Eastern Mediterranean.[5]

## ENGAGEMENTS AT SEA

The prospect of ship-to-ship combat is hinted at in both *Iliad* and *Odyssey*. The former contains a more oblique reference, consisting of the *hapax legomenon* ναύμαχα 'sea-fighting':

οἳ δ' ἀπὸ νηῶν ὕψι μελαινάων ἐπιβάντες
μακροῖσι ξυστοῖσι, τά ῥά σφ' ἐπὶ νηυσὶν ἔκειτο
ναύμαχα κολλήεντα, κατὰ στόμα εἱμένα χαλκῷ.

the Achaeans high up on the decks of their black ships to which they had climbed, fought therefrom with long pikes that lay at hand for them upon the ships for sea-fighting—jointed pikes, shod at the tip with bronze. . .

*Iliad* XV, 387–389

Eumaios, Odysseus' swineherd, compares Penelope's suitors unfavorably to pirates (*Odyssey* xiv, 85–93). It is unsurprising, then, that the reference to shipborne ambush in the *Odyssey* involves the suitors as waterborne aggressors—specifically, their plot to intercept Telemakhos' vessel at sea:

ἀλλ᾽ ἄγε μοι δότε νῆα θοὴν καὶ εἴκοσ᾽ ἑταίρους,
ὄφρα μιν αὐτὸν ἰόντα λοχήσομαι ἠδὲ φυλάξω
ἐν πορθμῷ Ἰθάκης τε Σάμοιό τε παιπαλοέσσης,
ὡς ἂν ἐπισμυγερῶς ναυτίλλεται εἵνεκα πατρός. . .
μνηστῆρες δ᾽ ἀναβάντες ἐπέπλεον ὑγρὰ κέλευθα
Τηλεμάχῳ φόνον αἰπὺν ἐνὶ φρεσὶν ὁρμαίνοντες.
ἔστι δέ τις νῆσος μέσση ἁλὶ πετρήεσσα,
μεσσηγὺς Ἰθάκης τε Σάμοιό τε παιπαλοέσσης,
Ἀστερίς, οὐ μεγάλη· λιμένες δ᾽ ἔνι ναύλοχοι αὐτῇ
ἀμφίδυμοι· τῇ τόν γε μένον λοχόωντες Ἀχαιοί.

But come, give me a swift ship and twenty men, that I may watch in ambush for him as he passes in the strait between Ithaca and rugged Samos. Thus shall his voyaging in search of his father come to a sorry end. . .
But the wooers embarked, and sailed over the watery ways, pondering in their hearts utter murder for Telemachus. There is a rocky isle in the midst of the sea, midway between Ithaca and rugged Samos, Asteris, of no great size, but therein is a harbor where ships may lie, with an entrance on either side. There it was that the Achaeans tarried, lying in wait for Telemachus.

*Odyssey* iv, 656–674, 842–847

Such a scene may be reflected in the kraters from Bademgediği Tepe and Kynos kraters, each of which appears to depict a naval battle between spear-wielding warriors who are pictured aboard antithetic oared galleys. The more fragmentary representation from Liman Tepe, with its one remaining rower belowdecks and partial figure atop the deck, may also follow in this tradition. Interestingly, if the hedgehog helmets of the warriors on the Bademgediği and Kynos vessels do in fact mark them as Sea Peoples, then these may not only be Sea Peoples vessels, but participants in a battle scene portraying combat between ships manned by Sea Peoples. The corpus of Sea Peoples in combat is limited to these representations and those at Medinet Habu, and the naval battle relief at the latter is the only such representation from this period that includes non-Sea Peoples participants. This may be evidence that only Egypt was able to successfully defend against these foes at sea, though their victory was short-lived, as the events of this period set the Egyptian empire on a course toward inexorable decline. The scenes on Late Helladic pottery, on the other hand, may depict that turmoil on a smaller scale, between (or even within) local Aegean communities.[6]

It should also be noted, though, that the iconography of warfare throughout the Mycenaean period frequently depicted similarly attired and equipped warriors engaged in combat with each other. In other words, whether read thematically or as representations of actual events, war in Mycenaean iconography was almost exclusively depicted as being fought between individuals or groups from within the Aegean milieu.[7] The nature of the scenes pictured on the Kynos and Bademgediği kraters, then, is consistent with the preceding phases of the Late Helladic period, even if the figures' appearance and the presence of ships represented radical developments.

## BOAR'S TUSKS, HORSEHAIR CRESTS, AND HORNS

Given the stylistic differences between Helladic pictorial vase painting and Egyptian art, it may be that the soldiers in horned helmets on the obverse of the Warrior Vase were intended to represent something akin to the Sherden, who are depicted in horned helmets in the reliefs of Ramesses II and Ramesses III. Only shown in relief (never, at least in examples found to date, on papyrus), the first pictorial representations of warriors we identify by this name appear in the commemorations of Ramesses II, at Abu-Simbel, Abydos, Karnak, Luxor, and the Ramesseum, of his Qidš "victory" over the Hittites.[8] Sherden are generally differentiated from their native counterparts in Egyptian art by three key features. The first two are their circular shields and the swords or dirks they sometimes wield either instead of, or as a supplement to, the spears carried by their Egyptian counterparts. The third, and most distinctive, are horned helmets that, with two possible exceptions, feature a protrusion at the crest with a disc or other circular accouterment mounted atop it. The exceptions to the latter guideline include a group of helmet-wearing warriors from Luxor, shown fighting alongside the forces of Ramesses II in an assault on Dapur in Amurru, and two ships of warriors fighting against Ramesses III in the naval battle pictured at Medinet Habu.[9] Also of interest are two additional horn-helmed figures featured elsewhere in the Dapur reliefs, at least one of which may be a Sherden shown either from a different angle than seen in other images, or in a style that was abandoned as the depiction of these warriors became more standardized.[10]

Though the identification of Sherden has been considered "one of the few sartorial certainties in the complicated history of Egypt's friends and attackers," it is important to note that our visual identification of this people is solely dependent on a small number of horn-helmed individuals who appear as determinatives in Egyptian inscriptions.[11] The first is seen in the phrase *Š3rdn3 n ḫ3q ḥm.f* 'Sherden of his majesty's capture,' a phrase in Ramesses II's Qidš "Poem" in which a figure wearing a helmet with horns and disc serves as the determinative for the term *Š3rdn3*. This text is replicated at Abydos, Luxor, the Ramesseum, and twice at Karnak.[12] The second exemplar is a single captioned image from the front pavilion wall at Medinet Habu, which shows a monumental series of captive foreign princes or chieftains acting as determinatives for their accompanying hieroglyphic descriptors. The latter representation seems problematic at first: while this lone figure at Medinet Habu who bears the label *Š3rd3n3 n p3 ym* 'Sherden of the Sea' is wearing the distinctive helmet associated with this people, his aquiline nose and earring are distinctive among the numerous warriors who are pictured in Egyptian reliefs wearing the standard horned headgear (Fig. 1.3). His long beard is also unique, though the remaining decoration on another Sherden at Medinet Habu shows that beards were depicted *in paint* on at least some of these individuals (Fig. 7.4). Short beards may also appear *in relief* on two other Sherden—one from Medinet Habu, and the other from the Qidš reliefs of Ramesses II at Luxor.[13]

Though they are the most obvious and the most discussed examples, horns and a central protrusion are not the only distinctive aspects of Sherden head-wear. On at least two occasions—on one individual in the land battle, and on a group of at least nine victims lying prostrate beneath the feet of Ramesses III in the naval battle scene—the Medinet Habu artists chose to give *texture in relief* to these horned helmets, creating what has been called a "laminated" effect (Fig. 7.5). Why would this be the case, particularly on such a small scale? The answer, helpfully informed also by the painted beard noted above, may lie in further explanation of Egyptian visual representation. While they

**Figure 7.4.   At left, the lead Sherden in the victory procession of Ramesses III with remnants of painted beard and textured helmet; at right, the remnant in relief of this Sherden and others in the procession**
Epigraphic Survey. 1930. *Medinet Habu I: Earlier Historical Records of Ramses III*. After plates 62 and 65c. Courtesy of the Oriental Institute of the University of Chicago.

**Figure 7.5. Sherden warrior with beard and textured helmet shown in relief, from the land battle of Ramesses III against the Sea Peoples at Medinet Habu (*emphasis added*)**
Epigraphic Survey. 1930. *Medinet Habu I: Earlier Historical Records of Ramses III*. After plate 34. Courtesy of the Oriental Institute of the University of Chicago.

primarily exist as unadorned reliefs now, at the time of their composition the representations at Medinet Habu followed Egyptian artistic tradition in combining *both relief and paint* to make a complete picture. Settings, actions, and even individuals could be augmented or even portrayed in their entirety through painting, a medium that may even have taken precedence over relief in some cases.[14] The millennia since the composition of the Medinet Habu images have stripped them almost completely of pigment, leaving behind largely unadorned reliefs. These remnants may seem to tell a clear story, and to hold within them clear and critical details that can aid in our interpretation of their meaning; however, it is critical to consider that "[once] painted details have disappeared, though the sculptured design may remain in fairly good condition, much of the life of the original scene is gone and many aids to its interpretation are lost."[15]

With this in mind, a hint of what is no longer there, but which might have been visible in antiquity, may be found in these outliers among the carved scenes—specifically, the "laminated" helmets and beards on Sherden individuals, each of which is depicted only twice in relief. The Sherden individual on whom a painted beard can still be seen also wears a helmet on which paint has survived. Perhaps unsurprisingly, given the clues provided thus far, it also shows evidence for texture. This may confirm that both textured helmets and beards were standard features of Sherden in Egyptian iconography, despite the small sample size remaining in the absence of paint. Interestingly, the painted Sherden individual also retains skin pigment: he is painted reddish brown in similar fashion to the *K3ftiw* 'Keftiu' (= Cretans) last seen in the tomb of the 18th dynasty Egyptian official Rekhmire (Theban tomb (TT) 100), as well as in similar fashion to the warriors in the well-known battle fresco from Pylos. Remaining pigment on a feather-hatted warrior at Medinet Habu shows that these individuals' skin was similarly reddish, and their kilts red and blue.[16]

Now we return to the Mycenaean Warrior Vase to consider the possible connection between Egyptian representations of Sherden warriors at Abu-Simbel, Luxor, Karnak, Abydos, and Medinet Habu, and the representation on painted Mycenaean pottery of horn-helmed warriors marching into battle. Warrior headgear in the Aegean Late Bronze Age took many different forms, from relatively straightforward bronze helmets to the famous boar's tusk headgear associated with Odysseus himself:

Μηριόνης δ᾽ Ὀδυσῆϊ δίδου βιὸν ἠδὲ φαρέτρην
καὶ ξίφος, ἀμφὶ δέ οἱ κυνέην κεφαλῆφιν ἔθηκε
ῥινοῦ ποιητήν: πολέσιν δ᾽ ἔντοσθεν ἱμᾶσιν
ἐντέτατο στερεῶς: ἔκτοσθε δὲ λευκοὶ ὀδόντες
ἀργιόδοντος ὑὸς θαμέες ἔχον ἔνθα καὶ ἔνθα
εὖ καὶ ἐπισταμένως: μέσσῃ δ᾽ ἐνὶ πῖλος ἀρήρει.
τήν ῥά ποτ᾽ ἐξ Ἐλεῶνος Ἀμύντορος Ὀρμενίδαο
ἐξέλετ᾽ Αὐτόλυκος πυκινὸν δόμον ἀντιτορήσας,
Σκάνδειαν δ᾽ ἄρα δῶκε Κυθηρίῳ Ἀμφιδάμαντι:
Ἀμφιδάμας δὲ Μόλῳ δῶκε ξεινήϊον εἶναι,
αὐτὰρ ὁ Μηριόνῃ δῶκεν ᾧ παιδὶ φορῆναι:
δὴ τότ᾽ Ὀδυσσῆος πύκασεν κάρη ἀμφιτεθεῖσα.

And Meriones gave to Odysseus a bow and a quiver and a sword, and about his head he set a helm wrought of hide, and with many a tight-stretched thong was it made stiff within, while without the white teeth of a boar of gleaming tusks were set thick on this side and that, well and cunningly, and within was fixed a lining of felt. This cap Autolycus on a time stole out of Eleon when he had broken into the stout-built house of Amyntor, son of Ormenus; and he gave it to Amphidamas of Cythem to take to Scandeia, and Amphidamas gave it to Molus as a guest-gift, but he gave it to his own son Meriones to wear; and now, being set thereon, it covered the head of Odysseus.

*Iliad* X, 260–271

Both bronze and boar's tusk helmets are known from as early as the 16th century BCE. An early example of the former can be found in a 15th century warrior burial at Knossos, while the latter appear in significant numbers in battle, ceremonial, and funerary contexts. Examples (among many) include the Dendra panoply; the northern and southern wall friezes from Room 5 of the West House on Akrotiri, where they appear on land-based warriors and displayed on flotilla vessels (Fig. 7.6); and the "Battle Krater" from Shaft Grave IV at Mycenae (Fig. 1.1). The endurance of the boar's tusk helmet through the centuries is widely attested in paint, including on the aforementioned papyrus from el-Amarna and in the battle fresco at the Palace of Nestor at Pylos;[17] in sculptures, sealings, and physical remains, as seen, for example, in the LH IIIC Tomb B at Kallithea and warriors' heads from Mycenae (LH IIIA–IIIB; Fig. 7.7) and Enkomi (LC IIB–IIIA), both sculpted of ivory; and, of course, in Homeric epic.[18] Given the age of this tradition, it is perhaps unsurprising that Odysseus' own helmet had a detailed history—it had attained great age before the hero first laid hands on it.

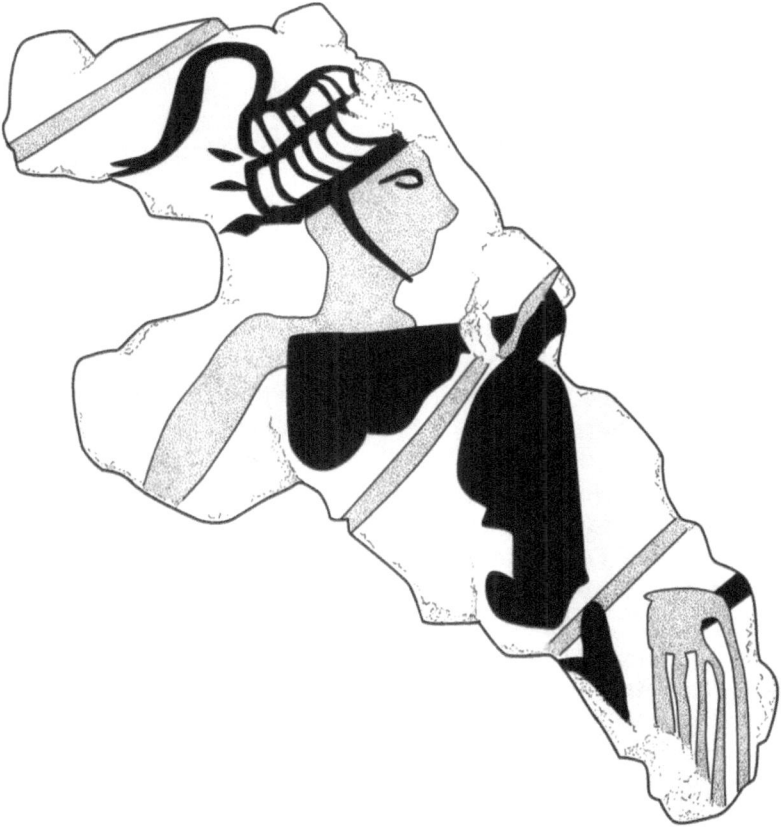

**Figure 7.6.  Warrior with boar's tusk helmet and plume, from the Miniature Fresco in Room 5 of the West House at Akrotiri**
Drawing by Valerie Woelfel.

**Figure 7.7. Sculpted ivory head from Mycenae featuring a boar's tusk helmet**
Tsountas, Ch. and Manatt, J. I. 1897. *The Mycenaean Age: A Study of the Monuments and Culture of Pre-Homeric Greece.* London. Figure 85.

The characteristic feature of the boar's tusk helmet, whose base of material was most likely leather, was the antithetic rows of cut boar's tusks that encircled it. From bottom to top, these rows of cut tusks were made up of progressively smaller pieces, until the crown itself was covered in the pointed tips. While the number and size of the rows could vary, along with the general shape, this construction seems generally uniform across the existing evidence for these helmets. However, in both boar's tusk and bronze helmets, many differences in accompanying accoutrement can be seen in both iconography and material remains. For example, some helmets featured ear- (and sometimes cheek-) guards, in similar fashion but, on boar's tusk helmets, manufactured from leather and perhaps additional cut tusks. The most heavily customized zone of both types of Mycenaean helmet appears to have been the crest, atop which a knob was frequently mounted, to which could be attached a vertical tusk, or crests and plumes of various shape, size, color, and texture.[19] The variety of this helmet adornment even within a single representation is striking; for example, in both the north wall frieze of the miniature fresco at Akrotiri (eight examples) and the Mycenaean Battle Krater (seven remaining examples), no two boar's tusk helmets feature identically depicted accoutrements.

ὣς εἰπὼν οὗ παιδὸς ὀρέξατο φαίδιμος Ἕκτωρ·
ἂψ δ᾽ ὁ πάϊς πρὸς κόλπον ἐϋζώνοιο τιθήνης
ἐκλίνθη ἰάχων πατρὸς φίλου ὄψιν ἀτυχθεὶς
ταρβήσας χαλκόν τε ἰδὲ λόφον ἱππιοχαίτην,
δεινὸν ἀπ᾽ ἀκροτάτης κόρυθος νεύοντα νοήσας.

So saying, glorious Hector stretched out his arms to his boy, but back into the bosom of his fair-girdled nurse shrank the child crying, affrighted at the aspect of his dear father, and seized with dread of the bronze and the crest of horsehair, as he marked it waving dreadfully from the topmost helm.

*Iliad* VI, 466–470

The most common accoutrements attached to the crest of these helmets appear to have been horsehair plumes or large, circular crests with feathered appearance (though the circular crests also seem to have been placed on the front and sides of the helmets at times, resulting in an appearance very similar to horns). With its circular shape, the latter provides an interesting analogue to the disc mounted atop the crest of Sherden helmets in Egyptian relief. One of the most remarkable helmets in this style known to date includes both horsehair plume and circular accoutrement—along with, perhaps most interestingly, horns (Fig. 7.8).[20] This image, which has generally been accepted as

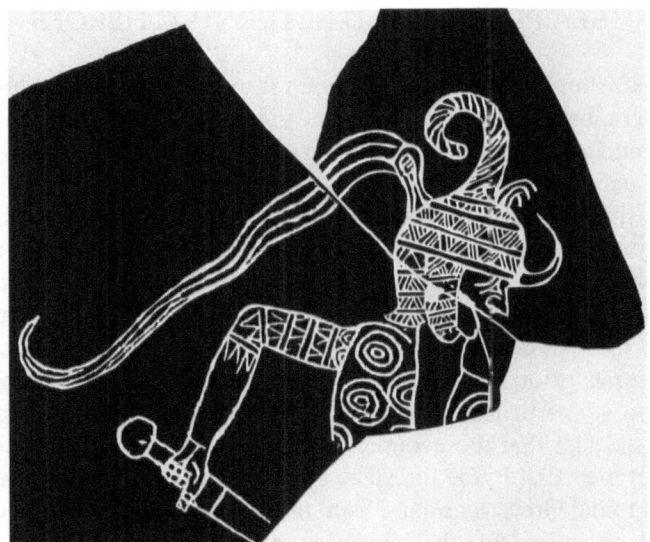

**Figure 7.8.  Aegean-style warrior on a bowl from Boğazköi, ca. 1400 BCE**
Bittel, K. 1976. "Tonschale mit Ritzzeichnung von Boğazköy." *Revue Archéologique* 1: 9–14. Figure 3.

representing an Aegean warrior, is inscribed into a bowl from Boğazköi that has been dated to *circa* 1400 BCE. Expected stylistic differences aside, the warriors represented on this Hittite bowl and on a slightly earlier fragment of a faience figurine from Mycenae are strikingly similar to the horn-helmed soldiers depicted on the Warrior Vase from Mycenae, which, as noted earlier, dates to LH IIIC Middle.

It is interesting to consider the Boğazköi bowl and the Warrior Vase in light of the as many as three centuries that separate them (from the 15th/14th to the 12th centuries BCE). On one hand, this seems to further demonstrate the intergenerational continuity of some aspects of Mycenaean warrior dress and equipment, as has already been discussed with regard to the boar's tusk helmet. On the other hand, leaving aside the highly fragmentary faience figurine from Mycenae, these are the only two examples in an Aegean context of this type of dress—in particular, the horned helmet. Further, it is of particular interest that an association with Anatolia can be argued in both cases. While this is obvious in the case of the Boğazköi bowl due to its provenience, the representation of horn-helmed warriors on the Warrior Vase is connected to Anatolia more indirectly: via the image on the reverse of the vase, the hedgehog-helmed warriors whose antecedents are found at Bademgediği Tepe (and perhaps Kos) in the East Aegean-West Anatolian Interface.

## SEA PEOPLES AND RETURNING HEROES

Rather than simply a sign of a westward movement by Anatolian warriors, the iconography seen in Egypt and on Cyprus early in the 12th century, and in mainland Greece a few decades later, may demonstrate the emergence of a class of people from the Interface at the end of the Late Bronze Age. Certainly, as shown above, the "feather-hatted" warriors appear in the Eastern Mediterranean in the late 13th century and become widespread across the Aegean through the 12th century, while the horn-helmed warriors on the obverse of the Warrior Vase are both new to LH III imagery, and highly similar to the "Mycenaean" warrior pictured on the Boğazköi bowl two to three centuries prior. Further support for this area as an origin point for the people and styles that appear slightly later in the Aegean proper may be found in the fact that the ceramics that mark the LH IIIC period seem to have developed first in the Interface or even on Cyprus, and to have spread westward to the Greek mainland from there.[21] An origin within—or, at very least, with close ties to—the Interface may also be supported by the material culture of the Philistines, whose Cypro-Aegean affinities have already been discussed.[22]

Such an association provides a subtle but interesting twist to our present consideration, in light of Homer's *Odyssey*, of the Sea Peoples movements and other events of the Late Bronze-Early Iron Age transition. While Odysseus was posing as a Cretan within the micronarrative of the Second Cretan Lie, his character in the macronarrative of the *Odyssey*, though a native of Ithaca, was engaged in his ten years of trials and tribulations in search of a *nostos* from Troy. In geographic terms, Odysseus was undertaking a dangerous and circuitous journey westward from the northernmost point in the East Aegean-West Anatolian Interface to the Greek mainland. Thus, he may be a *Sea Person* in the truest sense: an involuntary "nomad of the sea"[23] who has arisen from within the Interface and who is, over the course of a most turbulent decade, making his way west toward permanent settlement in the Aegean, all the while engaging in extracurricular activities around the Eastern Mediterranean, including piracy, raiding, trading, and outright warfare. Odysseus references just this situation in the narrative he tells to the Phaiakians:

ἡμεῖς τοι Τροίηθεν ἀποπλαγχθέντες Ἀχαιοὶ
παντοίοις ἀνέμοισιν ὑπὲρ μέγα λαῖτμα θαλάσσης,
οἴκαδε ἱέμενοι, ἄλλην ὁδὸν ἄλλα κέλευθα
ἤλθομεν: οὕτω που Ζεὺς ἤθελε μητίσασθαι.

We, thou must know, are from Troy, Achaeans, driven wandering by all manner of winds over the great gulf of the sea. Seeking our home, we have come by another way, by other paths; so, I ween, Zeus was pleased to devise.

*Odyssey* ix, 259–262

This was true not only for Odysseus, of course. As we noted earlier, the activities of other heroes in the aftermath of the collapse of Troy—and amidst the larger collapse of Bronze Age civilization as a whole—are also similar, as can be seen in the case of Menelaos' eight-year journey home.

A similar, though more limited, parallel was drawn between the *Odyssey*, the Interface and Near East, and the Sea Peoples (specifically, Merneptah's *Ekwesh*) with the suggestion that the latter "*are* Achaeans of some kind, probably not from the mainland but from Rhodes, Cyprus, or the Levant— one reason being that the Odyssey contains a probable reminiscence of one such raid on Egypt."[24] As we have seen, the connection between Ekwesh and Achaeans is highly problematic at best, although the lack of one-to-one identification between individual groups does not render the connection between the Sea Peoples phenomenon and Homer's wandering heroes entirely inapt. In light of Merneptah's reference to the Libyan incursion of which some Sea Peoples were part, and of their Cypriot and Levantine connections, it is worth noting that Menelaos' stopovers were not just contained to Egypt, but also included time spent in Phoenicia, Cyprus, and Libya:

ἦ γὰρ πολλὰ παθὼν καὶ πόλλ᾽ ἐπαληθεὶς
ἠγαγόμην ἐν νηυσὶ καὶ ὀγδοάτῳ ἔτει ἦλθον,
Κύπρον Φοινίκην τε καὶ Αἰγυπτίους ἐπαληθείς,
Αἰθίοπάς θ᾽ ἱκόμην καὶ Σιδονίους καὶ Ἐρεμβοὺς
καὶ Λιβύην, ἵνα τ᾽ ἄρνες ἄφαρ κεραοὶ τελέθουσι.

For of a truth after many woes and wide wanderings I brought my wealth home in my ships and came in the eighth year. Over Cyprus and Phoenicia I wandered, and Egypt, and I came to the Ethiopians and the Sidonians and the Erembi, and to Libya, where the lambs are horned from their birth.

*Odyssey* iv, 81–85

Late in the 20th century, British archaeologist Hector Catling sought to identify wealthy burials in four Subminoan (ca. 1050 BCE) tombs at Knossos with the wandering heroes described in Homer's *Odyssey*.[25] The tombs in question, numbered 186, 200, 201, and 202 (the latter two of which consisted of separate "caves" dug into a single pit), were found with cremation burials and grave goods largely intact, in a cemetery that continued in use into the early Christian period. These burials are unique in no small part because inhumation predominated during the era of the Aegean palaces, with cremation not becoming widespread until the 8th and 7th centuries BCE.[26] Two tombs in particular—T186 and T201—follow in the "warrior burial" tradition, containing a significant number of bronze and iron weapons, including spears and arrowheads and perhaps fragments of boar's-tusk headgear, which Catling suggested was an heirloom of the type worn by Odysseus in book ten of the *Iliad*.[27] The presence of these burials, and the continuity of settlement at Knossos across the Late Bronze-Early Iron transition (as at other large Cretan sites, like Chania and Kastelli Pediada), stands in sharp contrast to the aforementioned refuge settlements that marked much of the 12th century Late Minoan IIIC civilization. Because of this, Catling suggested Homer's "heroes returned" were simultaneously the source of the wealthy burials at Knossos and the cause of the refuges high above.[28]

A notable burial in this tradition is found at the Toumba '*heroön*' at Lefkandi on Euboea, where a cremated man was entombed alongside an inhumed woman. The man's ashes were wrapped in cloth, laid in a krater topped with a bowl, both of which were bronze imports from Cyprus, and placed next to an iron sword, whetstone, and spear head. The woman was adorned in gold and faience, and her grave goods included an Old Babylonian pendant, which was nearly a millennium old at the time of her burial, and a dagger. The *heroön* also features four horses, which seemed to have been thrown headfirst into the burial pit.[29] These burials were beneath an apsidal building, constructed around 1000 BCE, which may have served either as a monumental grave marker or as the home of the deceased, prior to being covered by a massive tumulus.[30] The man's grave goods seem to point to a role in feasting and entertaining, an interpretation which may be supported by the structure of the building under which he was buried. As archaeologist Jan-Paul Crielaard notes:

> [W]hile the weapons symbolize the man's capacity for violence and aggression connected to a distinct warrior ideology, the drinking equipment represents the socialized, political side of his activity, which presumably included ritualized leadership, sacrifice, inter- and intra-group negotiation. etc. What is more, these objects have symbolic content that relates to the man's position and functioning within his own, local community. On top of that, the burial gifts show that he maintained connections with the eastern Mediterranean.[31]

Crielaard further suggests that the approximate age of the bronze krater that served as a portion of the cremated male's urn—150 years old—may suggest that it had an "object biography" similar to valuable items seen in the Homeric epics, like the boar's tusk helmet discussed above (the Old Babylonian pendant buried with the woman can be viewed similarly). Perhaps similar to Homer's κειμήλια 'valuable object, treasure, heirloom,' these objects begin with intrinsic value, based on their material(s), geographic origin, maker, or previous owner(s), and their stories grow with each change of location and ownership until reaching their ultimate conclusion, when they are taken to the grave by their final owners.[32]

Material connections to Cyprus seem to be a characteristic of these burials, as can also be seen, for example, in 11th century "warrior burials" at Knossos and Pantanassa on Crete.[33] Further, an analogue to these tombs can be found in mid-12th century (Late Cypriot IIIB) cremation burials at Kourion-Kaloriziki on Cyprus (Tomb 40, which may have contained a male and a female).[34] Along with being located at major sites, each of these is among the earliest graves at a new cemetery. Several have multiple additional features in common, including weapons and defensive armor. Their grave goods also contain similarly alien elements that may suggest time spent in a foreign cultural milieu, and the adoption of non-local traits.[35] While this may be the result of structured interactions like trade and other forms of long-distance communication, it is also suggestive of Homer's wandering heroes, whose travels and travails following the fall of Troy included lengthy stays in foreign locales, where they assumedly adopted local customs and *materiel* as necessary. This knowledge, and a taste for these objects (or the objects themselves) would then have accompanied the individual home to Cyprus or the Aegean.[36]

The co-interment of women with the "warrior" males in each of these tombs (save T186 at Knossos) is interesting to consider in light of epic references to human sacrifice at the tombs of heroes. Particularly noteworthy examples include the slaughter of Polyxena on the tomb of Achilles in *Ilioupersis* 21, and the sacrifice of twelve Trojans on the pyre of Patroklos in the *Iliad* (along with four horses, which is reminiscent of the Lefkandi burial mentioned above):

ἐν δ' ἐτίθει μέλιτος καὶ ἀλείφατος ἀμφιφορῆας
πρὸς λέχεα κλίνων: πίσυρας δ' ἐριαύχενας ἵππους
ἐσσυμένως ἐνέβαλλε πυρῇ μεγάλα στεναχίζων.
ἐννέα τῷ γε ἄνακτι τραπεζῆες κύνες ἦσαν,
καὶ μὲν τῶν ἐνέβαλλε πυρῇ δύο δειροτομήσας,
δώδεκα δὲ Τρώων μεγαθύμων υἱέας ἐσθλοὺς
χαλκῷ δηϊόων: κακὰ δὲ φρεσὶ μήδετο ἔργα
ἐν δὲ πυρὸς μένος ἧκε σιδήρεον ὄφρα νέμοιτο.
ᾤμωξέν τ' ἄρ' ἔπειτα, φίλον δ' ὀνόμηνεν ἑταῖρον:
'χαῖρέ μοι ὦ Πάτροκλε καὶ εἰν Ἀΐδαο δόμοισι:
πάντα γὰρ ἤδη τοι τελέω τὰ πάροιθεν ὑπέστην,
δώδεκα μὲν Τρώων μεγαθύμων υἱέας ἐσθλοὺς
τοὺς ἅμα σοὶ πάντας πῦρ ἐσθίει: Ἕκτορα δ' οὔ τι
δώσω Πριαμίδην πυρὶ δαπτέμεν, ἀλλὰ κύνεσσιν.

Against the bier he leaned two-handled jars of honey and unguents; four proud horses did he then cast upon the pyre, groaning the while he did so. The dead hero had had house-dogs; two of them did Achilles slay and threw upon the pyre; he also put twelve brave sons of noble Trojans to the sword and laid them with the rest, for he was full of bitterness and fury.

Then he committed all to the resistless and devouring might of the fire; he groaned aloud and called on his dead comrade by name. 'Fare well,' he cried, 'Patroklos, even in the house of Hades; I am now doing all that I have promised you. Twelve brave sons of noble Trojans shall the flames consume along with yourself, but dogs, not fire, shall devour the flesh of Hektor son of Priam.'

*Iliad* XXIII, 175–182

While we have evidence for captive women in the Late Bronze Age Aegean, though, there is no clear indication that they carried the status of either chattel slave or burial sacrifice. In fact, the grave goods with which these women were interred seem to suggest the opposite. Catling himself admits that "the woman represented by the ashes of Tomb 200 was equipped more richly than any contemporary Subminoan or Submycenaean burial known to me."[37] The female in the *heroön* was interred in a wooden coffin, and her orientation within the south shaft placed her nearer the aforementioned horses, who were buried in the north shaft, than the male burial. This may suggest that the horses transported her bejeweled body to its (and their own) final resting place—an unlikely case if she were simply viewed as another good accompanying the male warrior to his grave.[38]

The appearance in Aegean iconography at this time of the new type of warrior discussed above—which begins a trend in pictorial representation, specifically with regard to headwear, that lasts into the Geometric period—may both support this theory, and shed light upon the subjects of these warrior burials. The common genre to which the tombs at Knossos, Lefkandi, Perati, and elsewhere on the Greek mainland, Aegean islands, and Cyprus may signal internal developments in post-palatial society. As noted previously, the 12th and 11th centuries in the Aegean saw the devolution of power and prestige from the centers into the peripheries—or, as Aegean prehistorian Thomas Palaima has suggested, a reversion from the Minoan-inspired palatial system led by the still somewhat mysterious *wanax* (*wa-na-ka* = ἄναξ) to a more traditional, loosely knit, and localized mainland Helladic system wherein the local leader (*qa-si-re-u* = βασιλεύς) held power.[39] This period would be recalled much later by Thucydides as a time of insecurity and shifting power structure, when "the richest soils were always most subject to . . . change of masters" and the "goodness of the land favored the aggrandizement of certain individuals" (1.2.3–4).

The loss of writing at the end of the Mycenaean period shifted Greek culture from the realm of history to that of prehistory. This combined with the reduction in settlements and abandonment of the palatial centers to fuel the long-held assumption that the centuries between the Late Helladic and Archaic periods were an impoverished and inward-looking "Dark Age":

> The collapse of the Bronze Age civilisations at the beginning of the period meant the end of a sophisticated system of social organisation that had dominated the leading regions of the Aegean for centuries, and it has generally been taken to involve a good deal more, the uprooting and dispersal of whole populations and the reduction of surviving communities throughout the Aegean to small and impoverished villages, which at best had only intermittent contact with a wider world.[40]

Put more briefly, it was long believed that, "During the Dark Age, the Greeks had little archaeologically measurable contact with the outside world . . . [instead, they] appear to have kept to themselves and to have attracted little attention."[41] Homer, of course, recognizes no such "Dark Age." As historian Oliver Dickinson has noted:

> Although Greek tradition generally spoke of an age of heroes in the past, most vividly described in the Homeric epics, when kings ruled wide lands from palaces full of fabulous treasures, and great deeds were performed, it recognised no period of catastrophic decline intervening between this and more recent times.

Rather, it presented the age of heroes as shading, after the Trojan War, into a period of less striking deeds that ended with the migrations by which, supposedly, the later map of mainland and Aegean Greece was largely created.[42]

Recent archaeological evidence has also helped demonstrate that this period was far less dark than modern scholars previously thought, both domestically and in terms of foreign contacts. Instead, in the words of Greek archaeologist Ioannis Moschos:

> [We must now] approach the course of a post-palatial extroverted culture with a fine political and military organization, which was not unilateral, as it was in the palatial period, but capable of changing, transforming and evolving, in order to attend, adapt to and have the lead in the demands and conditions of each era.[43]

It now seems that while power and property across the mainland were left to be seized by those who could take and hold them, the removal of the topmost stratum of Late Bronze Age society provided room for those outside the palatial centers to flourish—particularly coastal areas that had previously been limited or exploited by the palaces.[44] Such development would have been marked by the ascent of charismatic leaders—in this case, Submycenaean and Protogeometric "big men" whose physical strength, cunning, and force of will allowed them to achieve and maintain power, and to hold a population of some size together in general order. This description fits Odysseus very nicely, with his combination of physical prowess and cunning.[45] Catling christened these big men "*grandees*," and suggested that they were indeed heroes in the mold of Odysseus, wandering the Eastern Mediterranean in search of a *nostos* from the wars of the final Late Bronze Age and, upon their return, having to assert themselves in a social order that now recognized no indisputable right to rule.[46] It may also be, though, that the individuals in Tombs 186 and 200–202 at Knossos, along with their analogs across the Greek mainland, the Aegean islands, and Cyprus, represent what another scholar has referred to as "warrior princes"—our charismatic leaders—in whose hands rested the transference of power and whatever order there was to be found in the post-palatial period, all of whom, like Penelope's suitors at Ithaca, were "out to seize what they could for themselves."[47]

In anthropological terms, post-palatial Aegean society seems to have been broken up into a number of "big-man societies" or "chiefdoms," perhaps led by those who had been identified in the Late Bronze Age by the term *qa-si-re-u*, and in the post-palatial period with the term βασιλεύς. [48] These local leaders would likely have acquired more power and responsibility through a combination of force, of charisma, and of claims to legitimacy via hereditary connection to the preceding order.[49] The former may have manifested itself in part in the command of vessels and rowing crews, as we shall see below, while the latter could have taken the form of the manipulation of objects and symbols tied to elite status, be they luxury items or images like chariots, which, as we have already seen, their Bronze Age predecessors may have been able to muster in significant numbers.[50]

As Tomb 40 at Kourion attests, the post-palatial rise of the warrior-leader seems to have been projected east of the Aegean, to Cyprus. Terminologically, this is further supported by the fact that βασιλεύς served as official title for the leaders of most Cypriot states until the fourth century BCE.[51] It also seems clear that the island absorbed a portion of the displaced Aegean population in the 12th century BCE, although the long-standing view that "Mycenaean colonists and conquerors were the lords of [Cyprus]" in the Early Iron Age has been discarded in favor of a more measured approach. As historian Claude Baurain noted, Mycenaean civilization was not simply transplanted to—nor transposed upon—Cyprus in the 12th century. After all, "none of those essential elements [of Mycenaean civilization], absent in Cyprus before the end of LC IIC, are sufficiently present during the LC IIA and LC IIIB: tholos tombs, palaces of a continental type, seals and Linear B archives."[52] (The great Cypriot archaeologist Vassos Karageorghis replied to this by noting that, "if these strict criteria were applied to indicate the presence of Mycenaeans elsewhere, they would be confined to the Peloponnese and to certain other centers of mainland Greece throughout the Bronze Age and beyond. . . . We have [Mycenaean] seals in Cyprus, but should we expect every immigrant to build a tholos tomb?").[53]

Instead, among the most important things Aegeans brought with them to Cyprus were their language, which became the Greek dialect of Cyprus,[54] and pottery and domestic implements like the Aegean-style cooking jug—in other words, signals of the aforementioned "deep change" we would expect from the presence of migrants. The absence of writing and similar trappings of the Helladic palace system, on the other hand, including the position of the *wanax* itself, suggests that the topmost stratum of Mycenaean civilization was not included in this limited migration. Instead, the movement eastward to Cyprus may have weighed heavily in the other direction, toward society's non-elites.[55] As we shall see, nautically oriented leaders may have been among this migratory population, bringing not just people, but a major instrument of maritime technology along with them at the end of the Bronze Age, in the form of the Helladic oared galley.

*Chapter Eight*

# Mariners and Their Ships: Vessel Types, Capacity, and Rigging

ἐννέα νῆας στεῖλα, θοῶς δ᾽ ἐσαγείρατο λαός.

Nine ships I fitted out, and the host gathered speedily.

*Odyssey* xiv, 248

When evaluating the makeup of Odysseus' fleet of nine ships against the magnitude of his undertaking, it is important to consider both the *type* and the *potential capacity* of the hero's vessels. This is particularly true in light of new maritime technology that appears to have been introduced in the Aegean and Eastern Mediterranean at this time.

## THE HELLADIC OARED GALLEY AND THE BRAILED SAIL

Until the last century or so of the Bronze Age, ship design in the Mediterranean seems to have been typified by the sailing vessels found in Minoan and Egyptian relief, such as the craft depicted on the south wall of Room 5 of the West House at Akrotiri and the "Byblos ships" (*kbn*) shown in the commemoration of an expedition to Punt at Queen Hatshepsut's mortuary temple at Deir el-Bahri.[1] The construction and use of these ships carried over into the Mycenaean period, with iconography providing evidence for their adoption by polities on the Greek mainland. This can be seen in particular in an early 14th century fresco from Iklaina and late 14th–early 13th century painted ship representations from Hall 64 of the southwestern building in the palace complex at Pylos.[2] Alongside this, though, the 13th century in the Aegean saw the development and introduction not just of the first distinctly Mycenaean craft, but an altogether new type of vessel: the oared galley. A long, narrow, light craft propelled primarily by rowers and designed specifically for speed, the galley was a vessel well suited for martial purposes, including raiding, piracy, and naval warfare. Called "the single most significant advance in the weaponry of the Bronze Age Eastern Mediterranean," the galley was lighter and more maneuverable than Minoan-style vessels, and could be quickly beached and refloated as needed.[3]

The first depictions of this vessel type are found in the late 13th century, with the majority appearing in the 12th century (LH IIIC). It is important to emphasize how significant a break the galley represents with the shipbuilding tradition to that point, which had been traceable along a linear path from Cycladic longboats via the earliest known Minoan vessels. Unlike these earlier "oared sailing ships," whose primary form of propulsion was downwind sails, the galley was built around a human "motor"—its rowers—and the process behind its seemingly abrupt appearance in the known typology of sailing vessels is still not fully understood.[4]

Iconographic evidence from both Egypt and the Aegean suggests that, sometime between the end of the 13th and middle of the 12th centuries BCE, the oared galley began to be outfitted with the brailed rig and loose-footed sail. The brailed rig consisted of lines attached to the bottom of a sail and run vertically through rings called "brails" (also called "fairleads," possibly Homeric κάλοι; see, for example, *Odyssey* v, 260), which were sewn into the front of the sail. From there, they were run vertically over the yard and aft to the stern, where they were controlled by the steersman. Using this system, sails could be easily raised, lowered, and otherwise manipulated in a manner similar to a set of Venetian blinds.[5] As we shall see, this combination, which would become a mainstay of Eastern Mediterranean sailing vessels for the next two millennia, was most likely developed in the area of the Syro-Canaanite littoral and diffused from there to the south and west via the aforementioned "raiders and traders" of the Late Bronze Age.[6]

If the development of the Helladic oared galley was "a strategic inflection point in ship architecture," as one scholar has termed it, the adoption of the loose-footed, brailed squaresail was no less than a technological revolution in Mediterranean seafaring.[7] Until this time, sailing craft had relied on large square sails held fast by upper and lower yards, referred to as the "yard" and the "boom," respectively (hence the term "boom-footed squaresail"). The sail on these vessels was furled by lowering the yard to the boom, at which time the former was held in place by topping lifts. The boom, on the other hand, was affixed to the mast and supported by lifts connected to the mast cap, an aspect of ancient vessels which, Wachsmann has noted, "were one of the most conspicuous elements of [the boom-footed] rig and almost always appeared in iconographic depictions of ships carrying this type of rig."[8] This can be seen in representations of boom-footed vessels in media as diverse as the aforementioned Akrotiri fresco,[9] Punt reliefs,[10] and Pylian representations,[11] as well as a small 14th century cylinder seal from Tell Miqne-Ekron,[12] among many other examples. At least 33 representations of vessels with boom-footed squaresails are known from the Bronze Age Aegean, and while they clearly provided advantage over oared propulsion alone, this rig largely limited seafarers to downwind travel.[13]

The existence of a brailing system for boom-footed vessels has also been hypothesized.[14] In such an "all-around" system, brailing lines would be looped around both yard and boom before being passed aft to the stern of the vessel, theoretically allowing the sail to be shaped for better maneuverability by adjusting the angle of the yard and boom relative to each other (an adjustment from their standard positioning, which was parallel to each other and perpendicular to the mast), rather than by simply shaping the windward edge of the sail itself, as with a loose-footed sail. However, while this type of adjustment may have been made on Bronze Age vessels, such a system would likely have been too unwieldy to have been worth the minor benefits, particularly on large merchantmen. Further, no secure evidence from the Mediterranean world currently exists to support the use of brails with a boom-footed sail in this "all-around" manner.

Other depictions which have been held to be representations of brails on boom-footed vessels feature sails affixed only to the upper yard (supposedly "brailed up"), rather than around both yard and boom. An Abydos boat from the late 18th dynasty tomb of Neferhotep (TT 50), an Egyptian official during the reign of the final pre-Ramesside pharaoh, Horemheb (1319–1292 BCE), shows a sail which may be interpreted as being brailed to an upward-curving yard. However, the boom is still present, no brailing lines are explicitly shown, and the ship appears elsewhere in the same relief with the sail secured to both upper and lower yards. Turin Papyri 2032 and 2033, which date to the early Ramesside period, likewise show riverine vessels whose sails appear similarly brailed-up to upward-curving upper yards, but which still carry booms.[15]

In part because of the boom-footed squaresail's limitations, merchantmen in the Late Bronze Age Eastern Mediterranean are believed to have generally traveled in a counterclockwise circuit. In this system, a ship sailing from the Aegean would likely begin its international journey on Crete, perhaps at the southern port of Kommos, a key node in the international trade network until the mid-13th century, whose combination of imports from Anatolia, the Levant, Cyprus, Egypt in the east, the Greek mainland to the north, and Sardinia to the west provide the greatest evidence for inter-cultural exchange of any site in the Aegean.[16] From there, they would either sail directly to Egypt (as seen in the *Odyssey*), or make a shorter journey south to Marsa Matruh or the Ramesside fortress site of Zawiyet Umm el-Rakham on the Marmarican coast before proceeding eastward to Egypt.[17] A ship departing Egypt, or seeking to travel in a westerly direction more generally, would likely have sailed up the Canaanite littoral to Ugarit, and then put in at Enkomi, Kition, or Hala Sultan Tekke on Cyprus before traveling along the Anatolian coast and entering the Aegean from the east. An example of the latter is the late 14th century Ulu Burun shipwreck, which was discussed in detail earlier.[18]

The manipulation of the sail made possible by the addition of brails and removal of the boom, on the other hand, allowed for much greater maneuver-ability, as well as the ability to sail much closer to the wind—not to mention the fact that, when it came to maritime warfare, the maneuverability of troops on deck would have been improved, as they no longer had to worry about the lower yard obstructing their movement.[19] Once outfitted with the brailed rig and loose-footed sail, then, the Helladic oared galley became an ideal vessel for rapid travel and lightning-fast raids on coastal settlements:

> In the beginning the brailable square sail allowed hull forms quite unsuited to propulsion by sail of the Thera-type [the traditional boom-footed squaresail] the opportunity to extend their cruising range due to the lightness of gear and ease of control. Skills learnt in handling the rig coupled with improvements in gear and fittings enabled effective courses to be sailed in a wide range of directions other than before the wind. The ability to conserve the strength of the rowing crew . . . and the ability to sail in most directions economically with small crews, given a slant of wind . . . opened greater horizons to military adventurers.[20]

### Sea Routes: From Crete to 'Fair-Flowing *Aegyptus*'

ἑβδομάτῃ δ᾽ ἀναβάντες ἀπὸ Κρήτης εὐρείης
ἐπλέομεν Βορέῃ ἀνέμῳ ἀκραέϊ καλῷ
ῥηϊδίως, ὡς εἴ τε κατὰ ῥόον· οὐδέ τις οὖν μοι
νηῶν πημάνθη, ἀλλ᾽ ἀσκηθέες καὶ ἄνουσοι
ἥμεθα, τὰς δ᾽ ἄνεμός τε κυβερνῆταί τ᾽ ἴθυνον.
πεμπταῖοι δ᾽ Αἴγυπτον ἐϋρρείτην ἱκόμεσθα,
στῆσα δ᾽ ἐν Αἰγύπτῳ ποταμῷ νέας ἀμφιελίσσας.

On the seventh [day] we embarked and set sail from broad Crete, with the North Wind blowing fresh and fair, and ran on easily as if downstream. No harm came to any of my ships, but free from scathe and from disease we sat, and the wind and the helmsman guided the ships. On the fifth day we came to fair-flowing Aegyptus, and in the river Aegyptus I moored my curved ships.

*Odyssey* xiv, 252–258

Though scholars have long held the belief that ancient sailors could (or would) *only* travel in sight of land, this is demonstrably incorrect.[21] For example, amidst the prevalent counterclockwise trade routes plied by boom-footed merchantmen, there existed a blue water route aided by the Etesian winds that could be taken by vessels seeking a direct (albeit riskier) path from the southern coast of Crete to Egypt. As can be seen from the reference to running before the wind, Odysseus' δολιχὴν ὁδόν 'far voyage' (*Odyssey* xvii, 426) to the Nile delta is likely an example of this route in action. This four-day sailing period from southern Crete to Egypt is identical to that reported by Strabo (10.4.5) a millennium later, which suggests both that this route and its duration were common long before the Classical period.[22] Sailors may have plied it with some frequency at least from the 15th century BCE, though the aforementioned circuitous return trip would still have been required.[23]

On the surface, such a reference to a downwind trip as that made by Odysseus might seem to offer no specific information about the type of vessel the hero employed in this expedition; in fact, given that the blue water route from Crete to Egypt likely predates the advent of the brailed rig and oared galley, this passage might even be read as suggesting the use of vessels equipped with the traditional boom-footed squaresail. However, a potentially important clue is embedded in the phrase ἀσκηθέες καὶ ἄνουσοι ἥμεθα, τὰς δ' ἄνεμός τε κυβερνῆταί τ' ἴθυνον (*Odyssey* xiv, 255–256): the fact that Odysseus finds it worthwhile to specifically mention that the wind and helmsman "guided the ships," while he and his men "sat . . . free of scathe," suggests that this stroke of good fortune (ἐσθλὸν ἑταῖρον 'goodly comrade'; *Odyssey* xii, 149) allowed for a crew *that would otherwise have been rowing* to instead rest in preparation for their assault on the Delta (cf. *Iliad* VII, 4–6). Support for this reading can be seen in Odysseus' other use of the phrase ἥμεθα: τὴν δ' ἄνεμός τε κυβερνήτης τ' ἴθυνε (*Odyssey* xii, 152), the context of which makes clear that the vessel would have been propelled primarily by rowers had Circe's "fair wind that filled the sail" not provided a fortuitous reprieve for the hero's crew:

ἑξῆς δ' ἑζόμενοι πολιὴν ἅλα τύπτον ἐρετμοῖς.
ἡμῖν δ' αὖ κατόπισθε νεὸς κυανοπρῴροιο
ἴκμενον οὖρον ἵει πλησίστιον, ἐσθλὸν ἑταῖρον,
Κίρκη ἐϋπλόκαμος, δεινὴ θεὸς αὐδήεσσα.
αὐτίκα δ' ὅπλα ἕκαστα πονησάμενοι κατὰ νῆα
ἥμεθα: τὴν δ' ἄνεμός τε κυβερνήτης τ' ἴθυνε.

So they went on board straightway and sat down upon the benches, and sitting well in order smote the grey sea with their oars. And for our aid in the wake of our dark-prowed ship a fair wind that filled the sail, a goodly comrade, was sent by fair-tressed Circe, dread goddess of human speech. So when we had straightway made fast all the tackling throughout the ship we sat down, but the wind and the helmsman guided the ship.

*Odyssey* xii, 147–152

Thus, it is likely that the "fleet" employed on Odysseus' Egyptian expedition may very well have been made up of the aforementioned oared galleys, and the chronology of events into which this seems to best fit suggests that those galleys were likely equipped with the loose-footed, brailed squaresail.

## DEVELOPMENT AND DEPICTION IN RAMESSIDE EGYPT

Brailed sails are first shown on galleys in the naval battle depiction from Medinet Habu, carved no later than Ramesses III's twelfth regnal year (*circa* 1171 BCE). This relief serves as a monumental "coming out party" for several other new features of maritime technology, as well, including the top-mounted crow's nest and partial decking, from which warriors could engage enemy vessels with spears, slings, and grapnels. Remarkably, these attributes—including sail and rigging—are depicted identically on both the Sea Peoples' and the Egyptian vessels, perhaps suggesting a common source of these technologies.

In the Medinet Habu depiction, rowers are only shown aboard the Egyptian ships. However, this does not mean that sail was the Sea Peoples ships' sole means of propulsion; in fact, given that these vessels were modeled after the oared galley prototype, this was almost certainly not the case.[24] The best analogue for the Medinet Habu ships seems to be "Kynos A," the nearly complete vessel at right on the aforementioned LH IIIC Middle krater from Pyrgos Livanaton in central Greece (mid-12th century BCE; Figs. 7.3 and 8.1). Kynos A lacks rigging, instead displaying only a forestay and two slack lines trailing to stern. However, the circular masthead with its two deadeyes demonstrates that this ship is equipped with the brailed rig.

This is also seen on another fragment from Kynos and a stirrup jar from Skyros, which similarly depict vessels without raised sail, but with the two deadeyes characteristic of the loose-footed brailed sail, along with forestay and, unlike Kynos A, backstay.[25] Further support for this identification comes from another remarkable fragment from Kynos, which does depict a loose-

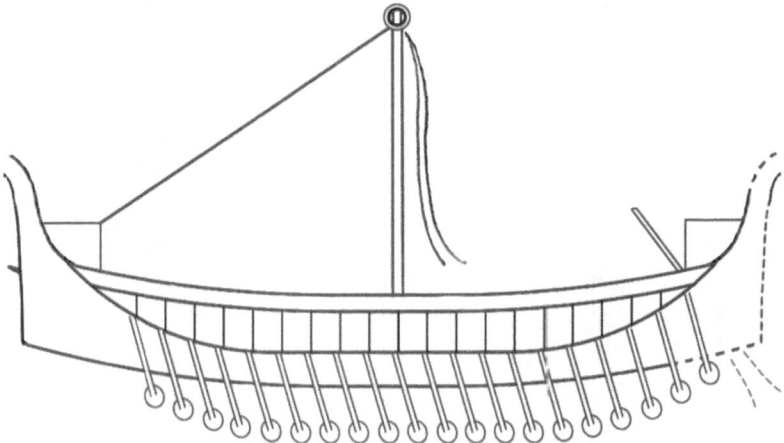

**Figure 8.1a.   'Kynos A' vessel from Pyrgos Livanaton, LH IIIC Middle**
Illustration by the author.

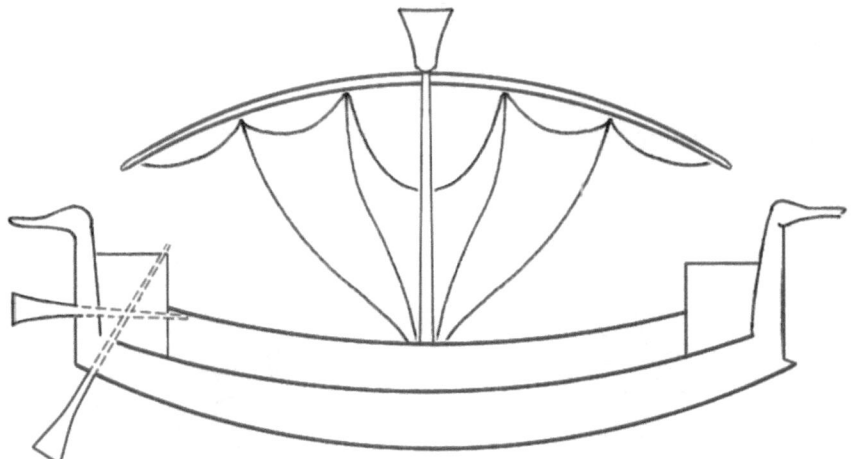

**Figure 8.1b.   Sea Peoples ship from the Medinet Habu naval battle**
Illustration by the author.

footed sail that is brailed up—the earliest secure representation from the Aegean region, and a *terminus ante quem* for its introduction there.[26]

As might be expected given their different authors, media, and intended audiences, there are significant differences between the Medinet Habu and Kynos representations. For example, while the single quarter rudder (or steering oar) depicted on Kynos A, characteristic of Mycenaean ships, is paralleled on two of the Sea Peoples' ships, two others feature two quarter rudders, and the fifth Sea Peoples ship has no quarter rudder.[27] On the former, both are on the starboard quarter, while the latter has a rudder on either quarter. Wachsmann has suggested multiple reasons for this inconsistency:

> Presumably, the normal complement was two steering oars, and those missing are attributable to loss during battle. In this matter they differ from contemporaneous representations of craft from the Aegean but seem to herald the use of the double steering oars that were to become common equipment on Geometric craft. Alternately, the Sea Peoples may have adopted the use of a pair of quarter rudders after encountering and capturing Syro-Canaanite and Egyptian seagoing ships that normally used two steering oars, one placed on either quarter.[28]

Aside from rowers, shown in stylized form on Kynos A, and the yard and sail which are absent from Kynos A but present at Medinet Habu (a representational gap that is filled in part by the aforementioned Kynos sherd depicting a brailed-up sail), the most notable difference between these ships may be the presence of crow's nests atop the masts of the Medinet Habu ships. Though we should, of course, keep in mind that the absence of a feature in iconography does not necessitate its physical or historical absence, it makes sense that the Kynos vessels would not feature crow's nests, as it is neither a feature of Helladic ships nor of Egyptian vessels in the pre-Medinet Habu period.[29] The earliest known crow's nests come from depictions of Syro-Canaanite vessels in two Egyptian tombs: the 18th dynasty tomb of Kenamun (Theban Tomb 162; Fig. 8.2) and the 19th or 20th dynasty tomb of Iniwia.[30]

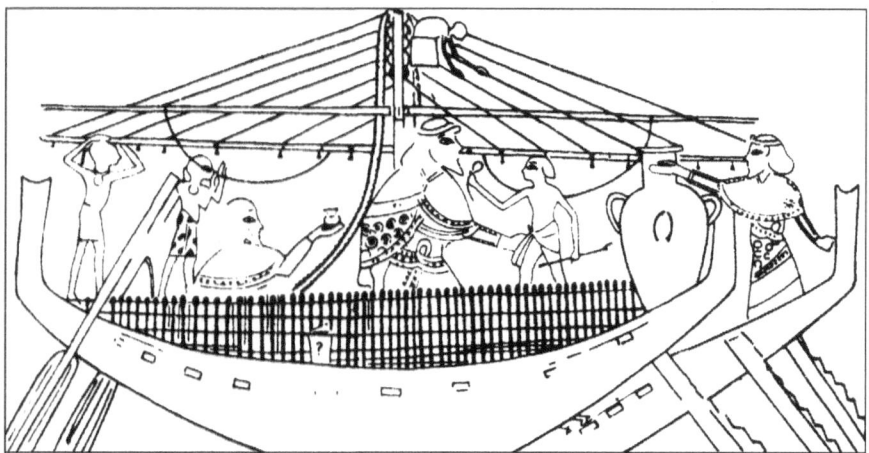

**Figure 8.2.   Crow's nest on a Syro-Canaanite trading vessel from the 18th dynasty Tomb of Kenamun (Theban Tomb 162)**
Davies, N. De G. and Faulkner, R. O. 1947. "A Syrian Trading Venture to Egypt." *Journal of Egyptian Archaeology* 33: 40–46. After plate VIII.

However, unlike the Medinet Habu vessels, the crow's nests depicted on these ships are side-mounted, either affixed to the forward face of the mast or hung from the masthead. A ship from the 18th dynasty tomb of Nebamun (TT 17; Fig. 8.3) features an implement atop its mast that has been called a top-mounted crow's nest, but which seems more likely, based on comparative iconography, to be a mast cap.

Ultimately, the appearance of the top-mounted crow's nest on Syro-Canaanite vessels depicted in Egyptian art (which is our only visual source of these ships prior to the 12th century BCE), and its absence from both Aegean and Egyptian maritime culture, suggest that it originated from this area.[31] Given their regular contact with the Syro-Canaanite littoral, as well as the clear value of a lookout on a raised platform for raiding and paramilitary functions, it is perhaps unsurprising that the Sea Peoples may have adopted the crow's nest from Levantine seafarers just as they seem to have adopted the brailed rig from this area.[32]

If correctly dated to the late 18th or early 19th dynasties (the first quarter of the 13th century BCE), a critically important but rarely cited portion of a relief from Saqqara may provide support for the Levantine origin of the crow's nest, loose-footed sail, and brailed rig, while providing a crucial missing link between Syro-Canaanite ship construction and the technology utilized by both sides of the naval battle.[33] The mast, furled sails, downward-curving yard, and top-mounted crow's nest of the seagoing ship depicted in this relief are identical to those from Medinet Habu (compare Figures 8.4 and 8.1b). Part of the yard, furled sail, and double backstay of a second, identically rigged vessel is partially visible on the left edge of the relief.

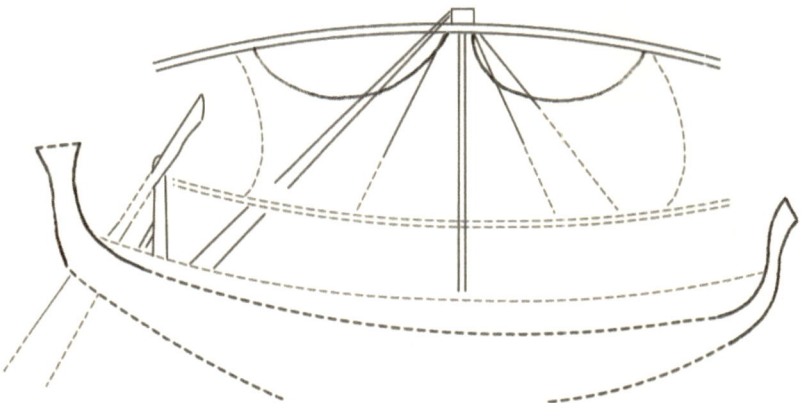

**Figure 8.3.   Syro-Canaanite ship with downward curving yard from the tomb of Nebamun (Theban Tomb 17)**
Illustration by the author.

Figure 8.4a. Late 18th or early 19th dynasty relief from Saqqara showing two vessels with downward-curving yards, brailed rigs, and top-mounted crow's nests
Capart, J. 1931. *Documents pour Servir à l'étude de l'art Égyptien* II. Paris. Plate 67.

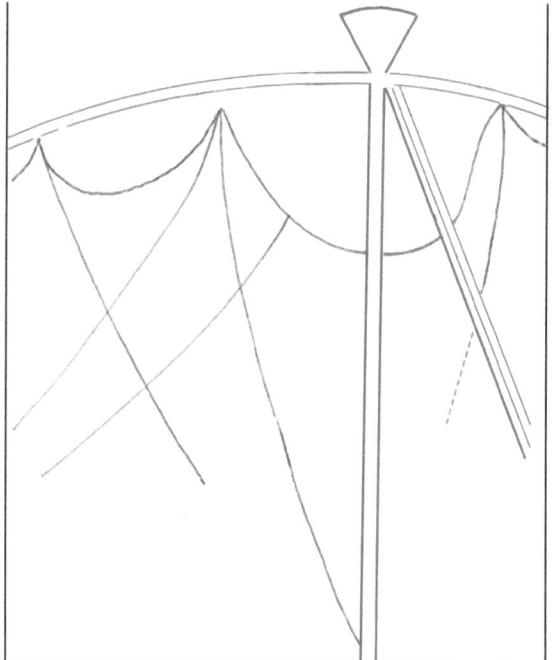

Figure 8.4b. Detail of the mast, yard, rigging, and crow's nest from the Saqqara relief
Illustration by the author.

Unfortunately, the mast and rigging are all that is shown of these ships; no hints are provided as to the hull design and shape. A date range between the late 18th and early 20th dynasties is supported by the ceramics visible in the sculpted scene—particularly the Canaanite amphorae being carried in the foreground, which are of a type that was in use from the 14th into the 12th centuries BCE (from the late 18th to the 20th dynasty in Egypt).[34] Such a range places the appearance of this vessel at the same general time as the first recorded appearance of the Sherden on Egypt's coast. While the scholar who initially published the Saqqara relief noted the similarity between the top-mounted crow's nest on this piece and the Medinet Habu ships, even among specialists very few people have noted these similarities in yard and rigging, and thus commented on the potential significance of this object for improving our understanding of both the geography and the chronology of this technological development.[35]

Unlike the brailed rig, the downward-curving yard is frequently seen in depictions of Syro-Canaanite seagoing vessels in the Late Bronze Age.[36] Likely the result of a light yard responding to downward pressure from the furled sails, this feature can be found on the aforementioned ship from the tomb of Nebamun and a 13th century scaraboid from Ugarit.[37] Along with the yard, brailed sail, and crow's nest, the Syro-Canaanite origin of this vessel is supported by the relief's aforementioned noted above depiction of the Canaanite amphorae being unloaded at an Egyptian port. As we have seen, its date, while perhaps roughly a century earlier than Medinet Habu, is consistent with late 18th and early 19th dynasty references to Sea Peoples in the Eastern Mediterranean, including Ramesses II's early 13th century defeat of "rebellious-hearted Sherden" off the Egyptian coast (more on this below).

A Syro-Canaanite provenience of the top-mounted crow's nest and downward-curving yard helps explain both their *absence* on galleys depicted in their native Aegean milieu and their *presence* on Sea Peoples' vessels of Helladic oared galley type that are shown in the area of the Levant and Egypt, while the development of the brailed rig in the area of the Canaanite littoral could also explain its nearly simultaneous appearance at a slightly later date, in the early-to-mid 12th century BCE, on both Egyptian and Aegean ships. The brailed sail's spread, in turn, can be credited without much difficulty to those aforementioned people whom we have seen referred to as "nomads of the sea" and "pirates, raiders, and traders," whose travels took them around the Aegean and Eastern Mediterranean, and whose lives and livelihoods alike were dependent on effective maritime technology.[38]

With that context in mind, we can now return to Kynos A and the Sea Peoples vessels at Medinet Habu. Relevant differences having been noted, it is clear that Kynos A, if not identical to the Sea Peoples ships, is an extremely close relative. Due to the style of the warriors and rowers depicted on them, as well as the medium, relative date of composition, and geographic provenance, we can cautiously suggest both that the vessels on the Bademgediği Tepe krater, and the fragmentary vessels shown on the sherds from Kos and Liman Tepe are of this type, as well, despite the highly schematic shape of the former and the fragmentary nature of the latter two representations. As can be seen in Figure 8.5, mounting the yard and furling the sail on Kynos A in

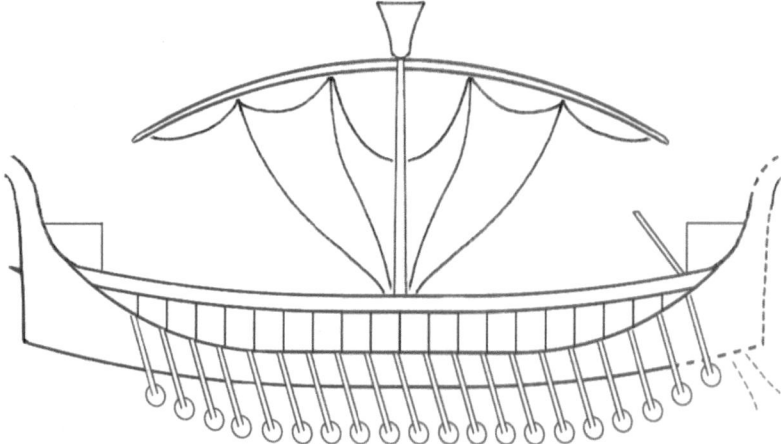

**Figure 8.5a.    'Kynos' A ship with oar detail and Medinet Habu rigging added**
Illustration by the author.

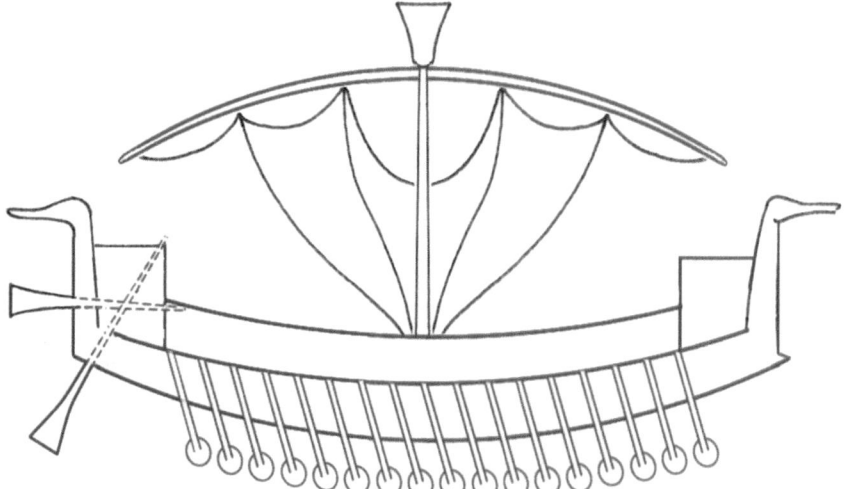

**Figure 8.5b.    Sea Peoples ship from Medinet Habu with oars added**
Illustration by the author.

the manner shown at Medinet Habu, and adding the missing oars to the Sea Peoples vessels, produces two nearly identical ships.

The above-noted Aegean association of at least some Sea Peoples, along with the importance of maritime technology to their lives and livelihoods, provides a logical basis for their adoption and use of the oared galley, while the well-documented travels of members of these groups throughout the Eastern Mediterranean may explain their exposure to the top-mounted crow's nest and brailed rig (only the latter of which appears on Aegean and Interface ships at this time). Further, while exceedingly few nautical references have been found in Philistine material culture, the connection between Sea Peoples and the brailed rig is further attested by ceramic evidence from Tel Miqne-Ekron. Sherds of a 12th century Philistine Monochrome krater feature the characteristic semi-circles of a brailed rig with furled sail, along with the horizontal line of the yard and three vertical lines, which likely represent a mast and halyards or brails.[39] Vertical lines below the deck may depict a rowers' gallery, further supporting the potential identification of this vessel as a galley (Fig. 8.6).

Two ship graffiti should also be noted, one from the Carmel coast of Israel and one from Cyprus. Sometime between the 13th and 11th centuries BCE, several boats were incised on the cliffs above the Me'arot River in northern Israel. One of these appears to display a brailed rig, furled sail, and downward curving yard, along with forward-facing ornamentation on the stempost and inward-curving sternpost, similar in form to the Kynos and Skyros vessels (Fig. 8.7).[40] On Cyprus, a similar, though much cruder, LC IIIA graffito from Enkomi also seems to depict a ship outfitted with the brailed rig, pictured with its sail furled.[41] Additionally, it has been suggested that a cryptic circular representation on the aforementioned bichrome pictorial krater fragment from Ashkelon may represent a brailed sail.[42]

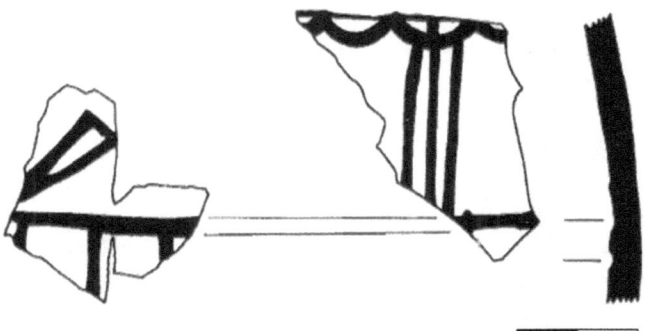

**Figure 8.6.   Philistine monochrome sherd from Ekron showing an oared vessel with a brailed sail**
Dothan, T. and Zukerman, A. 2004. "A Preliminary Study of the Mycenaean IIIC:1 Pottery Assemblages from Tel Miqne-Ekron and Ashdod." *Bulletin of the American Schools of Oriental Research* 333: 1–54. Figure 35.10.

**Figure 8.7.    Ship graffito from Nahal Me'arot on the Carmel Coast, likely of 13th–11th century date**
Artzy, M. 2013. "On the Other Sea Peoples." In Killebrew, A. E. and Lehmann, G., eds. *The Philistines and Other Sea Peoples in Text and Archaeology*. Atlanta. 329–344. Figure 4:5.

How exactly did Egypt come to acquire and adopt these innovative components of maritime technology, which appear on their ships at the same time as those of the Sea Peoples? A simple explanation may be that they were acquired through direct contact with those same "pirates, raiders, and traders"— groups like the Sherden and men like Odysseus—during the century prior to Ramesses III's famous battle.[43] The first direct mention of seaborne threats against Egypt during the Ramesside period can be found in the aforementioned Aswan and Tanis II stelae of Ramesses II, which refer to sea raiders and Sherden, respectively (see also EA 38 and the inscription of Amenhotep son of Hapu, discussed above, for prior references). If the early 13th century date is correct for several Ugaritic texts thought to refer to Sherden individuals in that coastal Syrian *emporion*, and if the *trtn(m)* and *srdnn(m)* found at Ugarit are in fact to be identified with the Ramesside Šrdn, then Tanis II in particular seems to support the contemporaneous movement and/or dispersion of these people along the Eastern Mediterranean coast early in the 13th century, albeit with widely differing levels of integration.[44]

As noted above, trade *emporia* dotted the region in this period, with shipping lanes and anchorages alike doubtless serving as tempting targets for skilled privateers and opportunities for similarly skilled swords-for-hire to defend those potential targets.[45] Thus, we should not be surprised to find warship-sailing "Sherden of the Sea" at various locations around the Eastern Mediterranean—particularly if their maritime exploits were by this time based in some part on piracy, as Ramesses II's inscriptions (along with those of Merneptah and Ramesses III) have traditionally been read as reporting, or on mercenary activities, as modern scholars have generally inferred. Further, if the encounter with the Sherden recorded in Tanis II took place while they were engaged in such marauding, then it stands to reason that they may have employed ships and/or sailing tactics that were similar in construction and nature to other sea raiders operating in the Eastern Mediterranean at this time. Certainly the characterization of the Sherden as those "whom none could ever fight against" suggests that they, like their fellow-travelers the Lukka (cf. EA 38, the Great Karnak Inscription, and the Athribis stele), had been engaging in such activities for some time by this point.

Some of the aforementioned Sherden living at Ugarit appear to have integrated into society to such a degree that they were able to own and bequeath land:

> [And next: the house] and the salt-producing field [of xxx]IM,
> son of the *sherdana*. Kurwanu bought [for x hund]red (shekels) of
> silver. This field [ of] Kurwanu will be forever.

RS 15.167+163, 12–15[46]

As we shall see, a number of those living in Egypt appear to have achieved a similar level of integration a century and a half later.

## A New Term for New Technology?

A noteworthy element of the Tanis II inscription is the fact, first observed by Jean Yoyotte and subsequently followed by Kenneth Kitchen, that the encounter it describes was unique enough that it apparently forced the Egyptians to invent a new term for "warship" in order to commemorate it.[47] The result was the somewhat clumsy *aḥaw aḥ3 m-ḥry-ib p3 ym* 'ships of fighting in the heart of the sea,' which Yoyotte glossed as "ships-of-warriors-on-the-sea" and Kitchen further distilled to "ships of fighting."[48] Seagoing ships had been used for some time in the Egyptian military, with one example being, the *imw n t3 aḥt* of Seti I and Thutmosis III, which have been glossed 'warship' or 'battleship' in modern scholarship.[49] Given this, the need to fabricate a new term suggests a certain lack of prior experience either with the *type* of vessel sailed by the Sherden, with the *capabilities* of those vessels, or with both. Thus, the term employed on Tanis II may have been intended to describe Sherden vessels as maritime fighting platforms (as the literal translation of the Tanis term may suggest), or it may have been a reference to a method of coastal marauding that made use of specialized ships or sailing techniques to conduct lightning-fast raids and then disappear back into the sea and over the horizon before military forces could be mobilized against them.

This absence of such fighting platforms from Egyptian maritime culture suggests, in turn, that the pharaoh's defeat of the Sherden may have taken place either on land or in the "river-mouths" of the Nile delta, which had been defended at least since the time of Amenhotep III (see above), and where the Egyptian army would have been better able to ensnare an enemy whose success was dependent on a combination of speed, stealth, and, above all, the avoidance of contact with professional soldiers.[50] It was here, of course, that Ramesses III would later famously claim to have defended the coast against another, much larger onslaught of Sea Peoples.

The introduction of a new vessel type, perhaps by Sherden raiders (see below), may also be supported by a comparative analysis of the determinatives used in the Tanis II inscription and in Ramesses III's Inscription of Year 8 at Medinet Habu (Fig. 8.8). The determinative utilized with *aḥaw* in Tanis II has the basic form of a typical Late Bronze Age Syro-Palestinian ship (Fig. 8.8g), similar in form, though far less detailed, to the trading vessels depicted in the Tomb of Kenamun and to the determinative used for *mnš* in the Tanis II inscription.[51] At Medinet Habu, on the other hand, the determinatives are dramatically different.

The Year 8 inscription mentions ships four times. The Sea Peoples' ships are referenced once, and three types of Egyptian vessels are said to have been "prepared like a strong wall . . . along the Nile mouth" against the assault.[52] Each reference to an Egyptian ship is accompanied by a distinct determinative, which seems related to that ship's function. As can be seen from Figures 8.8a and 8.8b, two vessel types—*b3r* and *mnš*—were primarily utilized for cargo or transport.[53] The third is the *aḥa* ship (*aḥawt*), familiar from Tanis II.[54] However, instead of being paired with a Syro-Palestinian cargo ship (as in Tanis II), the associated determinative is unmistakably a vessel of the same type as that manned by the Egyptians in the naval battle relief (Figs. 8.8c and 8.8e). Much like the Tanis II determinative's relationship to the vessels from TT 162, the Medinet Habu determinative for *aḥa* ships does not include the mast and rigging, but unlike the former, there are additional details besides the essentials of the hull shape—in particular, the forecastle and steering oar which are such integral parts of the Egyptian vessels shown in the relief. The mention of the Sea Peoples' vessels also utilizes the term *aḥawt*, with a determinative that is quite similar to that paired with the term in column 20 of the inscription, but with a castle amidships (Fig. 8.8d).[55] It is perhaps noteworthy that the determinative appearing as part of the mention of the Sea Peoples' *aḥawt* is much more similar in appearance to the Egyptian vessels than to those of the Sea Peoples in the naval battle relief (compare Figs. 8.8d and 8.8f). Additionally, in keeping with its slightly different presentation of the Sea Peoples narrative (and of his reign altogether), the Great Harris Pa-

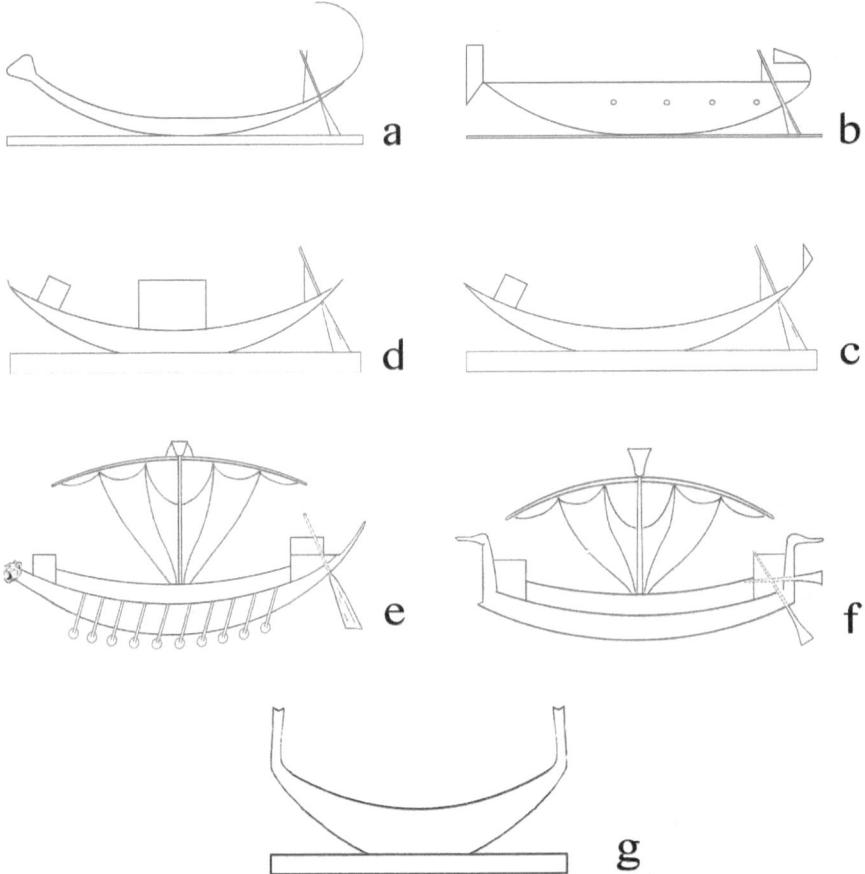

**Figure 8.8.** Ramesside ship determinatives and the vessels from Medinet Habu (MH): (a) *b3r* determinative, Great Inscription of Year 8, MH; (b) *mnš* determinative, MH; (c) *aḥawt* determinative, MH; (d) *aḥawt* determinative used in reference to Sea Peoples vessels, MH; (e) Egyptian warship from the naval battle relief, MH; (f) Sea Peoples vessel from the naval battle relief, MH; (g) *aḥaw* determinative, Tanis II rhetorical stele, Ramesses II
Illustrations by the author.

pyrus omits *aḥawt* from the catalogue of vessel types built by Ramesses III, replacing it instead with *qrr*-ships:

> . . . I made for thee [Amun of Karnak] *qrr*-ships, and *mnš*-ships, and *b3r*-ships, with bowmen equipped with their weapons on the Great Green Sea. I gave to them troop commanders and ship's captains, outfitted with many crews, without limit to them.

Great Harris Papyrus[56]

## Sherden as Drivers of Maritime Innovation?

The aforementioned change in Egyptian terminology (including determinatives) following their 13th century encounter with the Sherden suggests that the ships of war depicted at Medinet Habu were developed after the defeat of this "rebellious-hearted" foe early in the 13th century. Further, the striking similarity between the two fleets in the naval battle raises the possibility that Ramesses II's capture of Sherden warriors resulted not just in an increase in the ranks of Pharaonic conscripts, but in the transference of maritime technology as well. An example of such transference, during a military conflict that took place a millennium later, can be seen in Rome's ingenious reverse-engineering of Carthaginian warship design in the First Punic War. As Polybius tells it in his well-known account of the genesis of the Roman navy:

> ὅτε γὰρ τὸ πρῶτον ἐπεχείρησαν διαβιβάζειν εἰς τὴν Μεσσήνην τὰς δυνάμεις, οὐχ οἷον κατάφρακτος αὐτοῖς ὑπῆρχεν ναῦς, ἀλλ' οὐδὲ καθόλου μακρὸν πλοῖον οὐδὲ λέμβος οὐδ' εἷς, ἀλλὰ παρὰ Ταραντίνων καὶ Λοκρῶν ἔτι δ' Ἐλεατῶν καὶ Νεαπολιτῶν συγχρησάμενοι πεντηκοντόρους καὶ τριήρεις ἐπὶ τούτων παραβόλως διεκόμισαν τοὺς ἄνδρας. ἐν ᾧ δὴ καιρῷ τῶν Καρχηδονίων κατὰ τὸν πορθμὸν ἐπαναχθέντων αὐτοῖς, καὶ μιᾶς νεὼς καταφράκτου διὰ τὴν προθυμίαν προπεσούσης, ὥστ' ἐποκείλασαν γενέσθαι τοῖς Ῥωμαίοις ὑποχείριον, ταύτῃ παραδείγματι χρώμενοι τότε πρὸς ταύτην ἐποιοῦντο τὴν τοῦ παντὸς στόλου ναυπηγίαν, ὡς εἰ μὴ τοῦτο συνέβη γενέσθαι, δῆλον ὡς διὰ τὴν ἀπειρίαν εἰς τέλος ἂν ἐκωλύ.

> When they first took in hand to send troops across to Messene they not only had no decked vessels but no war-ships at all, not so much as a single galley: but they borrowed quinqueremes and triremes from Tarentum and Locri, and even from Elea and Neapolis; and having thus collected a fleet, boldly sent their men across upon it. It was on this occasion that, the Carthaginians having put to sea in the Strait to attack them, a decked vessel of theirs charged so furiously that it ran aground, and falling into the hands of the Romans served them as a model on which they constructed their whole fleet. And if this had not happened it is clear that they would have been completely hindered from carrying out their design by want of constructive knowledge.

Polyb. *Hist.* 1.20[57]

As can be seen in Figures 5.2, 8.8, and 8.9, the Egyptian ships depicted in the naval battle were neither Helladic galleys nor traditional Egyptian vessels. Instead, they seem to have been developed by combining elements of the new Sea Peoples vessels and old, familiar riverine "traveling ships" into a hybrid form of warship. Though a lack of hogging trusses, seen on earlier Egyptian

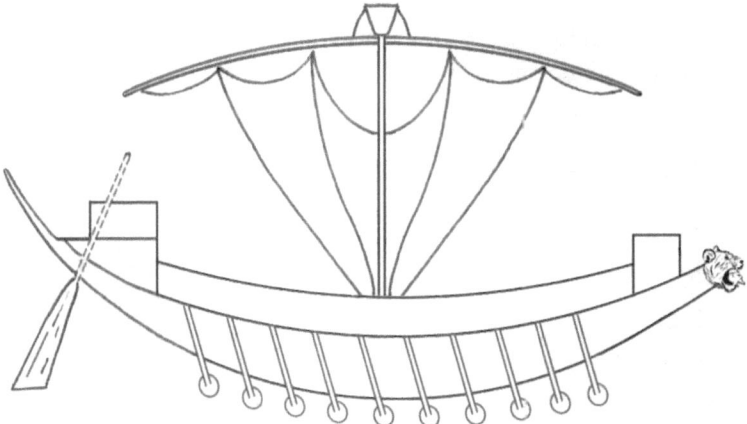

**Figure 8.9.  Egyptian warship from the Medinet Habu naval battle**
Illustration by the author.

vessels, points to a sturdier hull than previous Egyptian boats and ships, the shape (absent the papyriform stern), "shell-first" construction, fore- and aftercastles, and lion's head stem are consistent with the Egyptian shipbuilding tradition.[58]

As we have seen, the Sherden are the first Sea Peoples group to be specifically named as such in the Egyptian sources, as well as the first whose capture and impressment is documented, in Ramesses II's "Poem" and in Papyrus Anastasi II. As such, we may consider the possibility that elements of the ships sailed by the Sherden at the time of their initial defeat by Ramesses II may have been used as prototypes for the hybrid Egyptian vessels that were sailed against the maritime component of the latter invasion. There is precedent for Levantine influence on Egyptian ship design and construction: for example, a heavily Asiatic workforce at the 18th dynasty shipyard at *prw-nfr* on the Nile is strongly suggested by the worship of Semitic deities Ba'al and Astarte,[59] while the appearance at this time of the *mnš*-ship, a large, seagoing merchantman, provides evidence for the appropriation of Syro-Canaanite technology (and, like the ships sailed by the Sherden, the need for a new term to describe it).[60] The aforementioned Saqqara relief demon shows that Egyptians may have come into contact with this sail type and rigging system, as well as the top-mounted crow's nest, via Syro-Canaanite traders in the late 18th or 19th dynasties. However, it is possible that the full value of such a technological 'package' only truly became apparent when the Sherden and their *aḥaw aḥ3 m-ḥry-ib p3 ym* were encountered—and defeated—early in Ramesses II's reign.

Of course, as we have seen, the distinction need not be binary, as *both* the Sherden and those aboard the ship offloading Canaanite amphorae in the Saqqara relief may belong to the population elements variously referred to as "pirates, raiders, and traders" or as "nomads of the sea." Further, they may be related (or even identical) groups; we simply lack the evidence, at present, to make such clear identifications and to draw such fine distinctions between the various individuals and groups operating in such capacities at this time. However, appropriating this technology from these "rebellious-hearted" enemies in the first quarter of the 13th century would have allowed for a "breaking in" period of roughly a century prior to the seemingly flawless integration of these components seen in the Egyptian ships whose naval triumph is memorialized at Medinet Habu.

## *PENTEKONTORS* AND FLEET SIZES

Painted pottery and textual sources suggest the use of *pentekontors*, or galleys rowed by fifty men (twenty-five on each side), in the Aegean in the Late Bronze-Early Iron transition.[61] A 12th century pyxis from Tholos Tomb 1 at Tragana near Pylos features a ship with twenty-four vertical lines beneath the deck.[62] Wachsmann described this motif as a "horizontal ladder" and identified it with stanchions, or vertical support posts, which served in part to mark the divisions within an open rowers' gallery.[63] The Tragana ship has twenty-four of these vertical lines; thus, if they do represent stanchions between rowers, then, they serve to subdivide the gallery into twenty-five sections on each side of the vessel, for a total of fifty rowers, making this ship a *pentekontor* (Fig. 8.9). One side of a late 13th century (Late Minoan IIIB) larnax from Gazi on Crete features a large ship with twenty-seven vertical lines in this area, which could signify a ship crewed by even more than fifty men. However, as the horizontal ladder motif also seems to have served to address a certain *horror vacui* on the part of Mycenaean artists, it seems more likely that the Gazi painter intended to portray a *pentekontor* than a ship with fifty-four oarsmen.[64] Kynos A, on the other hand, features nineteen oars and schematically-rendered rowers. The odd number of rowers, combined with the need to fit two antithetic vessels onto a single side of a krater, may suggest that this vessel was also intended to be a *pentekontor* whose representation the artist was forced to abbreviate due to space constraints.[65]

The *Iliad* and *Odyssey* contain multiple mentions of *pentekontors*, as do other tales that touch on subjects addressed in Homer's epics. In the *Iliad*, for example, Philoloctes is said to have led a fleet of seven *pentekontors*, while Achilles is said to have led fifty (*Iliad* II, 719–720, XVI, 169–170). Additionally, while the *Iliad* makes mention of Herakles leading six ships of unknown size in a sack of Troy in the time of Priam's father Laomedon (*Iliad* V, 638–642), an alternate tradition instead assigns Herakles a fleet of eighteen *pentekontors*:

μετὰ δὲ τὴν λατρείαν ἀπαλλαγεὶς τῆς νόσου ἐπὶ Ἴλιον ἔπλει
πεντηκοντόροις ὀκτωκαίδεκα, συναθροίσας στρατὸν ἀνδρῶν ἀρίστων ἑκουσίως
θελόντων στρατεύεσθαι.

After his servitude, being rid of his disease [Herakles] mustered an army of noble volunteers and sailed for Ilium with eighteen ships of fifty oars each.

ps-Apollod. II, 6.4[66]

μετὰ δὲ ταῦτα ἐπανελθὼν εἰς Πελοπόννησον ἐστράτευσεν εἰς Ἴλιον, ἐγκαλῶν
Λαομέδοντι τῷ βασιλεῖ. οὗτος γὰρ Ἡρακλέους στρατεύοντος μετὰ Ἰάσονος ἐπὶ
τὸ χρυσόμαλλον δέρος, καὶ τὸ κῆτος ἀνελόντος, ἀπεστέρησε τῶν ὡμολογημένων
ἵππων, περὶ ὧν ἐν τοῖς Ἀργοναύτοις τὰ κατὰ μέρος μικρὸν ὕστερον διέξιμεν.
καὶ τότε μὲν διὰ τὴν μετ' Ἰάσονος στρατείαν ἀσχοληθείς, ὕστερον δὲ λαβὼν
καιρὸν ἐπὶ τὴν Τροίαν ἐστράτευσεν, ὡς μέν τινές φασι, ναυσὶ μακραῖς
ὀκτωκαίδεκα, ὡς δὲ Ὅμηρος γέγραφεν, ἓξ ταῖς ἁπάσαις. . .

After this Heracles, returning to Peloponnesus, made war against Ilium, since he had a ground of complaint against its king, Laomedon. For when Heracles was on the expedition with Jason to get the golden fleece and had slain the sea-monster, Laomedon had withheld from him the mares which he had agreed to give him and of which we shall give a detailed account a little later in connection with the Argonauts.
At that time Heracles had not had the leisure, since he was engaged upon the expedition of Jason, but later he found an opportunity and made war upon Troy with eighteen ships of war, as some say, but, as Homer writes, with six in all. . .

Diod. Sic. IV, 32.1–2[67]

The *Odyssey* attests to vessels rowed by fifty men, as well, with one being specifically attributed to the Phaiakians:

κούρω δὲ κρινθέντε δύω καὶ πεντήκοντα
βήτην, ὡς ἐκέλευσ', ἐπὶ θῖν' ἁλὸς ἀτρυγέτοιο.
αὐτὰρ ἐπεί ῥ' ἐπὶ νῆα κατήλυθον ἠδὲ θάλασσαν,
νῆα μὲν οἵ γε μέλαιναν ἁλὸς βένθοσδε ἔρυσσαν,
ἐν δ' ἱστόν τ' ἐτίθεντο καὶ ἱστία νηὶ μελαίνη,
ἠρτύναντο δ' ἐρετμὰ τροποῖς ἐν δερματίνοισι,
πάντα κατὰ μοῖραν, ἀνά θ' ἱστία λευκὰ πέτασσαν.

And chosen youths, two and fifty [fifty rowers, a captain or coxswain, and a helmsman], went, as he bade, to the shore of the unresting sea. And when they had come down to the ship and to the sea, they drew the black ship down to the deep water, and placed the mast and sail in the black ship, and fitted the oars in the leathern thole-straps, all in due order, and spread the white sail.

*Odyssey* viii, 48–54

Crews of roughly *pentekontor* size may also be attested in the aforementioned Rower Tablets from Pylos. Tablet An 610 records approximately 569 oarsmen, a number that Chadwick reconstructed as 600, while An 1 lists thirty *e-re-ta pe-re-u-ro-na-de i-jo-te* 'rowers to go to Pleuron' who are being summoned to man what seems likely to have been a single ship, a thirty-oar *triakontor*.[68] Interestingly, this crew size may have a parallel in a Ugaritic text (UT 83), which lists eighteen + *x* rowers from four locations to man a single vessel.[69]

When ship numbers are considered in light of likely crew sizes, the danger that raiding parties made up of small "fleets" could pose to unwary coastal settlements becomes clear. For example, if the ships crewed by the men of An 610 were *pentekontors*, the 600-rower force would be enough to man only twelve ships. Even if they were *triakontors*, like the vessel crewed by the An 1 rowers, there would only be enough to fully man twenty ships. Similarly, whether the ships sailed on Odysseus' Egyptian raid were in fact fifty-oared *pentekontors* or thirty-oared *triakontors*, his nine vessels may have carried between 360 and 450 combatants, while Herakles' raid on Troy, which, as we have seen, consisted of either six (*Iliad* V, 638–642) or eighteen (ps-Apollod. II, 6.4; Dio. IV, 32) vessels, would have carried between 300 and 900 combatants. This would have been far fewer than the number of ships and men that a seagoing state could have provided, of course. The Ugaritic text RS 20.141 mentions thirty ships, while a far larger number is referenced in RS 18.148, "kiln text" contains summaries of two letters that seem to discuss defenses against external threats:

The message of Yadinu [*ydn*] to the king [of Ugarit], his lord. Protect your country. Will, please, supply ships, will supply 150 ships . . . and 400 'Apiru [or "shipwrights"] and the king [. . .]
And the king who governs in his homeland to Yadinu the servant of the king, whom he has made commander of his army [or "who was placed over his children"]. Let the dynasty not go to ruin. The border patrol has taken *kws't*, let your army . . . border.

RS 18.148[70]

The context of this letter is unclear, as is the sender. Is it a military commander or a Hittite official? (The latter, Singer notes, would be "in a better position to mobilize the fleet of Ugarit.")[71] Why does the summarized response contain no mention of the requested ships, instead only referring to the king's family? At fully fifty percent more than the hundred Mycenaean vessels that made up the largest element of Homer's catalogue of ships (*Iliad* II, 576), the number of ships being requested by Yadinu is massive by ancient standards, regardless of the specific context of this text. If the fragmentary remnants of RS 18.148 are interpreted as saying that such a number of ships could be committed upon request, the Ugaritic navy may have been quite large indeed, even if most of its ships should be thought of as merchantmen rather than as potential combat vessels.

While they would have been small enough to be highly vulnerable to encounters with organized military units, though—as both Odysseus himself and his Cretan avatar would learn, much to his chagrin (*Odyssey* ix, 39–61 and xiv, 262–272)—the hundreds of combatants carried by Odysseus' nine ships, and by Herakles' six or eighteen, would certainly have been large enough to carry out a raid on a lightly defended coastal settlement. This is supported by two late 13th or early 12th century texts from Ugarit. The first is addressed to King 'Ammurapi from the prefect of Alašiya:

> But now, (the) twenty enemy ships—even before they would reach the mountain (shore)—have not stayed around but have quickly moved on, and where they have pitched camp we do not know. I am writing you to inform and protect you. Be aware!
>
> RS 20.18[72]

The second is addressed to the king of Alašiya from King 'Ammurapi of Ugarit:

> My father, now the ships of the enemy have been coming. They have been setting fire to my cities and have done harm to the land. Doesn't my father know that all of my infantry and [chariotry] are stationed in Ḫatti, and that all of my ships are stationed in the land of Lukka? They haven't arrived back yet, so the land is thus prostrate. May my father be aware of this matter. Now the seven ships of the enemy which have been coming have done harm to us. Now if other ships of the enemy turn up, send me a report somehow(?) so that I will know.
>
> RS 20.238[73]

The latter seems to have been a response to another letter, which was sent to 'Ammurapi by the king of Alašiya:

> Thus says the king. Speak to Ammurapi, king of Ugarit: May you be well! May the gods keep you in good health! Concerning what you wrote to me: 'They have

spotted enemy ships at sea'; if they have indeed spotted ships, make yourself as strong as possible. Now, where are your own troops (and) chariotry stationed? Are they not stationed with you? If not, who will deliver you from the enemy forces? Surround your towns with walls; bring troops and chariotry inside. (Then) wait at full strength for the enemy.

RSL 1[74]

Why were 'Ammurapi's ships "stationed in the land of Lukka" instead of at their home port at this time of need? Historian Michael Astour suggested that this was an attempt to preempt the attacks of the Sea Peoples:

We are in the presence of the first stage of the Sea Peoples' invasion. The main forces of the enemy are still in the Aegean, but their intentions are known, and the king of Ugarit, instead of passively waiting for their arrival, attempts to oppose their offensive at its very start. His entire fleet sails westward to Lycia to defend the passage from the Aegean to the Mediterranean main. . . . Meanwhile, small flotillas of the invaders take advantage of the situation to attack the unprotected coast of the Ugaritic kingdom.[75]

While this makes for an exciting story, the reality may instead have been more transactional in nature. AhT 27A and B (= RS 94.2530 and 94.2523), quoted earlier, describe a mission to Lukka to deliver a shipment of metal ingots to representatives of Aḫḫiyawa on behalf of the Hittites. Instead of standing like the last bulwark against an influx of Sea Peoples into the Eastern Mediterranean, does this (or a similar undertaking) explain their absence from Ugarit at this critical time?[76] If so, this seems to have been an extraordinarily poorly timed expedition, particularly because it evidently removed the entire Ugaritic fleet from its home port and abandoned the defense of their coastal waters. This situation is all the more perplexing if we accept RS 18.148 as indicating that Ugarit was capable of mustering 150 ships on command.

Regardless of the size of the Ugaritic fleet, the idea that it would have taken every serviceable ship at Ammurapi's disposal to carry out this venture is difficult to accept, particularly in light of the key role the Ugaritic fleet seems to have played in Ḫatti's maritime strategy (such as it was)—a fact recognized in Karkemiš, as evidenced by RS 34.138, a letter in which the queen of Ugarit is instructed that she may not send ships to places more distant than Byblos and Sidon on the Phoenician coast.[77] As we have seen, piratical activity was a significant threat at this time. Both merchants and polities may have attempted to mitigate this threat in part by placing armed individuals on heavily laden merchant ships, as is suggested by the Syrian, Aegean, and possibly Balkan or Italic weapons and armor on the Ulu Burun vessel.[78] Could vessels carrying precious cargo also have been provided with combat-equipped escorts? If this was the case, then 'Ammurapi's declaration that "all of my ships are stationed in the land of Lukka [and] haven't arrived back yet" may refer to a subset of the Ugaritic fleet that was better equipped for coastal defense—a subset that was, most inopportunely, away when the enemy ships were wreaking havoc on the city and its surrounding territory. Interestingly, Bryce has suggested that the purpose of this mission was to deliver payment from the Hittite king to Mycenaean (Aḫḫiyawan) mercenaries in exchange for their service.[79] While this casts the effort and its timing in a more logical light, such a case would mean that Ḫatti's determination to meet its financial obligation to the Ḫiyawa-men came at the cost of critically weakening an important coastal dependency.

The companion complaint that Ugarit's army—both infantry and chariotry—were "stationed in Ḫatti" may be related to events taking place elsewhere in northwestern Syria at this time. RS 16.402 and RS 34.143 address the king of Ugarit's unwillingness to send troops to the aid of the Hittite viceroy in Karkemiš, who was responsible for overseeing the vassal state on behalf of the Great King of Ḫatti. The ruler of Karkemiš was evidently dealing with an enemy that had established what Singer referred to as a "bridgehead" in Mukiš, a Hittite-controlled territory. In the Ugaritic letter RS 16.402, a representative informs the queen that the enemy is in Mukiš, while in RS 34.143, the king of Karkemiš accuses the king of Ugarit of misrepresenting the location of his army, which was evidently supposed to be aiding the combat effort in Mukiš, but which was positioned in the northern city of Apšuna instead.

Mukiš was located north of Ugarit, and consisted of the 'Amuq plain and its surrounding areas. Its major center was Tell Atchana (ancient Alalaḫ), a site which was previously discussed in the context of the possibly Philistine-related settlement at its neighbor, Tell Ta'yinat. It is possible that the enemy movement in Mukiš recorded in RS 16.402 and RS 34.143 is to be connected to the aforementioned settling of Tell Ta'yinat and the surrounding area by an intrusive people (or peoples) with Cypro-Aegean affinities. It is also possible that this land movement through Mukiš is related to the seaborne threats noted in RS 20.18 and RS 20.238, and that it should therefore be seen as the land component of a combined land and sea assault. Based on other evidence, like the Medinet Habu inscriptions and the Hittite claim to three sea battles and a land battle against the "enemies from Alašiya" (KBo XII 38, quoted above), this tactic seems to have been the *modus operandi* of at least some groups at this time—perhaps one or more of the Sea Peoples. In his Year 8 account of the Sea Peoples' rampage across the Near East, Ramesses III declares that they set up camp in Amurru, Ugarit's southern neighbor. Another Ugaritic text, RS 20.162, is a letter from Parṣu of Amurru to the king of Ugarit which couples a request for information about an enemy with an offer of ships:

Speak to the king of the land of Ugarit: thus says Parşu, your servant. I fall at the feet of my lord. May you be well. My lord, has the king of Amurru not spoken to you in the following terms: 'As soon as you hear a report about the enemies: write to my country.' But now, why has my lord not written to us as soon as you had learned about the enemies? Furthermore, my lord, the land of Amurru and the land of Ugarit are one! If you, my lord, hear a report about the enemies, then my lord should write to me. My lord, herewith I am writing to you: I will surely send the ships which are with us, for your inspection. My lord should know (this)!

RS 20.162[80]

Whatever the reason for Ugarit's dire defensive situation, the seven ships 'Ammurapi mentions in RS 20.238 seem to have been sufficient to cause significant damage to the lands under his control. If they were composed of *triakontors*, *pentekontors*, or some combination thereof, then the seven ships mentioned in this letter may have contained between 210 and 350 rowers (and, therefore, potential warriors), while the twenty mentioned in RS 20.18 may have contained between six hundred and one thousand. Thus, as with Odysseus' small fleet, the number of rowers aboard the enemy ships mentioned in these Ugaritic texts were clearly sufficient to strike fear in the heart of one of the major coastal polities of the age.

## Unit Cohesion and the 'Galley Subculture'

Beyond simply opening up new maritime possibilities, the development of the oared galley likely created a significant *social* impact, as well. The development of a community that specialized in seafaring and maritime technology organization, and the organization and cohesion of this community that resulted from the unique requirements that came along with the organization of personnel into crews, and the importance of unit cohesion to effective rowing, led to the development of a "galley subculture" in the coastal territories of the Aegean and the Interface.[81] This phenomenon resulted from the fact that "rowing a galley led to the fusing of rowers into a team, creating an *esprit de corps*, further enhanced by the virile activities in which rower-warriors usually engage. The enhanced position of the helmsman and the aeonian authority of the captain provided two leader-figures for the crew."[82] The subculture that resulted from such cohesive communities may have resulted in power bases for maritime leaders, who, as we discussed previously with regard to intermediaries in the Late Bronze Age trade network, had "peculiar expertise: capital in the form of a boat and knowledge of navigation."[83]

Sauvage may be correct that very few mariners technically owned their own ships during the Late Bronze Age, instead operating them as an agent of the palace(s) on whose behalf they were doing business.[84] After all, though the documentary evidence is largely biased in favor of the royal perspective, textual references demonstrate a significant state interest in ship numbers, status, and control.[85] However, even if this is true, the legal owner of a vessel would have been less important to those crewing it than their immediate leader, while the collapse of the palatial system may have effectively caused ownership of these vessels to default to their operators regardless of who actually possessed the ancient equivalent of the "pink slip."

Thus, with oared galleys manned by seasoned rower-warriors whose primary allegiance was to their captain and to each other, these leaders would have had at their disposal not just a means of travel, trade, and subsistence, but one of the most lethal weapons of the age, in terms of both humans and hardware. These growing power bases may have played a role in the increased maritime threats to the Eastern Mediterranean trade network as 1200 BCE approached. Even more importantly, though, they may have morphed into discrete but powerful threats to the major Aegean polities of the age, as well as to each other, as the Kynos, Bademgediği Tepe, and Liman Tepe examples may show.[86]

As previously discussed, the Rower Tablets have been seen by some scholars as reflective of an attempt to sortie a fleet of galleys against a seaborne threat. While this threat may have been external, it is also worth considering, in light of the coastal power bases that could have resulted from the galley subculture, that the threat may ultimately have been of the palatial structure's own creation. Odysseus himself acts in this role throughout much of the *Odyssey*: though still a "noble," he is, as the Phaiakians note, an ἀρχὸς ναυτάων 'captain of sailors' with a πολυκλήϊδι 'many-benched ship' as his property, and its crew as his subjects (*Odyssey* viii, 161–162). Much as Homer's Odysseus can be viewed as a 'Sea Person' in the historical and archaeological sense, traveling circuitously from Troy in the east to the westernmost point of the Greek world (Ithaka) amidst the chaos of a transforming age—while, it must be noted, playing a role in the disruptions—he also acts in the capacity of a naval captain who has at his disposal the power base and maritime capability associated with this subculture. As such, he represents a component of society that seems to have proved most durable in the centuries following the palatial collapse.

As briefly noted above, warriors in Geometric art are frequently represented with hair or headdresses similar to the LH IIIC "hedgehog" style. Along with this, the Helladic oared galley is a mainstay of Geometric art, reappearing on painted pottery around 800 BCE in a form that clearly represents continuity of style and, perhaps more importantly, continuous development from the 12th century onward.[87] But how did this happen? It has been argued that the cost associated with building, maintaining, and manning even a single galley would have been prohibitive during the Submycenaean and Proto-Geometric "Dark Age" of Greece, which was long viewed as a time of severe depopulation and economic depression. Even if the knowledge of ship construction did not altogether die out in the Aegean, as Wachsmann has suggested, it does seem unlikely that a significant number of these vessels could have been manufactured, supported, and further developed both stylistically and technologically across the intervening generations between the 12th and 9th centuries.

Archaeologist Michael Wedde has proposed that galleys, like chariots, were just important enough to those who wished to "keep the flame of the epic past alive" by maintaining a connection to their palatial history to make it seem worthwhile to undertake the necessary expenditures to keep one or more around, as a status symbol if nothing else.[88] Wachsmann, on the other hand, argues that the tradition of the Helladic galley continued unabated not on the Greek mainland, nor even in the Aegean, but on Cyprus, where the 12th and 11th centuries BCE were a time of forward-looking political reorganization, increased importance as a hub of trade, and economic growth.[89] As we have seen, Cyprus was the beneficiary of a number of Aegean migrants, who would naturally have arrived by ship. Could at least some of these immigrants have arrived by galley, with their vessels' captains amongst the new population's authority figures? If so, their integration into the local society may explain the adoption and development of this vessel type on Cyprus, and its reintroduction into the Aegean society from this location. The relative stability of Cypriot culture, its prominent role in maritime travel and exchange, and its relationship with the Aegean, certainly make it a candidate not only to have been the keeper of the flame, to use Wedde's vivid metaphor, of the Helladic galley tradition, but also to have pushed this craft's development forward into the Iron Age.

Additionally, though the Greek dark age was not a time of economic surplus, the warrior burials discussed above seem to suggest that there were leaders at this time who could, in fact, have commanded the resources necessary to field and crew one or more galleys. As we have seen in RS 20.238 from Ugarit, which references "the seven ships of the enemy," and *Odyssey* xiv, 248, in which Odysseus describes his fleet of nine vessels, a large number of ships was not necessarily a requirement for maritime effectiveness.

The question of the galley's survival and development does not require a solitary answer. As we have seen in our study of the transmission of maritime technology across seas and political boundaries in the Late Bronze Age, the use and development of a vessel type need not be confined to one region or polity—in fact, it almost certainly *could not* have been so confined. For example, we already know that the Phoenician bireme is a descendant of the Bronze Age galley, and that strong contacts existed between Cyprus and Phoenicia in the Iron Age. However, the evolution of this vessel on the Levantine coast in the Iron Age seems to have progressed independent of both Cyprus and the Aegean, where the galley developed into the Geometric *dieres* of the late 8th century. Further, this continuous development of maritime technology reinforces the likelihood that, whatever their role in the fate of the Late Helladic palaces and the palatial structure, the "galley subculture" was able to remain intact throughout the period that followed the Mycenaean collapse, both in the Aegean and on Cyprus. This may have been achieved through the localized actions of these maritime leaders, acting as the "big men" discussed above, who mobilized their coastal power bases and took charge of peoples and territories in the post-palatial world through charisma and force. It may also have been accomplished by a combination of piracy, itinerance, and migration—in other words, through actions that have been associated in large part with the Sea Peoples.

## The Gurob Ship-Cart Model

Further evidence for the use of fifty-oared galleys in the years surrounding the Late Bronze-Early Iron transition (and for the employment of such a vessel by *Sherden* sailors, discussed below) may be found in a recently republished ship model from Tomb 611 at Gurob in Middle Egypt.[90] Incorrectly assembled but perceptively labeled "Pirate Boat?" by Flinders Petrie and recently republished by Shelley Wachsmann, the model was paired with a wheeled cart, and its cultic affinities are suggested both by its cart and by its hole for a *pavois*, to which bars were attached for priestly porters to shoulder as they carried a cultic ship over land.[91] Like the vessels shown on LH IIIB and IIIC pottery, the ship-cart model features stanchions and a stempost with an upturned finial.[92] Flanking the model just below the caprails are rows of black dots, which have been interpreted as oarports, whose number and spacing make it probable that the vessel after which the model was patterned was also a fifty-oared *pentekontor.* Also present is a bow projection at the junction of stempost and keel, shown on some depictions of Late Helladic ships, which would become a standard feature of oared galleys in the Iron Age.

Radiocarbon dating of the Gurob ship-cart model returned a 2σ calibrated age range of 1256 to 1054 BCE, and its appearance is most similar to iconography from the 13th and 12th centuries.[93] In all, seven pigments were detected,[94] including a base layer of white, over which a stripe of red paint just below the caprail and above the oarports, and a coating of black asphalt covering the bottom half of the full, were added.[95] This preserved polychrome schema not only makes the model unique among known representations of Helladic ships, but it aligns with Homer's description of the Achaeans' ships as μέλας 'black' and, remarkably, with the poet's description of Odysseus' ships specifically as μιλτοπάρῃος 'red-cheeked' (*Iliad* II, 637 and *Odyssey* ix, 125).[96] Odysseus' ships are also referred to as φοινικοπάρῃος 'purple-cheeked' (*Odyssey* xi, 124, xxiii, 271) but most noteworthy is the fact that *only* Odysseus' ships are identified by the "red-" and "purple-cheeked" epithets.

The phrase μέλαινα ναῦς 'black ship' is a common epithet in Homer, appearing eighty-one times in *Iliad* and *Odyssey* combined,[97] while ναῦς κυανόπρωρος, commonly glossed 'dark-prowed ship,' appears a further thirteen times.[98] The former alludes to the coating of hull planking with dark pitch or asphalt, a practice which, though known from at least the Bronze Age, is found in physical representation for the first time on the Gurob ship-cart model.[99] References to the use of pitch or asphalt to seal wooden ships can be seen in such diverse ancient examples as the biblical instructions for building Noah's Ark (Gen. 6:14) and the more chronologically relevant letter from Ramesses II to Ḥattušili III referring to the apparent transfer of ships for study and replication, discussed earlier, which instructs the Hittite king to ensure that vessels be coated with asphalt so that they will remain seaworthy (KUB III, 82).

Ναῦς κυανόπρωρος, on the other hand, has multiple possible meanings. As noted above, it is typically glossed "dark-prowed ship," and its uses in Homer suggest that this and μέλαινα ναῦς are interchangeable terms. However, κύανος and κυάνεος can also refer either to the color blue or to a dark blue substance used in works of metal.[100] Traces of blue paint on the forecastle of the Gurob ship-cart model provide for the possibility, suggested by Wachsmann, that the model once incorporated a blue-painted forecastle screen, thus creating a blue prow to go along with an epithet that may hint at the use of the color blue on Helladic ships.[101] Although the ship-cart model's publishers may be correct in their acceptance of the traditional use of Homeric κυανόπρωρος as 'dark-prowed,' it is easy to imagine seeing an oncoming galley painted in a fashion similar to the Gurob model, with its red stripes, blue forecastle screen, and pitch-coated hull, as being *blue-prowed*, *red-cheeked*, and *black-hulled*, in a physical embodiment of Homer's epithets.[102]

## THE NEED FOR SPEED (AND STEALTH)

The combination of small raiding parties and heavily militarized targets meant that success in piratical endeavors was dependent on a combination of speed, stealth, and—above all—the avoidance of conflict with professional soldiers. For this reason, "raiders and pirates in the Aegean and else-where . . . historically tended to operate in relatively small groups, whose basic tactic would be fast sweeps to gather up what could be easily taken, whether human captives, livestock, or other plunder."[103]

Success in piratical endeavors—and the very survival of raiding parties—required not only the adoption of new sailing technology, but also the development of tactics that could satisfy such a life-and-death need for stealth and celerity. One such tactic was the deliberate beaching of vessels, which allowed attackers to disembark and conduct their raid as quickly as possible. The fastest way to land, and disembark from, a vessel is to row it bow first directly up onto the beach. The aforementioned keel extensions seen on some depictions of Helladic ships (Figs. 8.9 and 8.10), on the Sea Peoples vessels in the naval battle at Medinet Habu (Fig. 5.2), and on the Gurob ship-cart model may have served as beaching aids, allowing raiders' ships to sail more easily up onto land for the purpose of facilitating a rapid disembarkation.[104] These prominent extensions would become a standard feature of oared galleys in the Iron Age. These are seen, in concert with the shift of the stempost finial from outward-curving to inward, as key delineating features in the development of the galley as a vessel type from the Late Bronze into the Geometric periods.[105] The shift in sternpost orientation from vertical or outward-curving to inward-curving can be seen as early as LH IIIC on the Skyros vessel, as well as on the Helladic ship model graffiti from the Dakhla Oasis in central Egypt.[106]

The technique of beaching a galley is described elsewhere in the *Odyssey*, when the Phaiakians, returning Odysseus to Ithaca, run their vessel aground for the purpose of quickly offloading their human cargo:

ἔνθ᾽ οἵ γ᾽ εἰσέλασαν, πρὶν εἰδότες. ἡ μὲν ἔπειτα
ἠπείρῳ ἐπέκελσεν, ὅσον τ᾽ ἐπὶ ἥμισυ πάσης,
σπερχομένη· τοῖον γὰρ ἐπείγετο χέρσ᾽ ἐρετάων

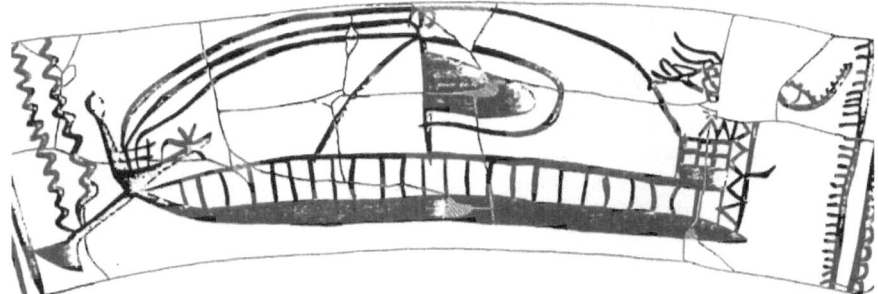

Fig 8.10.   **LH IIIC pyxis from Tholos Tomb 1 at Tragana featuring a ship with 24 vertical stanchions dividing the rowers' gallery to two groups of 25**
Wedde, M. 2000. *Toward a Hermeneutics of Aegean Bronze Age Ship Imagery.* Mannheim. Number 643.

The ship, hard-driven, ran up onto the beach for as much as
half her length, such was the force the hands of the oarsmen
gave her.

*Odyssey* xiii, 113–115[107]

The overall importance of *speed* in raiding is likewise reinforced in the
epic, as Odysseus clearly explains the catastrophe that could befall a raiding
party that lingered too long on an objective, as well as that which could result
from contact with regular troops:

Ἰλιόθεν με φέρων ἄνεμος Κικόνεσσι πέλασσεν,
Ἰσμάρῳ. ἔνθα δ᾽ ἐγὼ πόλιν ἔπραθον, ὤλεσα δ᾽ αὐτούς:
ἐκ πόλιος δ᾽ ἀλόχους καὶ κτήματα πολλὰ λαβόντες
δασσάμεθ᾽, ὡς μή τίς μοι ἀτεμβόμενος κίοι ἴσης.
ἔνθ᾽ ἦ τοι μὲν ἐγὼ διερῷ ποδὶ φευγέμεν ἡμέας
ἠνώγεα, τοὶ δὲ μέγα νήπιοι οὐκ ἐπίθοντο.
ἔνθα δὲ πολλὸν μὲν μέθυ πίνετο, πολλὰ δὲ μῆλα
ἔσφαζον παρὰ θῖνα καὶ εἰλίποδας ἕλικας βοῦς:
τόφρα δ᾽ ἄρ᾽ οἰχόμενοι Κίκονες Κικόνεσσι γεγώνευν,
οἵ σφιν γείτονες ἦσαν, ἅμα πλέονες καὶ ἀρείους,
ἤπειρον ναίοντες, ἐπιστάμενοι μὲν ἀφ᾽ ἵππων
ἀνδράσι μάρνασθαι καὶ ὅθι χρὴ πεζὸν ἐόντα.
ἦλθον ἔπειθ᾽ ὅσα φύλλα καὶ ἄνθεα γίγνεται ὥρῃ,
ἠέριοι: τότε δή ῥα κακὴ Διὸς αἶσα παρέστη
ἡμῖν αἰνομόροισιν, ἵν᾽ ἄλγεα πολλὰ πάθοιμεν.
στησάμενοι δ᾽ ἐμάχοντο μάχην παρὰ νηυσὶ θοῇσι,
βάλλον δ᾽ ἀλλήλους χαλκήρεσιν ἐγχείῃσιν.
ὄφρα μὲν ἠὼς ἦν καὶ ἀέξετο ἱερὸν ἦμαρ,
τόφρα δ᾽ ἀλεξόμενοι μένομεν πλέονάς περ ἐόντας.
ἦμος δ᾽ ἠέλιος μετενίσσετο βουλυτόνδε,
καὶ τότε δὴ Κίκονες κλῖναν δαμάσαντες Ἀχαιούς.
ἓξ δ᾽ ἀφ᾽ ἑκάστης νηὸς ἐυκνήμιδες ἑταῖροι
ὤλονθ᾽: οἱ δ᾽ ἄλλοι φύγομεν θάνατόν τε μόρον τε.

From Ilios the wind bore me and brought me to the Kikones, to Ismarus. There
I sacked the city and slew the men; and from the city we took their wives and
great store of treasure, and divided them among us, that so far as lay in me no
man might go defrauded of an equal share. Then verily I gave command that we
should flee with swift foot, but the others in their great folly did not hearken.
But there much wine was drunk, and many sheep they slew by the shore, and
sleek kine of shambling gait.
Meanwhile the Kikones went and called to other Kikones who were their neighbors, at once more numerous and braver than they—men that dwelt inland and

were skilled at fighting with their foes from chariots, and, if need were, on foot. So they came in the morning, as thick as leaves or flowers spring up in their season; and then it was that an evil fate from Zeus beset us luckless men, that we might suffer woes full many. They set their battle in array and fought by the swift ships, and each side hurled at the other with bronze-tipped spears. Now as long as it was morn and the sacred day was waxing, so long we held our ground and beat them off, though they were more than we. But when the sun turned to the time for the unyoking of oxen, then the Kikones prevailed and routed the Achaeans, and six of my well-greaved comrades perished from each ship; but the rest of us escaped death and fate.

*Odyssey* ix, 39–61

οἱ δ' ὕβρει εἴξαντες, ἐπισπόμενοι μένεΐ σφῷ,
αἶψα μάλ' Αἰγυπτίων ἀνδρῶν περικαλλέας ἀγροὺς
πόρθεον, ἐκ δὲ γυναῖκας ἄγον καὶ νήπια τέκνα,
αὐτούς τ' ἔκτεινον· τάχα δ' ἐς πόλιν ἵκετ' ἀϋτή.
οἱ δὲ βοῆς ἀΐοντες ἅμ' ἠοῖ φαινομένηφιν
ἦλθον· πλῆτο δὲ πᾶν πεδίον πεζῶν τε καὶ ἵππων
χαλκοῦ τε στεροπῆς· ἐν δὲ Ζεὺς τερπικέραυνος
φύζαν ἐμοῖς ἑτάροισι κακὴν βάλεν, οὐδέ τις ἔτλη
μεῖναι ἐναντίβιον· περὶ γὰρ κακὰ πάντοθεν ἔστη.
ἔνθ' ἡμέων πολλοὺς μὲν ἀπέκτανον ὀξέϊ χαλκῷ,
τοὺς δ' ἄναγον ζωούς, σφίσιν ἐργάζεσθαι ἀνάγκῃ.

But my comrades, yielding to wantonness, and led on by their own might, straightway set about wasting the fair fields of the men of Egypt; and they carried off the women and little children, and slew the men; and the cry came quickly to the city. Then, hearing the shouting, the people came forth at break of day, and the whole plain was filled with footmen, and chariots and the flashing of bronze. But Zeus who hurls the thunderbolt cast an evil panic upon my comrades, and none had the courage to hold his ground and face the foe; for evil surrounded us on every side. So then they slew many of us with the sharp bronze, and others they led up to their city alive, to work for them perforce.

*Odyssey* xiv, 262–272 and xvii, 431–441

These descriptions are remarkably similar to the inscription accompanying the naval battle relief from Medinet Habu, which described the Sea Peoples as being "capsized and overwhelmed where they are," saying, "Their heart is taken away, their soul is flown away. Their weapons are scattered upon the sea. His arrow pierces whom of them he may have wished, and the fugitive is become one fallen into the water."[108]

As noted above, the Sea Peoples vessels battling Ramesses III's navy are not shown actively utilizing any means of propulsion, as no oars are visible and the sails are clearly brailed up. Rather than being engaged in open water—even in a riverine environment—the Sea Peoples' ships were most likely at anchor when Ramesses III "capsized and overwhelmed" them.[109] The most likely reason that rowers are absent from this scene is that a surprise attack by the Egyptian army left the enemy no time to run out their oars and attempt to escape, thus "capsiz[ing] and overwhelm[ing them] where they" were. This is supported by the scene on the right side of the relief, which shows the Sea Peoples' vessels pinned against land, with the Egyptian fleet as waterborne aggressors and a supporting force on land both firing arrows and collecting prisoners at water's edge, who are then marched away for presentation to the pharaoh and to the Theban triad.[110]

It is possible that this signals migration rather than coastal raiding as an aim of those on board the Sea Peoples' ships, much like their land-based counterparts who traveled with ox-carts. Certainly it makes little sense, if their intention was to conduct a surprise coastal raid, that they would have been entirely unprepared to depart the Egyptian coast at the first sign of arrival of military forces against whom they surely had little chance of martial success. However, Odysseus' tale of hubris on the part of his undisciplined crew members can account equally well for the raiding party's lack of readiness, and their resultant inability to escape the wrath of the pharaoh's army.

*Chapter Nine*

# Αἴγυπτόνδε: Life, Prosperity, and Health in the Land of the Pharaohs

ἔνθα μὲν ἑπτάετες μένον αὐτόθι, πολλὰ δ' ἄγειρα
χρήματ' ἀν' Αἰγυπτίους ἄνδρας· δίδοσαν γὰρ ἅπαντες.

There then I stayed seven years, and much wealth did I gather among the Egyptians, for all men gave me gifts.

*Odyssey* xiv, 285–286

## MYTH AND HISTORY, ONCE AGAIN

Like all epic products of oral tradition, the "master myth" of the Homeric *Odyssey* is a tapestry woven from many fascinating micronarratives, each of which has its own origin, development, and—in some cases, at some point in time—individual grounding in historical truth. Though the specific stories told by Odysseus to Eumaios and Antinoos, respectively, are portrayed as fiction within the Homeric macronarrative, several of their elements have precedent in archaeological and literary records dating to the Late Bronze Age and the Late Bronze–Early Iron Age transition, or the end of the Late Helladic IIIB period and the succeeding Late Helladic IIIC and Submycenaean periods. As Martin West has noted:

Almost everyone accepts that the Greek epic tradition goes back at least to late Mycenaean times. In fact . . . there is reason to assume its existence as early as the fifteenth century, and before that an ancient tradition of poetry, which may have been in some sense heroic, going back to an Indo-European setting. In one sense, then, the rise of the Greek epic will have to be dated no later than the middle of the second millennium.[1]

151

Homer's epics are themselves songs of the deeds of heroes (κλέα ἀνδρῶν), and, in meta fashion, they also feature scenes within them wherein such songs are performed:[2]

Μυρμιδόνων δ᾽ ἐπί τε κλισίας καὶ νῆας ἱκέσθην,
τὸν δ᾽ εὗρον φρένα τερπόμενον φόρμιγγι λιγείῃ
καλῇ δαιδαλέῃ, ἐπὶ δ᾽ ἀργύρεον ζυγὸν ἦεν,
τὴν ἄρετ᾽ ἐξ ἐνάρων πόλιν Ἠετίωνος ὀλέσσας·
τῇ ὅ γε θυμὸν ἔτερπεν, ἄειδε δ᾽ ἄρα κλέα ἀνδρῶν.

The two of them reached the shelters and the ships of the Myrmidons, and they found Achilles diverting his heart as he was playing on a clear-sounding lyre, a beautiful one, of exquisite workmanship, and its cross-bar was of silver. It was part of the spoils that he had taken when he destroyed the city of Eëtion, and he was now diverting his heart with it as he was singing the glories of men.

*Iliad* IX, 185–189[3]

αὐτὰρ ἐπεὶ πόσιος καὶ ἐδητύος ἐξ ἔρον ἕντο,
μοῦσ᾽ ἄρ᾽ ἀοιδὸν ἀνῆκεν ἀειδέμεναι κλέα ἀνδρῶν,
οἴμης τῆς τότ᾽ ἄρα κλέος οὐρανὸν εὐρὺν ἵκανε

But when they had put from them the desire of food and drink, the Muse moved the minstrel to sing of the glorious deeds of warriors, from that lay the fame whereof had then reached broad heaven

*Odyssey* viii, 72–74

The method of performance described by Homer seems to follow a tradition extending at least to the Mycenaean period, as evidenced by the Lyre Player Fresco from the throne room at Pylos and by references to *ru-ra-ta-e* 'lyre players' on Linear B tablets from Thebes.[4] This is not to say that the Homeric epics in their current (or classical) form were composed in, or are entirely reflective of, this period. Continuing the quote above, West writes, "it is scarcely to be supposed that the Homeric epics are simply late examples of something that had existed in much the same state for seven or eight hundred years. This is surely a tradition that, however old its roots, burst spectacularly into flower within the last few generations before Homer." As we discussed in the introduction, the multitextual nature of the Homeric tradition dictates that the epics' contents remained simultaneously reflective and incorporative of *multiple* times, as well as multiple historical, linguistic, and poetic traditions. Further, the continued evolution of these epics into the 6th century BCE and beyond, via a "streamlining of variations," can be seen in the countless elements of both *Iliad* and *Odyssey* which are clearly anachronistic in their fictive setting, or which are wholly appropriate to various periods within the first millennium BCE.[5]

## Continuity and Change Across the Ages

The possible existence of epic in oral tradition from earliest Mycenaean times and even before, perhaps conveyed to us in art—like that seen in Miniature Fresco from the West House at Akrotiri, or on the Siege Rhyton from Shaft Grave IV—may help explain the strands of continuity and vague memories of people, places, and events that seem to have come down to the archaic composer(s) of Homer's epics from centuries long past.[6] Sarah Morris refers to these works of art as "a visual counterpart to early epic poetry," while Eric Cline and Assaf Yasur-Landau have suggested that "miniature narrative art, possibly relating to an early epic tradition . . . could serve as a unifying *epos* or epic cycle in the time of extended colonization and diaspora, for instance on Crete, Kea, and Santorini during the [Late Minoan] IA period, and it served somewhat as a membership card to a Mediterranean club of members who shared this tradition—a club which extended from the northern Cyclades to Crete and perhaps beyond."[7]

We should not underestimate the importance (and pride of place) that oral tradition held in societies that lacked their own literary tradition. As we have seen, writing in Mycenaean Greece was very limited in comparison to the literatures, legends, international correspondence, and enumerated deeds of kings known from Near Eastern texts. Further, Linear B was restricted to palatial administrators, with illiteracy being the rule, rather than the exception, throughout the Late Bronze Age Aegean and beyond. Thus, the incorporation of names and events into epics that are reminiscent of those known from centuries long past should not necessarily be surprising, and the conglomeration of such events and people from such a wide period of time may in fact support their basis in real events, chronologically scattered as they may have been in actual history. A prime example of this is the Trojan War, still a topic of intense importance and debate to Homerists and Bronze Age archaeologists alike.

In this vein, it is important to note that a later date of composition, and a reflection of geography and events that fit accurately in an earlier age (in this case, in the fictive period of the epic's setting), need not be mutually exclusive realities. As Singer has noted:

> . . . to be sure, [Homer's epics] had to be revised and adapted to contemporary needs, but [their] basic features had been remembered and kept alive in all probability *without* any written transmission. In evaluating the historicity of a story, a distinction should be made between its main structure and its secondary details. In other words, even if Odysseus's boar-tusk helmet were proven to be

late, there would still remain the general situation described by Homer, which fits much better the Mycenaean age than his own times.[8]

## ODYSSEUS AND THE SHERDEN OF THE SEA

In the case of the *Odyssey* and its hero's Second Cretan Lie, the experiences of the central character find a remarkable analogue in a very real and very specific group of sea raiders, the Š3rd3n3 n p3 *ym* 'Sherden of the Sea,' who set upon Egypt in their ships—likely many times over—around the same time Odysseus claims to have carried out his ill-fated raid.

As we have seen, the Tanis II rhetorical stele marks the first of many Ramesside claims to have defeated and captured named maritime foes. Various Sea Peoples groups, including Sherden, are also claimed by name as victims and captives by Ramesses II in the poem recounting his "victory" at Qidš over the forces of the Hittite king Muwatalli II; by Merneptah in the Great Karnak Inscription and Papyrus Anastasi II, as well as on his Aswan Stele, Cairo Column, and Heliopolis Victory Column; and by Ramesses III in multiple inscriptions at Medinet Habu in the Great Harris Papyrus, and on a stele at Deir el-Medineh. The treatment of Sherden as prisoners may be supported by the Papyrus Amiens, a ledger from the time of Ramesses V (ca. 1149–1145 BCE) or later which records transport ships and revenue in the form of grain collected from the domains of various temples. This document lists two "houses . . . founded for the people of the Sherden," one by Ramesses II and the other by Ramesses III, as well as a "House of the Sherden" whose founder is unknown (R. 4.9–10, 5.4, V. 2.x+10), alongside a "domain" established for "the people who were brought on account of their crimes," or convicted criminals (R 5.3–4), though this may refer to those sentenced to carry out agricultural labor.[9]

### In the Service of the Pharaoh

Despite typical Pharaonic bombast like that seen in Ramesses II's Tanis II inscription, not all of those Sherden who were "carried off to Egypt" after their initial capture early in the 13th century languished in prisons or spent the rest of their days serving the state as slave laborers, as many of the survivors of Odysseus' fictional raiding party are said to have done. Rather, like Odysseus himself, they appear to have been welcomed into Egypt and allowed to profit from the employment of their unique skills, which were utilized in the direct service of the pharaoh.

Already in the fifth year of Ramesses II's reign (1275 BCE), for example, Sherden are depicted as what is thought to be members of the Pharaonic bodyguard—surely a place of high honor among soldiers, as well as one requiring great trust.[10] Evidence for the place of honor afforded those *Sherden* who gave allegiance to Egypt may also be found in the Great Harris Papyrus, wherein Ramesses III addresses "the officials and leaders of the land, the infantry, the chariotry, the Sherden, the many bowmen, and all the souls of Egypt."[11] The term 'Sherden' is the only *ethnikon* employed in this Pharaonic salutation, if indeed it is meant as such; all others are grouped solely by rank, title, and occupation. This may signify that, in the century following their initial defeat at the hands of Ramesses II, Sherden had joined the Egyptian army in such great numbers, or to such great and distinctive effect, that they had earned specific mention among the more general list of military specialties.

It is, of course, also possible that this term had at some point become a military title, or had given its name to a martial specialty other than the aforementioned three (infantry, chariotry, and bowmen). However, later in the same document Ramesses III makes direct reference to the enemy "Sherden and the Weshesh of the Sea," as well as to the "Sherden and Kehek . . . in their towns," thus associating the Sherden once again with named groups. This supports the continued use of the term as an *ethnikon* or other avocational associative marker.

## Domestic Life in an Adopted Land

The Great Harris Papyrus also provides the first evidence for this people in an Egyptian domestic setting, including a particularly noteworthy mention of Sherden *families* living together in Egypt:

> I made the infantry and chariotry to dwell [at home] in my time; the Sherden and Kehek were in their towns, lying the length of their backs; they had no fear, for there was no enemy from Kush [nor] foe from Syria [a reference to the southern and northern frontiers, respectively]. Their bows and their weapons were laid up in their magazines, while they were satisfied and drunk with joy. *Their wives were with them, their children at their side* [for] I was with them as the defense and protection of their limbs.

Great Harris Papyrus [12]

Like Odysseus of the Second Cretan Lie, the importance of the *Sherden* within Egyptian military and society also earned them significant material benefits. This can be seen in particular in the Wilbour Papyrus, a monumental land registry from the reign of Ramesses V covering portions of the Fayum region of Middle Egypt.[13] Among those listed in this text as land-owners and occupiers are 109 *Sherden*, "standard-bearers of the *Sherden*," "retainers of the *Sherden*," a "herdsman of the Sherden," and even one "tender of the crocodiles of the Sherden."[14] These allocations take various forms: some land seems to have belonged to others and been cared for by Sherden, some seems to have been shared by families (brothers are specifically mentioned), and some Sherden seem to have been allotted multiple areas to own or maintain.

Of the 59 plots assigned to *Sherden* in this document, 42 are five *arourae, or slightly under four acres* in size. This allocation was commensurate with priests, standard bearers, stablemasters, and others of similarly high rank. Soldiers, on the other hand, were generally allotted three *arourae*, or approximately two acres.[15] In some cases, the wealth bestowed on the pharaoh's *Sherden* in the form of land was not limited to a temporary inhabitation of this Middle Egyptian oasis; rather, their significant contributions were repaid with an equally significant reward: land they could pass down through the generations. This can be seen, for example, in entries that refer to land belonging to deceased *Sherden* being "cultivated by the hand of [their] children":[16]

The standard-bearer of Sherden Ptaḥemḥab, who is dead, (cultivated) by the hand of <his> children                        10 __| 5. *I*, mc. *1* $^2/_4$

$\S150.59.9–10$[17]

The retainer of the Sherden Mesman, (cultivated) by the hand of (his) children                        10 __| 5. *I*, mc. *1* $^2/_4$

$\S150.59.25–26$[18]

The inclusion of Sherden in the Wilbour Papyrus's register of landowners has been seen as evidence that those fighting in the service of Egypt by this time were mercenaries rather than prisoners of war.[19] It does seem likely that the landholding status of these Sherden was tied to their military service, and that it should be viewed either as a conditional grant exchanged for ongoing service to the pharaoh, or as an award presented after retirement for services rendered. However, the aforementioned references to Sherden land being cultivated by their descendants demonstrate that at least some of these people came into possession of territory through hereditary tenure. Needless to say, this would be an unlikely situation if continuous military service were required in exchange for the right to occupy land. Another suggestion is that some of these landholders came to own their territory through purchase rather than through military service.[20] Additionally, P. Wilbour makes a clear distinction between land ownership and indentured servitude, as the references to individuals—including Sherden—living on and cultivating land belonging

to others are clearly distinguished from references to the landowners themselves:

The Sherden Tjarobu                                         . 10 __| 5. *I*, mc. *I* $^{2}/_{4}$

Another measurement (made) for him land-cubits                     5.45

Another measurement (made) for him                                 5.45

Another measurement (made) for him                           50 resting

§32.17.40–43[21]

*T* Measurement made to the north of [Pen-Shō]s (in) the Lake of Iryut:

The retainer of the Sherden Pḳaha (?), together with his brethren
.10 __| 5. 2 ar., mc. *I* $^{2}/_{4}$

Another measurement (made) for him, in vegetables, land-cubits 20.80

Another measurement (made) for him                          .50 resting

§118.44.33–35[22]

His Majesty's charioteer Merenptaḥ, (cultivated) by the hand of | the Sherden
Siptaḥ arouras 20. *I*, mc. *I* $^{2}/_{4}$

§123.48.45[23]

The Mansion of King Menma'rē' in Abydus.

*T* Measurement made in [the] New land of Neby east of Sakō:

The scribe Setnakhte, (cultivated) by the hand of the Sherden Tja'o
.10. ¼, mc. *I* $^{2}/_{4}$

§234.83.23–25[24]

The mentions of Sherden being assigned to work others' lands are significant because they provide evidence for different social statuses, and perhaps
different levels of integration, enjoyed by Sherden individuals within Egyptian society, as some were either forced or allowed to work land belonging
to non-Sherden owners, while others among them not only owned land, but
were evidently able to pass it along to their children.

Aside from owning land, which was itself of significant value, it would be
far from surprising if, much like Odysseus, *Sherden* fighters also accumulated

additional material wealth as a result of their exploits. Papyrus Anastasi I, a 19th dynasty text that discusses proper preparation and provisioning for a military mission to Canaan, lists 520 *Sherden* among a mixed force of 5,000 soldiers. This suggests that, by midway through Ramesses II's reign, they had already become a standard component of Egypt's northern expeditionary forces. With regular exposure to warfare most likely came regular opportunities for plunder, which could be taken individually or divided among the conquering forces after a successful siege or battle, much in the way that *Sherden* pirates and Odysseus' raiding crews likely divided the plunder after their own successful raids:[25]

τῶν ἐξαιρεύμην μενοεικέα, πολλὰ δ᾽ ὀπίσσω
λάγχανον· αἶψα δὲ οἶκος ὀφέλλετο, καί ῥα ἔπειτα
δεινός τ᾽ αἰδοῖός τε μετὰ Κρήτεσσι τετύγμην.

Of this I would choose what pleased my mind, and much I afterwards obtained by lot. Thus my house straightway grew rich, and thereafter I became one feared and honored among the Cretans.

*Odyssey* xiv, 232–234

Rather than being a benefit of Egyptian generosity, it seems likely that the wealth he characterizes as being amassed via gifts from the Egyptians (δίδοσαν γὰρ ἅπαντες; *Odyssey* xiv, 286, quoted above) was likewise gained through a division of plunder from further raids in which Odysseus, acting essentially as a privateer on behalf of the pharaoh, was now a "legitimate" participant.

As noted above, Gurob is located within the territory recorded in the Wilbour Papyrus, and the text's date of composition falls directly within the chronological range of the ship-cart model found in Tomb 611 at that site. If it belonged to one of the *Sherden* mentioned in this text or to one of their descendants, as Wachsmann has proposed, then the ship-cart model provides support for the theory that members of this group, like Odysseus himself, may have been sailing oared galleys as they plundered the coasts of the Eastern Mediterranean.[26]

While the seafaring nature of the Sherden is clear, documentary evidence hints at an effort to downplay the nautical affinities of those who had entered Egyptian service and society. As noted above, Sherden in the Egyptian military and society are never referred to as being "of the Sea," an epithet that appears to be reserved for those fighting against Egypt. Thus, the ship-cart from Gurob, if properly attributed to a Sherden (or to the descendant of one), can be seen as evidence not only for this group's association with the type of ship represented at Medinet Habu, but also for at least one Sherden's attempt to maintain his foreign identity during a period of perhaps forcibly accelerated acculturation into Egyptian society (for an opposite example, see the Padjesef stele below). If such is the case, this may compare favorably to the self-representations like the Beth Shean coffins and seals from Enkomi and Tell el-Far'ah (S) discussed in Chapter 3, which perhaps memorialized in traditional Egyptian media the (foreign) ethnic identities of their commissioners.

Our dwindling evidence for the Sherden in the years following the Papyrus Amiens suggests a state of accelerating integration and assimilation into Egyptian society. In the "Adoption Papyrus" (Papyrus Ashmolean Museum 1945.96), a document from Spermeru in Middle Egypt that dates to the reign of Ramesses XI (ca. 1107–1078 BCE), an Egyptian woman named Nenūfer recounts her adoption as her stablemaster husband's legal child and heir.[27] Seven witnesses to the procedure are listed, two of whom, Pkamen and Satameniu, are identified as Sherden, with a third listed as Satameniu's wife. Though this legal action is local and essentially private in nature, the presence of Sherden among the witnesses demonstrates their legal and social ability to act in that capacity, while the inclusion of Satameniu's wife reinforces the theme of Sherden marrying and settling in Egypt, though the ethnicity (or ethnicities) of their spouses is never explicitly stated.

The final references, including perhaps the most intriguing of all, come in the form of three dedicatory stelae. The latest of these, the Donation Stele of Djedptahiuefankh (Cairo Journal d'Entrée 45327), which dates to the reign of Osorkon II in the 22nd dynasty (mid-9th century BCE), mentions "the fields of the Sherden, under the control of the prophet Hor."[28] While this inscription provides evidence of the term's endurance into the first millennium, its context does not allow us to draw any conclusions about its meaning at this point. The other stelae come from the Temple of Heryshef at Herakleopolis, and have been dated anywhere from the 19th to the 22nd dynasties.[29] The first of these mentions "the three fortresses of the Sherden" while the second claims "Padjesef . . . Sherden soldier of the great fortress" as its dedicator (Fig. 9.1).

While these inscriptions reinforce the Ramesside theme of Sherden being associated with strongholds or fortresses, the latter is also noteworthy for the image above its text, which appears to show Padjesef himself bringing offerings to Heryshef and Hathor. The unique importance of this stele stems from its status as the only known self-identification and self-representation of a Sherden individual, and from the fact that the scene it presents is entirely Egyptian, including the portrayal of Padjesef himself. It has been argued that the lack of a distinctive horned helmet in this image should be seen to be evidence of settlement and integration.[30] While the Egyptian nature of the scene certainly suggests acculturation, the lack of horned helmet should not

*Chapter Nine*

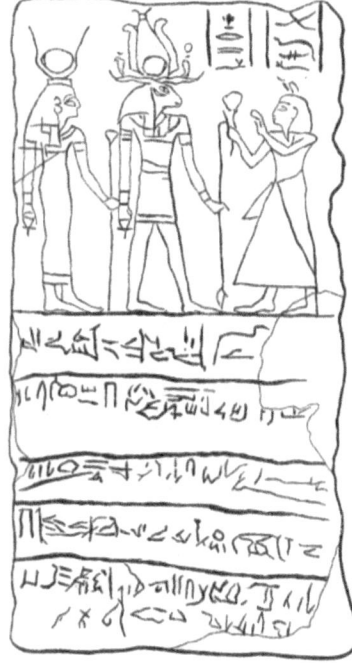

**Figure 9.1.** Dedicatory stele of "Padjesef . . . Sherden soldier of the great fortress" from the Temple of Heryshef at Herakleopolis
Petrie, W. M. F. 1905. *Ehnaysia, 1904*. London. Plate 27.2.

be surprising. We do not know how Sherden identified themselves internally or vis-à-vis other groups, either militarily or in civilian life. Even if Sherden like Padjesef considered this accoutrement to be their primary identifying mark, the date and dedicatory nature of the scene would make its presence much more surprising than its absence. Thus, the level to which Padjesef, and perhaps other Sherden, had been integrated into Egyptian society by this time is not demonstrated so much by what is *not* there—the distinctive Sherden helmet—as by what *is* there: a self-portrait in which the dedicator appears—in dress, action, and the location of the dedication itself—to be entirely Egyptian.[31]

## CONCLUSION

The Sherden of the Sea are named as a participant in maritime raids against Egypt from the earliest years of Ramesses II in the early 13th century to the reign of Ramesses III a century or more later. While the geographic origin of these people is uncertain, circumstantial evidence allows us to connect them to polychromatic, fifty-oared galleys of the type described by Homer—in one case, in terms reserved specifically for Odysseus' ships. Further, their story is extraordinarily similar to the tales that make up Odysseus' Second Cretan Lie, as well as the portion of this tale retold later in the epic: years of successful maritime raiding, at least one ill-fated attempt on the Nile delta, and a subsequent sojourn in Egypt, during which they were valued as a part of society and made prosperous for their efforts.

The two stories diverge as Odysseus' seven-year stay in Egypt draws to a close: while the *nostos* that makes up the *Odyssey*'s macronarrative dictates that its hero move on, those Sherden who settled in Egypt were able to create a new home for themselves in the land of the pharaohs, complete with wives, children, and land they could pass down through generations.

# Notes

## CHAPTER ONE

1. All passages of *Odyssey* are from Murray 1919, unless otherwise indicated.

2. Nagy 2013, 12 writes, "deep concerns about the human condition are organized by Homeric poetry in a framework of heroic portraits, with those of Achilles and Odysseus serving as the centerpieces of the *Iliad* and the *Odyssey* respectively."

3. Butler 1898; cf. Sherratt 1990, 810–12.

4. Sherratt 2010, 16.

5. Nagy 1990, 57–58; 1996a, 29–64; 1996b, 50; 2001.

6. Reece 1994, 157; Sherratt 2010, 3–4.

7. Reece 1994, 165.

8. Further evidence for a "Cretan *Odyssey*" has been discussed by Levaniouk 2011, 105, who notes the presence of the Cretan King Idomeneus on a red-figure *stamnos* that depicts Odysseus and his companions escaping the cave of the Cyclops, and by Nagy 2015a.

9. Among many, see Horrocks 1980; Janko 1982; Vermeule 1987; West 1988, esp 152–59; 2012; Sherratt 1990; 2010; Jamison 1994; Nagy 2010, 232–33, 308–310; additionally, West 1988, 169–70 and Bryce 2002, 261–68 in particular note Homeric poetry's Near Eastern and Mesopotamian affinities, while the Luwian text dubbed the *Wilusiad* by Watkins 1986, which begins "When they came from steep Wilusa . . . ," has been seen as a possible Anatolian tale that also focuses on Troy—another fascinating (potential) thread in the Bronze Age tapestries of epic and history alike.

10. Nagy 2007, 80–81.

11. Muhly 2010, 4.

12. Singer 2013a, 24–25.

13. Elements of the Hittite empire continued into the Iron Age, but its base of power largely shifted to northern Syria, where (among a collection of "rump states") a dynasty of "Great Kings" thought to have connected Bronze Age Ḫattuša to the Neo-Hittite

first millennium ruled from Karkamiš, which had been the seat of the Hittite viceroy in Syria in the preceding Late Bronze Age; Hawkins 1988; Beckman 1992, 43–44, 49; Güterbock 1992; Singer 2000; Bryce 2006, 134–35; Harrison 2009, 187.

14. Cf. Emanuel 2012 for a much briefer treatment of the subject.

15. Previously addressed in Emanuel 2015a.

16. Emanuel 2014.

17. Mountjoy 1998; 1999, 985–86; 2014; "the Interface," as the latter region will be referred to from this point forward, developed in the 15th century BCE and continued, in expanded form, into the 12th century, and is most visibly connected by a ceramic *koine* across the Aegean islands, including the Dodecanese (but excluding Rhodes during the Bronze Age), and into the western territories of Asia Minor.

18. The evidence for the Sherden was briefly reviewed in Emanuel 2013a, but the incorporation of *Odyssey* xiv, 248–72 into the analysis once again provides a complement to the primary historical sources that can help further our understanding of this group and its role in Egyptian society.

## CHAPTER TWO

1. Kitchen 2007; 2013; Bietak 2013; Höflmayer 2016.

2. Betancourt 1998, 295.

3. Deger-Jalkotzy 2010, 393.

4. See Toffolo et al. 2013 for the results of a recent effort to shore up the chronology of the Aegean Iron Age, including the LH IIIC, via the radiocarbon of seeds, bones, and wood from Corinth, Kalapodi, and Lefkandi.

5. Hankey 1967, 127–28; cf. Sherratt and Mazar 2013, who note the clear Cypriot affinities displayed by the "Mycenaean"-style ceramics from Beth Shean, thus highlighting the risks inherent in tying pottery of Aegean appearance directly to that region.

6. See especially Furumark 1941 and Mountjoy 1999, among many.

7. Nims 1976; Lesko 1992; Redford 2000, 11; Manassa 2013, 250.

8. S. Morris 2003, 8.

9. Redford 2000, 5.

10. Tilley and Johnstone 1976, 292.

11. Wachsmann 1998, 4–5.

12. Sauvage 2012, 227 English translation: "These iconographic representations raise the question of accuracy, as well as the possibility of reconstructing an object type from a drawing. A priori, a graffito should be able to give us more information, and be closer to reality, than an artistic representation, the artists not always being completely familiar with the marine environment. On the other hand, the sailors who had to engrave these ships were not necessarily endowed with an immense artistic talent and certain 'works' are therefore very difficult to understand and to interpret because of their rudimentary and schematic character."

13. Gardiner 1947, 200*–205.*

14. Among many, Weinstein 1992; Singer 2000; Stager 1995.

15. Wilson 1974b, 262–63; MH I, pl 46.

16. Yasur-Landau 2012a, with references; also see now Maeir and Hitchcock 2017. A recent paper by Jesse Millek (2017) pushes back against the former conventional wisdom, arguing that very few of the destructions in the southern Levant at the end of the Bronze Age were actually the result of hostile acts at all (let alone of attacks by the Sea Peoples).

17. Contrast, for example, Stager 1991 and 1995 and Stone 1995 with Maeir, Hitchcock and Horwitz 2013 and Maeir and Hitchcock 2017.

18. Drews 1998 39; for a less extreme version of the argument against the Philistines and other Sea Peoples as migrants from farther than the northern Levant and Anatolia, see now Ben-Dor Evian 2017.

19. Kitchen 2012 15.

20. Among recent studies are Karageorghis and Kouka 2011 and Fischer and Bürge 2017; a recent oppositional view can be seen in Middleton 2015, although his argument focuses on the outdated view of the Philistines as Mycenaeans who migrated *en masse* from the Aegean to southern Canaan (e.g., Stager, 1991; 1995), and overlooks studies that are more reflective of current views on the topic (e.g., Maeir, Hitchcock and Horwitz 2013).

21. Yasur-Landau 2010a, 15–16.

22. On "deep change," see especially Yasur-Landau 2010a 13–26. For the latest on the transcultural nature of the Philistines, see now Maeir and Hitchcock 2017.

23. Cline 1994 9–10; Burns 2010 137.

24. Van Wijngaarden 2002, 323–29.

25. Ben-Shlomo, Nodarou and Rutter 2011.

26. Karageorghis 1992, 17, 20; Sherratt and Sherratt 1991.

27. Birney 2007, 102–86; Lehmann 2013.

28. Nuñez 2017, 266.

29. Stager 1995, 334–35; Maeir 2012, 20.

30. Huertly 1936.

31. Wilson 1974a, 26; King 2009.

32. Gilboa 2006–7 210.

33. Tubb 2000, 182.

34. King 2009.

35. Dor: Stern 2013; Akko: e.g., Dothan and Dothan 1992; Stager 1995; Nuñez 2017, 265; el-Ahwat: Zertal 2012, with the merits of the case briefly addressed in Emanuel 2013b (cf. also Jung 2017, 35).

36. Gilboa 2005, 69; 2006–7, 211, 233; Gilboa and Sharon 2017, 292; also Boyes 2012, 107–8; Artzy 2013, 344.

37. Papyrus Louvre N3136, attributable either to Merneptah or to Ramesses III, refers to both Philistines and Sherden in the context of a Libyan invasion, saying, "*We caused 100 of the Philistines to go forth [. . .] at the time ... 200 Sherden of the great strongholds*"; Spalinger 2002, 359–62.

38. Barth 1969; *contra* Petrakis 2004, 4, who suggests that the concept of ethnicity at any time prior to late Medieval Europe is an anachronism.

39. For recent studies on the heterogeneity of the Philistines in particular, see Maeir, Hitchcock and Horwitz 2013 and Maeir and Hitchcock 2017.

## CHAPTER THREE

1. Moran 1992, xviii.
2. Redford 1984.
3. EA 3, 4, 10, 16, 19, etc.
4. EA 16.
5. EA 1.
6. Malamat 1971, 24.
7. Zaccagnini 1983; Gordon 1992; Niemeier and Niemeier 1998; Cline and Yasur-Landau 2007; Koehl 2013, 177; Feldman 2014, 346–47; additionally, see now Cline, Yasur-Landau and Koh 2017 for radiocarbon results that may suggest the "Minoan-style" frescoes at Kabri appeared well before their counterparts in the Aegean.
8. Caubet 1998; Feldman 2002, 17; 2006, 71, 89.
9. Pulak 1998; Vagnetti and Lo Schiavo 1989, 222–23; Knapp 1990, 120; Bachhuber 2006.
10. Cline 2014, 77.
11. Snodgrass 1991, 18; Cline 2014, 75.
12. Pulak 1998, 201.
13. Bass 1986, 282–85; Weinstein 1989; Pulak 1998, 204; Wachsmann 1998, 306, 373, nn44–53; Jackson and Nicholson 2010.
14. Bass 1998 188; Pulak 1998; 2005.
15. Hitchcock and Maeir 2014.
16. Bass 1990.
17. Fitzgerald 1998, 141.
18. Mallowan 1966, 278.
19. Bryce 2002, 69.
20. Shear 1998.
21. Artzy 1997; Sherratt and Sherratt 1998, 341; Bachhuber 2006, 355; Sauvage 2012, 161, 208–10; Papadimitriou 2015, 437.
22. Breasted 1906–7, §916.
23. Moran 1992, 111 (emphasis added).
24. Beckman, Bryce and Cline 2011, 95; AhT 3 = *Catalogue des Textes Hittites* [CTH] 147 = *Keilschrifttexte aus Boğazköi* [KBo] 14.1.
25. Beckman, Bryce and Cline 2011, 81.
26. West 2001.
27. Horden and Purcell 2000, 157.
28. E.g., Spalinger 2002, 361, who writes, "As for the ubiquitous Sherden, who were 'pirates' in the true sense of trading or despoiling as expedient"; on the uncertain prospect of Sherden in the Amarna Letters, see (briefly) Emanuel 2013a, 14, 23–24, nn10–14.
29. Kitchen 1996, 120.
30. Hitchcock and Maeir 2014; 2016; 2017.
31. Karraker 1953, 15; Baruffi 1998, 10; de Souza 1999, 16.
32. Wachsmann 1998, 317.
33. Wachsmann 1998, 320.

34. de Souza 1999, 16–17.
35. de Souza 2010, 290; 2014 24.
36. de Souza 2002, 180–81.
37. via de Souza 2002, 185.
38. Hall 1890, 253.
39. Moran 1992, 11.
40. Hall 1890, 256.
41. Braudel 1972, 866.
42. Starkey 1990, 13, 19.
43. Cf. Richard 2010.
44. de Souza 1999, 32, 36–37.
45. Keegan 1993, 9.
46. Buffaloe 2006, 17.
47. Liverani 200, 109.
48. See also, e.g., *Odyssey* iii, 71–74 and *Homeric Hymn to Apollo*, 452–455.
49. Jung 2009, 79.
50. Artzy 2003, 445; Sherratt and Sherratt 1998, 340–41.
51. Sherratt and Sherratt 1998, 339; Earle 2008, 133; Sauvage 2012, 290; Tartaron 2013; cf. Cherry and Davis 1982, 338–40.
52. Sauvage 2012, 208; Kramer-Hajos 2016, 144.
53. Earle 2008, 133; Horden and Purcell 2000, 143–52, 347; Tartaron 2013.
54. Van Wees 1992, 208; Baruffi 1998, 72.
55. French 1996, 280; Sherratt and Sherratt 1991, 359.
56. Artzy 1997, 12.
57. Georgiou 2012, 527.
58. Artzy 1997.

## CHAPTER FOUR

1. Niemeier 1998, 20–23; Beckman, Bryce and Cline 2011, 1–6; the full corpus of Aḫḫiyawa texts is presented with transliteration, translation, and commentary in Beckman, Bryce and Cline 2011.

2. Redford 1992, 242–43; Dickinson 1994, 253, though this assertion was later softened (2006, 29).

3. For linguistic arguments in favor of *Aḫḫiya(wa)* > Ἀχαιοι, cf. Finkelberg 1988 and Nagy 2015b.

4. Bryce 1989, 3–5; Kelder 2004–5, 158; Beckman, Bryce and Cline 2011, 5–6.

5. Beckman, Bryce and Cline 2011, 257; also Singer 2006 and Lackenbacher and Malbran-Labat 2005, who rendered PAD.MEŠ '*rations alimentaires.*'

6. Beckman, Bryce and Cline 2011, 261.

7. Beckman, Bryce and Cline 2011, 265; Bryce 2016, 72.

8. Bryce 2016, 74.

9. Jones 1924.

10. Yonge 1854.

11. Dinçol et al. 2015.

12. Hawkins 2000, 45–71; Singer 2009; 2013b, 322–25.

13. Oreshko 2013, 31; Lehmann 2017, 246–47; cf. Hawkins 2015; Yakubovich 2015a; 2015b.

14. Redford 2003, 96–98.

15. Cline 1998.

16. For color photographs of this base, see Cline and Stannish 2011.

17. Cline 2014, 47.

18. Cline and Stannish 2011, 7.

19. Rehak and Younger 1998, 102, 163.

20. Kelder 2010, 126.

21. Cline 1998, 244–48; 2014, 44–51.

22. Moran 1992, 238–39.

23. Bryce 1998, 343.

24. Beckman, Bryce and Cline 2011, 50.

25. AhT 4 = CTH 181 = KUB 14.3.

26. Hoffner 2009, 311; Beckman, Bryce and Cline 2011, 2, 101, 115.

27. Beckman 1996, 82–87; Bryce 1998, 244–45, 326–60.

28. Niemeier 1998, 27–40, 46; Bryce 1998, 343–44.

29. Bittel 1976; Salvini and Vagnetti 1994, 219–25.

30. Beckman, Bryce and Cline 2011, 63.

31. Bryce 2010, 50; 2016 ,70.

32. Schofield and Parkinson 1994; Kelder 2010, 127, 137.

33. Jones 1924; also Bacchylides *Epinician* XI, 77–80 and Pausanias II 25.8.

34. Bryce 1992, 126–28.

35. Sandars 1985, 65–67, figs 35–36; Niemeier 1998 43; Maran 2010, 726–29.

36. Frazier 1921.

37. Shelmerdine 1997, 567.

38. Halstead 1992, 72; Kramer-Hajos 2016, 144.

39. Dickinson 2006, 30.

40. Yasur-Landau 2010, 41–42, 55, table 2.1, fig 2.3; AhT 27A and B (=RS 94.2530 and 94.2523).

41. Sherratt and Sherratt 1998, 339; Tartaron 2013.

42. Kantor 1947, 79; Sjöqvist 1940, 183–84; Daniel 1942, 241.

43. Wachsmann 1987; Bass 1998.

44. Bass 1997.

45. Bass 1998 185.

46. Bass 2010.

47. Bass 2010; Sherratt 2000, 87; Singer 2006, 254.

48. Peltenburg 2012, 346.

49. Bass 1967; Pulak 1996; Zukerman 2010, on the other hand, has rightly cautioned against pushing back too hard against the concept of 'thalassocracy' by removing Aegeans from the international trade equation al together.

50. Billigmeier and Turner 1981, 6.

51. S. Morris 2001, 426; Michailidou and Voutsa 2005, 19.

52. Chadwick 1988, 80, 83; for an opposing view, see Billigmeier and Turner 1981, 6.

53. Olsen 2014, 94, 107.

54. Sasson 1966, 137.

55. Van Soldt 2010, 201.

56. S. Morris 2003, 7; Kirk 1965, 55; Gilan 2013, 53.

57. Beckman, Bryce and Cline 2011, 159.

58. Beckman, Bryce and Cline 2011, 8, 160.

59. Güterbock 1983, 134; Houwink ten Cate 1994, 251; Cammarosano 2010, 47, 56.

60. Yon 1992.

61. *MH* I, pl 46, col 16; Wilson, 1974, 262.

62. Cline 2014, 11.

63. Hallo 1992, 2; Drews 1993; on the tumultuous transition from the Late Bronze to the Early Iron Age, see (among many) Gitin, Mazar and Stern 1998; Oren 2000; Harrison 2006–7; Bachhuber and Roberts 2009; Killebrew and Lehmann 2013; Cline 2014; Knapp and Manning 2016; Fischer and Bürge 2017.

64. Killebrew and Lehmann 2013, 6–7; Sharon and Gilboa 2013, 463–67; Nuñez 2017. As noted earlier, Gilboa and Sharon (2017) have suggested that one of the Sea Peoples groups, the *Sikils* or *Tjeker*, were simply Phoenicians all along, thus partially explaining the lack of evidence for a foreign influx in this location.

65. Sherratt and Crouwel 1987. For a (very) brief gazetteer of "Mycenaean or Aegeanizing" pottery in Cilicia, see Lehmann 2017, 247–48; also Birney 2007, 102–36.

66. Venturi 2011, 144–45.

67. Ponchia 2011, 282; Venturi 2011, 150; 2013, 237–39.

68. Janeway 2006–7; 2011.

69. Birney 2007 427; 2008; Gates 2013; Ünlü 2005, 147–48.

70. Ben-Shlomo 2006–7; Maeir, Hitchcock and Horwitz 2013.

71. Mountjoy 2010; Maeir, Hitchcock and Horwitz 2013; Maeir and Hitchcock 2017; Yasur-Landau 2003; 2010; 2011; 2012a; Gilboa and Sharon 2017.

72. This rebuilding followed destruction that may have been caused by an earthquake; French 1996.

73. Iakovidis 1986, 259; Deger-Jalkotzy 2010, 388.

74. Deger-Jalkotzy 2010, 388; Lemos 2006, 524.

75. Van De Mieroop 2009, 80.

76. Deger-Jalkotzy 2010, 390.

77. As will be discussed below, short-lived attempts to continue the preceding order might be seen at Tiryns and at Cycladic sites like Koukounaries on Paros.

78. Whittaker 2017, 75, with references.

79. Kilian 1988, 134–45; Rutter 1992, 68–70; Walberg 1995, 89–91; Karageorghis and Morris 2001; French 2002, 135–40; Adrimi-Sismani 2006; Lemnos 2006, 524–25; Harrison and Spencer 2007; as Lantzas 2015, 467 notes, reasons for remaining in the areas around the palatial centers extend beyond the symbolic value of the former citadels, and include "a number of practical factors, such as access to arable land and water and the uncertainty and cost of moving."

80. For more on potential causes of collapse (with bibliography) see, among many, Dickinson 2006, 43–57 and Middleton 2010, 4–67; Knapp and Manning 2016.
81. Mountjoy 1997.
82. Palmer 1980, 143–67; Palaima 1995a 625; Shelmerdine 1999; Dickinson 2006, 43, 46, 55.
83. Hooker 1987, 264; Papadopoulos 2006, 131–32; Deger-Jalkotzy 2010, 389.
84. Palmer 1980, 143–144; Palaima 1991, 286; Wedde 2005, 33.
85. Shelmerdine 1999, 405–10.
86. Shelmerdine 1997, 547.
87. Zangger et al. 1997, 609–13.
88. This option is argued for by Baumbach 1983 and Wachsmann 1999.
89. Shelmerdine 1997, 584.
90. Karageorghis 2001, 5.
91. Schilardi 1984; 1992; 1999.
92. Earle 2008, 192.
93. Barako 2001, 136, n21.
94. Schilardi 1992 637.

# CHAPTER FIVE

1. Singer 1983, 217.
2. O'Connor 2000, 94–95.
3. Redford 2000, 8.
4. Stager 1995; Sweeney and Yasur-Landau 1999.
5. Yasur-Landau 2010, 175–79; 2012c.
6. Edgerton and Wilson 1936, 35; *MH* I pl. 29.
7. Edgerton and Wilson 1936, 35; *MH* I pls. 30–31.
8. Edgerton and Wilson 1936, 38–39; *MH* I pls. 32–34.
9. Edgerton and Wilson 1936, 39–40; *MH* I pl. 35.
10. Wilson 1974b, 263; *MH* I pls. 37–39.
11. Edgerton and Wilson 1936, 42; *MH* I, pl. 42.
12. Edgerton and Wilson 1936, 44–45; *MH* I pl. 43.
13. Wilson 1974b, 262–263; *MH* I pl. 46.
14. First Libyan campaign: *MH* I pls. 17–19, 24; second Libyan campaign: *MH* II, pls. 62, 65c, 72.
15. Second court; Kitchen 2008, 22; *MH* I pls. 27–28, 54c.
16. Face of the first pylon on the temple exterior; Edgerton and Wilson 1936, 130–31; *MH* II, pls. 107, 128a.
17. First court; Edgerton and Wilson 1936, 46–48; *MH* I pl. 44.
18. *MH* VIII 5.
19. Peden 1994, 65.
20. Wilson 1974b, 262.
21. Among many, see Albright 1932a, 57–58; Alt 1953, 227–28; Dothan 1982, 3; Singer 1985, 110.

22. E. Morris 2005, 731–33; Kahn 2011, 2–3; Ben-Dor Evian 2017, 269–70.

23. de Rougé 1877, 253.8; Kitchen 1996, 182.

24. An example of this is the site of Askut in Nubia; Smith 1991, 115; 1995, 41–43; E. Morris 2005, 641–45, 686–87.

25. Habachi 1980; Yurco 1999, 877; Snape 2010, 273–75.

26. White and White 1996, 29.

27. White 1986; 1999.

28. Snape 2010, 273, 286–87.

29. Snape 1997, 24; Thomas 2003; Ben-Shlomo et al. 2011, 336.

30. Bietak 2015.

31. Hulin and White 2002, 173.

32. Caminos 1954, 64.

33. Breasted 1906–7, §§254–255.

34. Kitchen 2003, 2–4.

35. Manassa 2003, 154–55.

36. *MH* I pl 22; Kitchen 2008, 15:10.

37. Sandars 1985, 107–11.

38. King James Version; see also Judg. 14:3, 15:18; 1 Sam. 14:6, 17:36, 31:4; 2 Sam. 1:20; 1 Chron. 10:4.

39. Hooker 2014 [1976] 161; also Page 1959, 21–22.

40. Kitchen 2003, 19, 29.

41. Caminos 1954, 45; Gardiner 1906–7, 210.

42. Kitchen 1996, 67.

43. Habachi 1980, 29.

44. Snape 2010, 286–87.

# CHAPTER SIX

1. Hoftijzer and Van Soldt 1998, 343.

2. Lehmann 1979; Redford 2006, 11.

3. Wachsmann 1982, 297; 1998; Stager 1991, 19, n23.

4. Rainey 1982, 134; Redford 2006–7.

5. "The 'Sea-Peoples' were essentially north Levantine (including western Anatolian) populations known as former allies of the Hittites"; Ben-Dor Evian 2017, 278.

6. Güterbock 1967, 78.

7. Edel 1994, H4, 283–85; also Basch 2009; Pomey 2009.

8. Basch 2009, 65–70; Monroe, personal communication.

9. Pomey 2009.

10. Beal 1992, 522.

11. Bryce 2016, 73.

12. Edel 1994b, 247.

13. Kanta 1980, 30; Andreadaki-Vlasaki 1991, 405; Rehak and Younger 1998, 166–68.

14. Nowicki 1987, 217; 2001, 25–36; 2002; 2011; Haggis and Nowicki 1993, 334.

15. Nowicki 2001, 29–30, 39; 1994, 268; 2000, 257–63; cf. Dickinson 2006, 69–72.

16. Schilardi 1992; Karageorghis 2001, 5.

17. Karageorghis 1985, 932; Symons 1987, 71.

18. Karageorghis and Demas 1988, 265; Yasur-Landau 2010a, 190.

19. Karageorghis 1992, 80; Yasur-Landau 2010a, 143–51.

20. Sandars 1985, 134; Vermeule and Karageorghis 1982, 132; Mountjoy 2005, 425; Yasur-Landau 2012b.

21. *MH I* pls, 19, 33–34, 37–39, 41–44, 46.

22. Oren 1973, 136–137, figs 7, 9, 18–19.

23. Moschos 2009, 356–57.

24. Furumark 1941, 240, n5.

25. Vermeule and Karageorghis 1982, 130–32, 222.

26. French 1998, 4.

27. Vermeule and Karageorghis 1982, pls XI.45–46.

28. Crouwel 1991, fig 7b.

29. Vermeule and Karageorghis 1982, pl XI.57.

30. Vermeule and Karageorghis 1982, pls XI.49, 16.1, 51.

31. Wardle and Wardle 2003, 154; Vermeule and Karageorghis 1982, pl XI.56.

32. Vermeule and Karageorghis 1982, pls XI.64, 64.1; Kanta 1980, fig 24.8.

33. Mountjoy and Gowland 2005, 165, 210.

34. Murray, Smith and Walters 1900, pl 1.

35. Crouwel 1981, 81; Knapp 2008, 271; the wheeled vehicles employed by the Sea Peoples in Ramesses III's land battle relief also featured six spokes per wheel.

36. Uehlinger 1988, 15–20; cf. Yasur-Landau, 2010, 209–11, who also notes a scaraboid from Stratum IV at Beth Shean that features a beardless, spiky-haired individual in long robes holding a lotus flower, perhaps in offering to a god.

37. Edgerton and Wilson 1936, 146.

38. *MH* I pl 28, col. 47; Redford 2007; Yasur-Landau 2012b, 33.

39. Stager and Mountjoy 2007; for a color plate, see Stager, Master and Schloen 2011, fig 15.40.

40. Also *Odyssey* v, 313–32; ix, 282–86; xii, 403–25; xxiii, 233–35; *Iliad* xv, 381–83, 624–28.

41. Janeway 2017, pl 9.15.

42. Janeway 2017, 87–91.

43. Harrison 2009; Hawkins 2009.

44. Kohlmeyer 2000; Hawkins 2009, 169.

45. Janeway 2017, 115–23; Harrison 2009, 183.

46. Janeway 2006–7, 140; 2017, 46–49.

47. Koehl 2005, 419; 2010, 83; Janeway 2017, 52, 65.

48. Janeway 2006–7, 138–39; 2017, 111–12.

49. Emanuel 2015b, 22–25.

50. Pritchard 1943, 39; Oren 1973, 129–30.

51. T. Dothan 1979, 100.

52. Fisher 1923, 234.

53. T. Dothan 1957; Weinstein 2012; Redford 1992 192–213; Higganbotham 1996; 2000.

54. Petrie 1930, 8; Wright 1959; 1966; E. Morris 2005, 702, n30.

55. Albright 1932b, 304.

56. Wright 1959, 54; 1966, 71; Dothan 1957, 163–64; 1958, 63–66; Kuchman 1977.

57. Brug 1985; Stager 1995, 341–42.

58. Oren 1973, 135–42, figs 1–19; Dothan 1982, 274.

59. Yasur-Landau 2010a, 152, 208–9; 2012b, 33.

## CHAPTER SEVEN

1. Meric and Mountjoy 2002, 82; Mountjoy 2014, 42, 75.

2. Meric and Mountjoy 2002, 92; Mountjoy 2006, 110–12; 2011, 484, 487; for LH IIIC Middle, Benzi 2013, 521.

3. Kos: Mountjoy 1999, 1075; Kynos: Dakoronia 1990; 1999; 2006; Liman Tepe: Aykurt and Erkanal 2017.

4. Mountjoy 2007, 226.

5. Yasur-Landau 2010a, 192; Hitchcock and Maeir 2014; 2016.

6. Mountjoy 2014, 67.

7. Blakolmer 2012.

8. Kuentz 1934, pls, 22, 28, 32, 35, 42.

9. *MH I* pls, 37–39, 41, 50c–d, 51g, 52a, 53d.

10. Youssef, Leblanc and Maher 1977, pls, XXXI–XXXII.

11. Sandars 1985, 106.

12. Kuentz 1929, pl 6.3; 1934, pl 220.26.

13. Kuentz 1934, pl 35.

14. Nelson 1929, 21–22; Wachsmann 1981, 191, 195.

15. Nelson 1929, 21.

16. *MH* II pl 100.

17. Schofield and Parkinson 1994, pl 22a; Parkinson and Schofield 1995.

18. Tsountas 188 pl 8.12; Yalouris 1960, 47; Krzyszkowska 1991, 119–20, pl 5.

19. Mylonas 1951, 143, fig 7.

20. Bittel 1976.

21. Mountjoy 1998.

22. Master 2005; Yasur-Landau 2010a.

23. This apt term originated with Artzy 1997.

24. Kirk 1965, 55–56.

25. Catling 1995; 1996, 645–49.

26. Crielaard 2016b, 45–51.

27. Catling 1995, 124–25. The term "warrior burial" is well-summarized by Deger-Jalkotzy 2006, 152 as "funerary monuments containing burials that are distinguished from other interments by a pronounced military character and symbolism of their burial gifts."

28. Catling 1995, 128; Nowicki 2000, 223–41.

29. Popham, Touloupa and Sackett 1982; Crielaard 2016b, 56–58.
30. Whitley 1991, 350; Crielaard 2016b, 56.
31. Crielaard 2016b, 56–57.
32. *Iliad* XI, 47, IX, 330, XI, 132, XVIII, 290, XXIII, 618, XXIV, 381; *Odyssey* i, 312, ii, 75, iv, 600, 613, x, 40, xiv, 326, xv, 91, 159, xvii, 527, xix, 272, 295, xxi, 9; Deger-Jalkotzy 2002, 59–62; Crielaard 2016b, 58–59.
33. Deger-Jalkotzy 2006, 141–42; Stampolidis and Kotsonas 2006, 340; Crielaard 2016b, 48.
34. McFadden and Sjöqvist 1954; Crielaard 2016b, 70.
35. Crielaard 2016a.
36. Crielaard 2016b, 77–78.
37. Catling 1995, 125.
38. Coldstream 1996, 142; Harrell 2014 99–101.
39. Palaima 1995b, 128; Crielaard 2006; 2011.
40. Dickinson 2006, x.
41. Tandy 1997, 59.
42. Dickinson 2006, 1; also Whitley 1991, 5, who declared that "the Dark Age of Greece is our conception."
43. Moschos 2009, 389.
44. Kramer-Hajos 2016, 4.
45. Qviller 1981, 109–17.
46. Catling 1995; Halverson 1986.
47. Muhly 2003, 31; Dickinson 2006, 242–50; cf. Deger-Jalkotzy 1994, 20.
48. Deger-Jalkotzy 2006, 174–76; 2010, 403; cf. Crielaard 2011; for a brief summary of the debate over the *qa-si-re-u* in Mycenaean society, see Tandy 1997, 91–92 (with references).
49. Whitley 1991; Maran 2006, 143; Arena 2015, 34–35; Middleton 2010, 94–97.
50. AhT 3 §12; Yasur-Landau 2010a, 95.
51. Iacovou 2006; 2012, 214–215.
52. Baurain 1989, 471.
53. Karageorghis 1992, 83.
54. Iacovou 2005, 127; 2012, 209–10.
55. Yasur-Landau 2010a, 150; Iacovou 2012.

# CHAPTER EIGHT

1. Doumas 1992, 68; Wachsmann 1998, 19–22.
2. Shaw 1980, 177–178; 2001; Cosmopoulos 2010, 3–4.
3. Wedde 1999, 465; 2005, 31–32.
4. Wedde 1999, 465; 2006, 256.
5. Roberts 1991, pls, XVIIa, XIX–XX; Wachsmann 1998, 251; Mark 2000, 130, fig 5.8. On brailed sails in *Odyssey*, see, for example, Monro 1886, 547; Seymour 1914, 314, n1; Kamarinou 2002, 451.
6. Artzy 1997; 2003, 245; Höckmann 2001, 228; Georgiou 2012, 527.

7. Wedde 1999, 465.

8. Wachsmann 1998, 248.

9. Marinatos 1974, pl 112.

10. Wachsmann 1998, 17–28.

11. Gittlen 2007.

12. Shaw 1980, 177–178.

13. Sølver 1936, 460; Casson 1971, 273–74; Wachsmann 1998, 330; Wedde 2000 ,80–85.

14. Georgiou 1991, 67–68.

15. Museo Egizio di Torino 1987, 195, fig 270; for a color illustration, see Vinson 1994, cover.

16. Watrous 1985; Tomlinson, Rutter and Hoffman 2010, 194; Day et al. 2011.

17. Vercoutter 1954, 17, 24–25, 173–74; Cline 1994, 131, 254, 290; Pulak 1988, 36–37; Watrous 1992, 176–77; Snape 2000, 18; White 2002, 24.

18. Pulak 1998; Watrous 1992, 175–76; Bass 1998, 184, 190.

19. Roberts 1991, 57–59.

20. Roberts 1991, 59.

21. McGrail 1996; Davis 2002.

22. Mark 2000, 148–49.

23. Lambrou-Phillipson 1991; Wachsmann 1998, 298–300.

24. Wachsmann 1981; 1982; 1998, 164–72; 2000 116–22.

25. Wachsmann 1998, 139; Dakoronia 2006, 29.

26. Dakoronia 2006, 27.

27. Wachsmann 1998, 157.

28. Wachsmann 1998, 175.

29. Wachsmann 1998, 253.

30. Wachsmann 1987, pls. V–VI.

31. Davies and Faulkner 1947 43; Wachsmann 1981, 214; 1998, 45–47, 51, 56, 253.

32. Raban 1989, 170; Wachsmann 1998, 252; 2013, 262, n135.

33. This object has traditionally been dated to the end of the 18th dynasty (late 14th or early 13th century BCE), with Egyptologist Alan Schulman assigning it specifically to the reign of Horemheb (1319–1292 BCE), with whose rule the 18th dynasty culminated; Capart 1931, 62; Schulman 1968, 33. Millet 1987; Vinson 1993, 136, n12, 138–39.

34. The Canaanite amphorae shown in the relief are consistent with Family 11 Form 22 of this ceramic type; Killebrew 2007, 167–73, figs 1.3, 4.6; compare also Amiran 1970, pls, 43:5, 9; Ben-Arieh and Edelstein 1977, pl XII:2; Pulak 1987, 39, 41.

35. Capart 1931, 62; Millet 1987; Vinson 1993, 138–39; 1994, 42.

36. Wachsmann 1982, 302 notes that a slight downward curve can be seen in the upper yards of boom-footed riverine vessels in the Theban tombs of Rekhmire (TT 100), Menna (TT 69), Amenemhet (TT 82), and Sennefer (TT 96B); Landström 1970, figs 316, 319, 399.

37. Wachsmann 1981, 214, fig 28; Roberts 1991, 55.

38. Artzy 1997; 1998; 2013; Georgiou 1991, 69; 2012, 527.

39. Dothan and Zukerman 2004, 41.

40. Artzy 2013.
41. Schaeffer 1952, 102; Wachsmann 1981, 206–9.
42. Stager and Mountjoy 2007.
43. See also Artzy 1988; Raban and Stieglitz 1991.
44. Liverani 1977, 212–16; Heltzer 1979, 9–16; Loretz 1995.
45. Pulak 1998, 219; Wachsmann 1998, 320; Hafford 2001, 199–202.
46. Heltzer 1979, 12.
47. Yoyotte 1949; Kitchen 1999.
48. Yoyotte 1949, 67; Kitchen 1999, 174.
49. Spiegelberg 1896, 82.5; Sethe 1909, 998.1; Jones 1988, 130.5, 131.13.
50. Ormerod 1924, 31; Wachsmann 1998, 320.
51. Wachsmann 1998, 47, 51, 349, n75.
52. *MH I* 1930, pl 46, col 20.
53. Artzy 1988, 184–85.
54. Yoyotte 1949, 67; Artzy 1988, 184.
55. *MH I* 1930, pl 46, col 24.
56. Wilson 1974b, 262.
57. Shuckburgh 1962.
58. Landström 1970, 98–115; Casson 1971, 37; Jones 1995, 59.
59. Baruffi 1998, 97.
60. Basch 1978; Baruffi 1998, 98; Wachsmann 1998, 47.
61. Barako 2001, 134.
62. Korres 1989, 200–202.
63. Wachsmann 1981. Greek archaeologist Vassilis Petrakis has vocally opposed this widely accepted interpretation, instead arguing that the horizontal ladder was simply artistic convention, perhaps meant to represent curved space on a
two-dimensional image. His primary evidence for this is the detailed appearance of
rowers on a sherd from Kos, which, he suggests, precludes other oared vessels in
the LH IIIC tradition from being shown without them. Artistic convention though it
undoubtedly was, Wachsmann has convincingly demonstrated that the evidence for
this motif suggests that it was, in fact, one of the key elements in depictions of the
oared galley, much as the boom was frequently used in artistic shorthand to represent squaresailed vessels; Petrakis 2004, 4; 2011 213; Wachsmann 1998, 130–33.
64. Wachsmann 1998, 138, figs 7.7, 7.27, 7.30–31. Also worth noting on the Gazi
vessel are parallel lines above the hull, the lower of which may represent a boom.
However, if the wavy lines beneath are intended to represent a sail, then the parallel
lines atop the mast are likely either a thick representation of a yard, or a combination
of yard and upper border of the image. The latter would fit with the motif, in which
borders appear to be present on the other three sides. If this is the case, then this vessel may carry a loose-footed, brailed rig that is "reefed," or furled to better allow for
oared propulsion; cf. Wachsmann 1998, 139.
65. Wachsmann 1998, 132.
66. Frazer 1921.
67. Oldfather 1935.
68. Chadwick 1973, 186–87, 431; 1987, 77.
69. Killen 1983.

70. The main translation is from Hoftijzer and Van Soldt 1998, 336, with parenthetical alternatives from Astour 1965, 256 and Lambrou-Phillipson 1993, 164.

71. Singer 2011, 116.

72. Hoftijzer and Van Soldt 1998, 343.

73. Hoftijzer and Van Soldt 1998, 343.

74. Hoftijzer and Van Soldt 1998, 343–44.

75. Astour 1965, 255.

76. The connection between AhT 27A–B and RS 20.238 was initially suggested by Singer 2006, 250.

77. Singer 2000, 22.

78. Pulak 1998, 207–208; Yasur-Landau 2010, 44.

79. Bryce 2016, 70–73.

80. Hoftijzer and Van Soldt 1998, 341.

81. Wedde 2005; Tartaron 2013, 132–33.

82. Wedde 2005, 32.

83. Artzy 2003, 445.

84. Sauvage 2012, 290.

85. E.g., Monroe 2009, 111–15, 160–63; Singer 2011, 65–66, 74, 81, 115.

86. Tartaron 2013, 69–70.

87. Wachsmann 1998, 133; 2013, 33; Wedde 1999, 471, pl XCII:E7–8; 2005, 36.

88. Wedde 2006.

89. Wachsmann 2013, 80–83.

90. Wachsmann 2013.

91. Petrie 1933, 74, fig 85; Wachsmann 2013, xviii, 20–21, 28, 202.

92. Compare to the stemposts on the ships in Figures 23 and 47; also see Wachsmann (2013, 78–80) for further discussion.

93. Prior 2013, 241; Wachsmann 2013, 28.

94. Siddall 2013, table 1.

95. Davis 2013, 219; Siddall 2013, 243.

96. Davis 2013, 219.

97. *Iliad* I, 141, 300, 329, 433, 485; II 1, 70, 358, 524, 534, 545, 556, 568, 630, 644, 652, 710, 737, 747, 759; V, 550, 700; VIII, 222, 528; IX, 235, 654; X, 74; XI, 5, 824, 828; XII, 126; XIII, 267; XV, 387, 423; XVI, 304; XVII, 383, 639; XIX, 331; XXIV, 780; *Odyssey* ii, 430; iii, 61, 360, 365, 423; iv, 646, 731, 781; vi, 268; viii, 34, 51, 52, 445; ix, 322; x, 95, 169, 244, 272, 332, 502, 571; xi, 3, 58; xii, 186, 264, 276, 418; xiii, 425; xiv, 308; xv, 218, 258, 269, 416, 503; xvi, 325, 348, 359; xvii, 249; xviii, 84; xxi, 39, 307; xxiii, 320; xxiv, 152.

98. *Iliad* XV, 693; XXIII, 852, 878; *Odyssey* iii, 299; ix, 482, 539; x, 127; xi, 6; xii, 100, 148, 354; xiv, 311; xxii, 465.

99. Davis 2013, 220.

100. For examples, see http://logeion.uchicago.edu/index.html#κυάνεος, http://logeion.uchicago.edu/index.html#κύανος.

101. Davis 2013, 218, 221.

102. Wachsmann 2013, 28; Davis 2013.

103. Dickinson 2006, 48.

104. Kirk 1949, 125–27; Wedde 1999, 469; Wachsmann 2013, 70.

105. Wedde 1999, 467; 2000, figs 15–17.

106. Wachsmann 2013, 82–83, fig 2.12.

107. Lattimore 1965.

108. Wilson 1974b, 263.

109. Nelson 1943, 46; Wachsmann 1981, 188; Dothan 1982, 7.

110. See especially Nelson 1943, fig 5.


# CHAPTER NINE

1. West 1988, 151.

2. *Iliad* IX, 524–528; Nagy 2013, especially 49–59, 256–64.

3. Nagy 2013, 56.

4. Meier-Brügger 2006, 418.

5. Nagy 2010, 313.

6. Vermeule 1964 x; 1987; S. Morris 1989; Blakolmer 2007; Vlachopoulos 2007.

7. S. Morris 1989, 515; Cline and Yasur-Landau 2007, 164.

8. Singer 2013a, 25.

9. Gardiner 1940, pl 7; 1941a, 41; Katary 1989, 186.

10. Breasted 1906, 2–3; Spalinger 2005, 256.

11. Wilson 1974b, 260.

12. Wilson 1974b, 262.

13. Gardiner 1941, 40; Faulkner 1953, 44–45; see now also Wachsmann 2013, 225–38, who provides a helpful distillation of Sherden and *Tjuk*-people mentioned in the Wilbour Papyrus.

14. Gardiner 1948b; *§§179.67.18*, 188.70.51.

15. Gardiner 1948b; Katary 1989, 49.

16. Also *§§59.27.19* and *150.59.8*; Gardiner 1948b, 28, 62.

17. Gardiner 1948b, 62.

18. Gardiner 1948b, 62.

19. Faulkner 1953, 44–45.

20. Menu 1970, 127.

21. Gardiner 1948b, 18.

22. Gardiner 1948b, 46.

23. Gardiner 1948b, 51.

24. Gardiner 1948b, 88.

25. Hasel 1996, 187, 251, 362; Lorton 1974, 56, 61–62.

26. Wachsmann 2013, 206.

27. Gardiner 1941b; Cruz-Uribe 1988, 220–23; Eyre 1992.

28. Ritner 2009, 346.

29. Petrie 1905, 22; Gardiner 1948a 80; Cifola 1994, 8; Sagrillo 2009, 347, n46.

30. Roberts 2009, 63.

31. As Franci 2013, 503 notes, adoption of Egyptian customs by foreigners is characteristic of the New Kingdom.

# Bibliography

Adams, M. J. and Cohen, M. E. 2013. "The Sea Peoples in Primary Sources." In Killebrew, A. E. and Lehmann, G., eds. *The Philistines and Other Sea Peoples in Text and Archaeology*. Archaeology and Biblical Studies 15. Atlanta. 645–664.

Adriml–Sismani, V. 2006. "The Palace at Iolkos and Its End." In Deger-Jalkotzy, S. and Lemos, I. S., eds. *Ancient Greece: From the Mycenaean Palaces to the Age of Homer*. Edinburgh Leventis Studies 3. Edinburgh. 465–481.

Aja, A. 2009. *Philistine Domestic Architecture in the Iron Age I*. Doctoral dissertation, Harvard University.

Albright, W. F. 1932a. *The Excavation at Tell Beit Mirsim in Palestine I: The Pottery of the First Three Campaigns (1930–1931)*. Annual of the American Schools of Oriental Research 12. New Haven.

———. 1932b. "An Anthropoid Clay Coffin from Sahab in Transjordan." *American Journal of Archaeology* 36: 295–306.

Alt, A. 1953. *Kleine Schriften zur Geschichte des Volkes Israel I*. Munich.

Amirell, S. E. and Müller, L. 2014. "Introduction: Persistent Piracy in World History." In Amirell, S. E. and Müller, L. (eds). *Persistent Piracy: Historical Perspectives on Maritime Violence and State Formation*. London. 1–23.

Anderson, J. L. 1995. "Piracy and World History: An Economic Perspective on Maritime Predation." *Journal of World History* 6: 175–199.

Arena, E. 2015. "Mycenaean Peripheries during the Palatial Age: The Case of Achaia." *Hesperia* 84: 1–46.

Artzy, M. 1988. "War/Fighting Boats in the Second Millennium BC in the Eastern Mediterranean." *Reports of the Department of Antiquities, Cyprus, 1988*: 181–186.

———. 1997. "Nomads of the Sea." In Swiny, S., Hohlfelder, R. L. and Swiny, H. W., eds. *Res Maritimae: Cyprus and the Eastern Mediterranean from Prehistory to Late Antiquity*. Atlanta. 1–16.

———. 1998. "Routes, Trade, Boats, and Nomads of the Sea." In Gitin, S., Mazar, A., and Stern, E., eds. *Mediterranean Peoples in Transition, Thirteenth to Early Tenth Centuries BCE*. Jerusalem. 439–448.

———. 2003. "Mariners and their Boats at the End of the Late Bronze Age and the Beginning of the Iron Age in the Eastern Mediterranean." *Tel Aviv* 30: 232–246.

———. 2013. "On the Other Sea Peoples." In Killebrew, A. E. and Lehmann, G., eds. *The Philistines and Other Sea Peoples in Text and Archaeology.* Archaeology and Biblical Studies 15. Atlanta. 329–344.

Astour, M. C. 1965. "New Evidence on the Last Days of Ugarit." *American Journal of Archaeology* 69: 253–258.

Aykurt, A. and H. Erkanal. 2017. "A Late Bronze Ship from Liman Tepe with Reference to the Late Bronze Age Ships from İzmir/Bademgediği Tepesi and Kos/Seraglio." *Oxford Journal of Archaeology* 36: 61–70.

Bachhuber, C. 2006. "Aegean Interest on the Uluburun Ship." *American Journal of Archaeology* 110: 345–363.

Bachhuber, C. and Roberts, R. G., eds. 2009. *Forces of Transformation: The End of the Bronze Age in the Mediterranean.* BANEA Themes from the Ancient Near East 1. Oxford.

Barako, T. 2001. *The Seaborne Migration of the Philistines.* Doctoral dissertation, Harvard University.

Barth, F. 1969. *Ethnic Groups and Boundaries: The Social Organization of Culture Difference.* London.

Baruffi, J. T. 1998. *Naval Warfare Operations in the Bronze Age Eastern Mediterranean.* Doctoral dissertation, University of Chicago.

Basch, L. 1978. "Le Navire *MNŠ* et Autres Notes de Voyage en Egypte." *The Mariner's Mirror* 64: 99–123.

———. 2009. "Were the Hittites Able to Build a Replica of an Egyptian Ship According to their own Drawings?" In Nowacki, H. and Lefévre, W., eds. Cre*ating Shapes in Civil and Naval Architecture: A Cross-Disciplinary Comparison.* History of Science and Medicine Library 11. Leiden. 65–72.

Basedow, M. 2007. "Troy Without Homer: The Bronze Age-Iron Age Transition in the Troad." In. Morris, S. P. and Laffineur, R., eds. *EPOS: Reconsidering Greek Epic and Aegean Bronze Age Archaeology.* Aegaeum 28. Liège. 49–58.

Bass, G. F. 1990. "A Bronze-Age Writing-Diptych from the Sea off Lycia." *Kadmos* 29: 169.

———. 1997. "Beneath the Wine-Dark Sea: Nautical Archaeology and the Phoenicians of the *Odyssey.*" In Coleman, J. E. and Walz, C. A., eds. *Greeks and Barbarians: Essays on the Interactions of Greeks and Non-Greeks in Antiquity and the Consequences for Eurocentrism.* Bethesda. 71–101.

———. 1998. "Sailing Between the Aegean and the Orient in the Second Millennium B.C." In Cline, E. H. and Harris-Cline, D., eds. *The Aegean and the Orient in the Second Millennium.* Aegaeum 18. Liège. 183–191.

———. 2010. "Cape Gelidonya Shipwreck." In Cline, E. H., ed. *The Oxford Handbook of the Bronze Age Aegean (ca. 3000–1000 BC).* Oxford. 797–803.

Baumbach, L. 1983. "An Examination of the Evidence for a State of Emergency at Pylos c. 1200 B.C. from the Linear B Tablets." In Heubeck, A. and Neumann, G., eds. *Res Mycenaeae: Akten des VII. Internationalen Mykenologischen Colloquiums.* Göttingen. 28–40.

Baurain, C. 1989. "Passé Légendaire et Archéologie Historique: L'Hellénisation de Chypre." *Annales Économies Sociétés Civilisations* 2: 463–477.

Beal, R. H. 1992. *The Organisation of the Hittite Military.* Texte der Hethiter 20. Heidelberg.

Beckman, G. M. 1992. "Hittite Administration in Syria in the Light of the Texts from Ḫattuša, Ugarit and Emar." In Chavalas, M. W. and Hayes, J. L., eds. *New Horizons in the Study of Ancient Syria.* Bibliotheca Mesopotamica 25. Malibu. 41–49.

———. 1994a. "Akkadian documents from Ugarit." In Wallace, P. W. and Orphanides, A. G., eds. *Sources for the History of Cyprus II: Near Eastern and Aegean Texts from the Third to the First Millennia B.C.* Nicosia. 26–28.

———. 1994b. "Hittite Documents from Ḫattuša." In Wallace, P. W. and Orphanides, A. G., eds. *Sources for the History of Cyprus II: Near Eastern and Aegean Texts from the Third to the First Millennia B.C.* Nicosia. 31–35.

———. 1996. *Hittite Diplomatic Texts.* Writings from the Ancient World 7. Atlanta.

Beckman, G. M., Bryce, T. R. and Cline, E. H. 2011. *The Ahhiyawa Texts.* Writings from the Ancient World 28. Atlanta.

Ben-Dor Evian, S. 2017. "Ramesses III and the 'Sea Peoples': Towards a New Paradigm." *Oxford Journal of Archaeology* 36(3): 267–285.

Ben-Shlomo, D. 2010. *Philistine Iconography: A Wealth of Style and Symbolism.* Orbis Biblicus et Orientalis 241. Göttingen.

Ben-Shlomo, D., Nodarou, E. and Rutter, J. B. 2011. "Transport Stirrup Jars from the Southern Levant: New Light on Commodity Exchange in the Eastern Mediterranean." *American Journal of Archaeology* 115: 329–353.

Benzi, M. 2013. "The Southeast Aegean in the Age of the Sea Peoples." In Killebrew, A. E. and Lehmann, G., eds. *The Philistines and Other Sea Peoples in Text and Archaeology.* Archaeology and Biblical Studies 15. Atlanta. 509–542.

Betancourt, P. P. 1998. "The Chronology of the Aegean Late Bronze Age: Unanswered Questions." In Balmuth, M. S. and Tykot, R. H., eds. *Sardinian and Aegean Chronology: Towards the Resolution of Relative and Absolute Dating in the Mediterranean.* Studies in Sardinian Archaeology 5. Oxford. 291–296.

Bietak, M. 2013. "Antagonisms in Historical and Radiocarbon Chronology." In Shortland, A. J. and Bronk Ramsey, C., eds. *Radiocarbon and the Chronologies of Ancient Egypt.* Oxford. 76–109.

———. 2015. "War Bates Island bei Marsa Matruth ein Piratennest? Ein Beitrag zur frühen Geschichte der Seevölker." In Nawracala, S. and Nawracala, R., eds. ΠΟΛΥΜΑΘΕΙΑ: Festschrift *für Hartmut Matthäus Anläßlich seines 65. Geburtstages.* Maastricht. 29–42.

Billigmeier, J.-C. and Turner, J. A. 1981. "The Socio-Economic Roles of Women in Mycenaean Greece: A Brief Survey from Evidence of the Linear B Tablets." *Women's Studies* 8: 3–20.

Birney, K. J. 2007. *Sea Peoples or Syrian peddlers? The Late Bronze Age-Iron I Aegean Presence in Syria and Cilicia.* Doctoral dissertation, Harvard University.

———. 2008. "Tracking the Cooking Pot à la Stéatite: Signs of Cyprus in Iron Age Syria." *American Journal of Archaeology* 112: 565–580.

Bittel, K. 1976. "Tonschale mit Ritzzeichnung von Boğazköy." *Revue Archéologique* 1: 9–14.

Blakolmer, F. 2007. "The Silver Battle Krater from Shaft Grave IV at Mycenae: Evidence of Fighting 'Heroes' on Minoan Palace walls at Knossos?" In Morris, S. P. and Laffineur, R., eds. *EPOS: Reconsidering Greek Epic and Aegean Bronze Age Archaeology.* Aegaeum 28. Liège. 213–224.

———. 2012. "The Missing 'Barbarians': Some Thoughts on Ethnicity and Identity in Aegean Bronze Age Iconography." *Talanta* 44: 53–77.

Boyes, P. 2012. *Social Change in 'Phoenicia' in the Late Bronze/Early Iron Age Transition.* Doctoral dissertation, University of Cambridge.

Braudel, F. 1972. *The Mediterranean and the Mediterranean World in the Age of Philip II.* New York.

Breasted, J. H. 1906. "Oriental Exploration Fund of the University of Chicago, First Preliminary Report of the Egyptian Expedition." *The American Journal of Semitic Languages and Literatures* 23: 1–64.

———. 1906–7. *Ancient Records of Egypt*, vol. 2. Chicago.

Brug, J. F. 1985. *A Literary and Archaeological Study of the Philistines.* BAR International Series 265. Oxford.

Bryce, T. R. 1989. "The Nature of Mycenaean Involvement in Western Anatolia." *Historia: Zeitschrift für Alte Geschichte* 38: 1–21.

———. 1992. "Lukka Revisited." *Journal of Near Eastern Studies* 51: 121–130.

———. 1998. *The Kingdom of the Hittites.* Oxford.

———. 2002. *Life and Society in the Hittite World.* Oxford.

———. 2006. *The Trojans and Their Neighbours.* Peoples of the Ancient World. London.

———. 2010. "The Hittite Deal with the *Ḫiyawa*-Men." In Cohen, Y., Gilan, A. and Miller, J. R., eds. *Pax Hethitica: Studies on the Hittites and their Neighbours in Honour of Itamar Singer.* Weisbaden. 47–53.

———. 2016. "The Land of Hiyawa (Que) Revisited." *Anatolian Studies* 66, 67–79.

Buffaloe, D. L. 2006. *Defining Asymmetric Warfare.* Land Warfare Papers 58. Arlington.

Caminos, R. A. 1954. *Late Egyptian Miscellanies.* Brown Egyptological Studies 1. London.

Cammarosano, M. 2010. "Tanuḫepa: A Hittite Queen in Troubled Times." *Mesopotamia* 45: 47–64.

Capart, J. 1931. *Documents pour Servir à l'étude de l'art* Égyptien *II*. Paris.

Casson, L. 1971. *Ships and Seamanship in the Ancient World.* Princeton.

Catling, H. W. 1995. "Heroes Returned? Subminoan Burials from Crete." In Carter, J. B. and Morris, S. P., eds. *The Ages of Homer: A Tribute to Emily Townsend Vermeule.* Austin. 123–130.

———. 1996. "The Subminoan Phase in the North Cemetery." In Coldstream, J. N. and Catling, H. W., eds. *Knossos North Cemetery: Early Greek Tombs II: Discussion.* London. 639–649.

Caubet, A. 1998. "The International Style: A Point of View from the Levant and Syria." In Cline, E. H. and Harris-Cline, D., eds. *The Aegean and the Orient in the Second Millennium.* Aegaeum 18. Liège. 105–114.

Chadwick, J. 1973. *Documents in Mycenaean Greek.* London.

———. 1987. "The Muster of the Pylian Fleet." In Ilievsky, P. H. and Crepajac, L., eds. *Tractata Mycenaea: Proceedings of the Eighth International Colloquium on Mycenaean Studies, Ohrid, September 15–20, 1985.* Skopje. 75–84.

———. 1988. "The Women of Pylos." In Palaima, T. G. and Olivier, J.-P., eds. *Texts, Tablets and Scribes: Studies in Mycenaean Epigraphy offered to Emmett L. Bennett, Jr.* Salamanca. 43–95.

Cherry, J. F. and Davis, J. L. 1982. "The Cyclades and the Greek Mainland in LC I: The Evidence of the Pottery." *American Journal of Archaeology* 86: 333–341.

Cifola, B. 1994. "The Role of the Sea Peoples at the End of the Late Bronze Age: A Reassessment of the Textual and Archaeological Evidence." *Oriens Antiqui Miscellanea* 1: 1–57.

Cline, E. H. 1994. *Sailing the Wine Dark Sea: International Trade and the Late Bronze Age Aegean.* BAR International Series 591. Oxford.

———. 1998. "Amenhotep III, the Aegean, and Anatolia." In O'Connor, D. and Cline, E. H., eds. *Amenhotep III: Perspectives on His Reign.* Ann Arbor. 236–250.

———. 2014. *1177 B.C.: The Year Civilization Collapsed.* Princeton.

Cline, E. H. and Stannish, S. M. 2011. "Sailing the Great Green Sea? Amenhotep III's 'Aegean List' from Kom el-Hetan, Once More." *Journal of Ancient Egyptian Interconnections* 3: 6–16.

Cline, E. H. and Yasur-Landau, A. 2007. "Poetry in Motion: Canaanite Rulership and Aegean Narrative Art at Tel Kabri." In. Morris, S. P. and Laffineur, R., eds. *EPOS: Reconsidering Greek Epic and Aegean Bronze Age Archaeology.* Aegaeum 28. Liège. 157–166.

Cline, E. H., Yasur-Landau, A., and Koh, A. 2017. "The Absolute Chronology of the Middle Bronze Age Palace at Tel Kabri: Implications for Aegean-Style Wall Paintings in the Eastern Mediterranean." *Journal of Ancient Egyptian Interconnections* 13: 43–47.

Coldstream, J. N. 1996. "Knossos and Lefkandi: The Attic Connections." In Evely, D., Lemos, I. S. and Sherratt, E. S., eds. *Minotaur and Centaur: Studies in the Archaeology of Crete and Euboea Presented to Mervyn Popham.* BAR International Series 638. Oxford. 133–145.

Cosmopoulos, M. B. 2010. *Iklaina Archaeological Project: 2010 Internet Report.* http://iklaina.files.wordpress.com/2011/11/2010report.pdf.

Crielaard, J. P. 2006. "*Basileis* at Sea: Elites and External Contacts in the Euboean Gulf Region from the End of the Bronze Age to the Beginning of the Iron Age." In Deger-Jalkotzy, S. and Lemos, I. S., eds. *Ancient Greece: From the Mycenaean Palaces to the Age of Homer.* Edinburgh Leventis Studies 3. Edinburgh. 271–297.

———. 2011. "The '*Wanax* to *Basileus* Model' Reconsidered: Authority and Ideology after the Collapse of the Mycenaean Palaces." In Mazarakis Ainian, A., ed. *The 'Dark Ages' Revisited: Acts of an International Symposium in Memory of William D. E. Coulson.* Volos. 83–111.

———. 2016a. "Hybrid Go-Betweens: The Role of Individuals with Multiple Identities in Cross-Cultural Contacts in the Late Bronze Age and Iron Age Mediterranean." Paper presented at the international conference *The Aegean and the Levant at the Turn of the Bronze and Iron Ages*, Warsaw.

———. 2016b. "Living Heroes: Metal Urn Cremations in Early Iron Age Greece, Cyprus and Italy. In Gallo, F., ed. *Omero: Quaestiones Disputata*. Ambrosiana Graecolatina 5. Milan. 43–78.

Crouwel, J. H. 1981. *Chariots and Other Means of Transport in Bronze Age Greece*. Studies in Ancient Civilization 3. Amsterdam.

———. 1991. *Mycenaean Pictorial Pottery*. Well Built Mycenae 21. Oxford.

Cruz-Uribe, E. 1988. "A New Look at the Adoption Papyrus." *Journal of Egyptian Archaeology* 74: 220–223.

Dakoronia, F. 1990. "War-Ships on Sherds of LH IIIC Kraters from Kynos." In Tzalas, H., ed. *TROPIS II: 2nd International Symposium on Ship Construction in Antiquity, Nauplia 1993*. Athens. 117–122.

———. 1999. "Representations of Sea-Battles on Mycenaean Sherds from Kynos." In Tzalas, H., ed. *TROPIS V: 5th International Symposium on Ship Construction in Antiquity, Nauplia 1993*. Athens. 119–128.

———. 2006. "Mycenaean Pictorial Style at Kynos, East Lokris." In Rystedt, E. and Wells, B., eds. *Pictorial Pursuits: Figurative Painting on Mycenaean and Geometric Pottery*. Stockholm. 23–29.

Dakoronia, F. and Mpougia, P. 1999. Τον καιρο των Μυκηναιων στη Φθιωτιδα. Lamia.

Davies, N. De G. and Faulkner, R. O. 1947. "A Syrian Trading Venture to Egypt." *Journal of Egyptian Archaeology* 33: 40–46.

Davis, D. 2002. "Maritime Space and Night-Time Sailing in the Ancient Eastern Mediterranean." In Tzalas, H., ed. *TROPIS VII: 7th International Symposium on Ship Construction in Antiquity, Pylos 1999*. Athens. 291–309.

———. 2013. "Ship Colors in the Homeric Poems." In S. Wachsmann, *The Gurob Ship-Cart Model and its Mediterranean Context*. College Station. 219–224.

Day, P. M., Quinn, P. S., Rutter, J. B. and Kilikoglou, V. 2011. "A World of Goods: Transport Stirrup Jars and Commodity Exchange at the Late Bronze Age Harbor of Kommos, Crete." *Hesperia* 80: 511–558.

de Rougé, E. 1877. *Inscriptions hiéroglyphices Copiées en Égypte Pendant la Mission Scientifique de M. le Vicomte Emmanuel de Rougé*. Paris.

de Souza, P. 1999. *Piracy in the Graeco-Roman World*. Cambridge.

———. 2002. "Greek Piracy." In Powell, A., ed. *The Greek World*. London. 179–198.

———. 2010. "Piracy." In Gagarin, M. and Fantham, E., eds. *The Oxford Encyclopedia of Ancient Greece and Rome* 5. Oxford. 290–291.

———. 2014. "'Piracy in Classical Antiquity: The Origins and Evolution of the Concept." In Amirell, S. and Muller, L., eds. *Persistent Piracy: Maritime Violence and State Formation in Global Historical Perspective*. London. 24–50.

Deger-Jalkotzy, S. 1994. "The Post-Palatial Period of Greece: An Aegean Prelude to the 11th Century B.C. in Cyprus." In Karageorghis, V., ed. *Cyprus in the 11th Century B.C*. Nicosia. 11–29.

———. 2002. "Innerägäische Beziehungen und Auswärtige Kontakte des Mykenischen Griechenland in Nachpalatialer Zeit." In Braun-Holzinger, E. A. and Matthäus, H., eds. *Die Nahöstlichen Kulturen und Griechenland an der Wende vom 2. zum 1. Jahrtausend v. Chr: Kontinuität und Wandel von Strukturen und Mechanismen Kultureller Interaktion*. Möhnesee. 47–74.

———. 2006. "Late Mycenaean Warrior Tombs." In Deger-Jalkotzy, S. and Lemos, I. S., eds. *Ancient Greece: From the Mycenaean Palaces to the Age of Homer*. Edinburgh Leventis Studies 3. Edinburgh. 151–180.

———. 2010. "Decline, Destruction, Aftermath." In Shelmerdine, C. W., ed. *The Cambridge Companion to the Aegean Bronze Age*. Cambridge. 387–415.

Dickinson, O. T. P. K. 1994. *The Aegean Bronze Age*. Cambridge.

———. 2006. *The Aegean from Bronze Age to Iron Age: Continuity and Change Between the Twelfth and Eighth Centuries B.C.* London.

Dinçol, B., Dinçol, A., Hawkins, J. D., Peker, H. and Öztan, A. 2015. "Two New Inscribed Storm-god Stelae from Arsuz (İskenderun): ARSUZ 1 and 2." *Anatolian Studies* 65: 59–77.

Dothan, M. 1986. "Šardina at Akko?" In Balmuth, M., ed. *Studies in Sardinian Archaeology II: Sardinia and the Mediterranean*. Ann Arbor. 105–115.

———. 1989. "Archaeological Evidence for the Movements of Early Sea Peoples in Canaan." In Gitin, S. and Dever, W. G., eds. *Recent Excavations in Israel: Studies in Iron Age Archaeology*. Annual of the American Schools of Oriental Research 49. Winona Lake. 59–70.

Dothan, T. 1957. "Archaeological Reflections on the Philistine Problem." *Antiquity and Survival* 2: 151–164.

———. 1958. "Philistine Civilization in the Light of Archaeological Finds in Palestine and Egypt." *Eretz-Israel* 5: 86.*

———. 1982. *Philistine Material Culture*. New Haven.

———. 1998. "Initial Philistine Settlement: From Migration to Coexistence." In Gitin, S., Mazar, A. and Stern, E., eds. *Mediterranean Peoples in Transition, Thirteenth to Early Tenth Centuries BCE*. Jerusalem. 148–161.

Dothan, T. and Zukerman, A. 2004. "A Preliminary Study of the Mycenaean IIIC:1 Pottery Assemblages from Tel Miqne-Ekron and Ashdod." *Bulletin of the American Schools of Oriental Research* 333: 1–54.

Doumas, C. 1992. *The Wall Paintings of Thera*. Athens.

Drews, R. 1993. *The End of the Bronze Age: Changes in Warfare and the Catastrophe ca. 1200 BC*. Princeton.

———. 1998. "Canaanites and Philistines." *Journal for the Study of the Old Testament* 81: 39–61.

Earle, J. W. 2008. *Trade and Culture in the Cycladic Islands during the Late Bronze Age*. Doctoral dissertation, New York University.

Edel, E. 1994. *Die Ägyptisch-Hethitische Korrespondenz aus Boghazköi*. Abhandlungen der Rheinisch-Westfälischen Akademie der Wissenschaften 77. Opladen.

Eder, B. and Jung, R. 2005. "On the Character of Social Relations Between Greece and Italy in the 12th/11th Cent. BC." In Laffineur, R. and Greco, E., eds. *Emporia: Aegeans in the Central and Eastern Mediterranean*. Aegaeum 25. Liège. 485–495.

Edgerton, W. F. and Wilson, J. A. 1936. *Historical Records of Ramesses III: Texts in Medinet Habu I–II*. Studies in Ancient Oriental Civilization 12. Chicago.

Emanuel, J. P. 2012. "Cretan Lie and Historical Truth: Examining Odysseus' Raid on Egypt in its Late Bronze Age Context." In Bers, V., Elmer, D., Frame, D. and

Muellner, L., eds. *Donum Natalicium Digitaler Confetium Gregorio Nagy Septua-genario a Discipulis Collegis Familiaribus Oblatum.* Washington, DC. 1–41.

———. 2013a. "Šrdn from the Sea: The Arrival, Integration, and Acculturation of a Sea People." *Journal of Ancient Egyptian Interconnections* 5: 14–27.

———. 2013b. Review of A. Zertal, "El-Ahwat: A Fortified Site from the Early Iron Age near Nahal 'Iron, Israel: Excavations 1993–2000." *Journal of Ancient Egyptian Interconnections* 5: 57–60.

———. 2014. "The Sea Peoples, Egypt, and the Aegean: Transference of Maritime Technology in the Late Bronze-Early Iron Transition (LH IIIB-C)." *Aegean Studies* 1: 21–56.

———. 2015a. "The Late Bronze-Early Iron Age Transition: Changes in Warriors and Warfare and the Earliest Recorded Naval Battles." In Lee, G., Whittaker, H. and Wrightson, G., eds. *Ancient Warfare: Introducing Current Research, Vol. 1.* Newcastle. 191–209.

———. 2015b. "King Taita and His 'Palistin': Philistine State or Neo-Hittite Kingdom?" *Antiguo Oriente* 13: 11–40.

———. 2016. "Maritime Worlds Collide: Agents of Transference and the Metastasis of Seaborne Threats at the End of the Bronze Age." *Palestine Exploration Quarterly* 148: 265–280.

Emlyn-Jones, C. 1986. "True and Lying Tales in the *Odyssey.*" *Greece & Rome* 33: 1–10.

Epigraphic Survey. 1930. *Medinet Habu I: Earlier Historical Records of Ramses III.* Oriental Institute Publications 8. Chicago. (= *MH* I)

———. 1932. *Medinet Habu II: Later Historical Records of Ramses III.* Oriental Institute Publications 9. Chicago. (= *MH* II)

———. 1970. *Medinet Habu VIII: The Eastern High Gate with Translations of Texts.* Oriental Institute Publications 94. Chicago. (= *MH* VIII)

Ergin, G. 2007. "Anatolian Women in the Linear B Texts: A General Review of the Evidence." In Alparslan, M., Doğan-Alparslan, M. and Peker, H., eds. *Belkis Dinçol ve Ali Dinçola Armağan: VITA: Festschrift in honor of Belkis Dinçol and Ali Dinçol.* Istanbul. 269–284.

Evans, A. J. 1900. "Mycenaean Cyprus as Illustrated in the British Museum Excavations." *Journal of the Royal Anthropological Institute* 30: 199–220.

Eyre, C. J. 1992. The Adoption Papyrus in Social Context. *Journal of Egyptian Archaeology* 78: 207–221.

Faulkner, R. O. 1953. "Egyptian Military Organization." *Journal of Egyptian Archaeology* 39: 32–47.

Feldman, M. H. 2002. "Luxurious Forms: Redefining a Mediterranean 'International Style,' 1400–1200 B.C.E." *The Art Bulletin* 84: 6–29.

———. 2006. *Diplomacy by Design: Luxury Arts and an 'International Style' in the Ancient Near East, 1400–1200 BCE.* Chicago.

———. 2014. "Beyond Iconography: Meaning-Making in Late Bronze Age Eastern Mediterranean Visual Culture." In Knapp, A. B. and van Dommelen, P., eds. *The Cambridge Prehistory of the Bronze and Iron Age Mediterranean.* Cambridge. 337–351.

Finkelberg, M. 1988. "From Ahhiyawa to Ἀχαιοι." *Glotta* 66: 127–134.

Fischer, P. M. 2017. "The 13th/12th Century BCE Destructions and Abandonment of Hala Sultan Tekke, Cyprus." In Fischer, P. M. and Bürge, T., eds. *'Sea Peoples' Up-to-Date: New Research on Transformation in the Eastern Mediterranean in the 13th–11th Centuries BCE*. Contributions to the Chronology of Eastern Mediterranean 35. Vienna: Austrian Academy of Sciences Press. 177–206.

Fischer, P. M. and Bürge, T., eds. 2017. *'Sea Peoples' Up-to-Date: New Research on Transformation in the Eastern Mediterranean in the 13th–11th Centuries BCE*. Contributions to the Chronology of Eastern Mediterranean 35. Vienna.

Fisher, C. S. 1923. "Bethshean: Excavations by the University Museum Expedition, 1921–1923." *Museum Journal* 14: 227–248.

Fitzgerald, R., trans. 1998. *Homer's 'The Iliad.'* Oxford World's Classics. Oxford.

Franci, M. 2013. "Being a Foreigner in Egypt, between Maintenance and Loss of Cultural Identity: The Archaeological Data." In Bombardieri, L., D'Agostino, A., Guarducci, G., Orsi, V. and Valentini, S., eds. *Identity and Connectivity Proceedings of the 16th Symposium on Mediterranean Archaeology, Florence, Italy, 1–3 March 2012*. BAR International Series 2581. Oxford. 501–507.

French, E. B. 1996. "Evidence for an Earthquake at Mycenae." In Stiros, S. and Jones, R. E., eds. *Archaeoseismology*. Fitch Laboratory Occasional Papers 7. Athens. 51–54.

———. 1998. "The Ups and Downs of Mycenae: 1250–1150 BCE." In Gitin, S., Mazar, A. and Stern, E., eds. *Mediterranean Peoples in Transition, Thirteenth to Early Tenth Centuries BCE*. Jerusalem. 1–5.

———. 2002. *Mycenae: Agamemnon's Capital: The Site and Its Setting*. Charleston.

Furtwängler, A. and Loeschcke, G. 1886. *Mykenische Vasen: Vorhellenische Thongefässe aus dem Gebiete des Mittelmeers*. Berlin.

Furumark, A. 1941. *The Mycenaean Pottery: Analysis and Classification*. Stockholm.

Gardiner, A. H. 1941a. "Adoption Extraordinary." *Journal of Egyptian Archaeology* 26: 23–29.

———. 1941b. "Ramesside Texts Relating to the Taxation and Transport of Corn." *Journal of Egyptian Archaeology* 27: 19–73.

———. 1948a. *The Wilbour Papyrus II, Commentary*. London.

———. 1948b. *The Wilbour Papyrus III, Translation*. London.

———. 1960. *The Kadesh Inscriptions of Ramesses II*. Oxford.

Gates, M.-H. 2013. "Early Iron Age Newcomers at Kinet Höyük, Eastern Cilicia." In Killebrew, A. E. and Lehmann, G., eds. *The Philistines and Other Sea Peoples in Text and Archaeology*. Archaeology and Biblical Studies 15. Atlanta. 485–508.

Georgiou, H. S. 1991. "Bronze Age Ships and Rigging." In Laffineur, R. and Basch, L., eds. *Thalassa: l'Egée Préhistorique et la Mer*. Aegaeum 7. Liège. 61–71.

———. 2012. "Bronze Age Sailing and Homeric Evidence." In Korres, G. S., Karadimas, N., and Flouda, G., eds. *Archaeology and Heinrich Schliemann: A Century After his Death*. Athens. 523–529.

Gettlen, B. M. 2007. "Sailing Up To Ekron: A Nautical Seal from Tel Miqne-Ekron." In White Crawford, S., Ben-Tor, A., Dessel, J. P., Dever, W. G., Mazar, A. and Aviram, J., eds. *Up to the Gates of Ekron: Essays on the Archaeology and History of the Eastern Mediterranean in Honor of Seymour Gitin*. Jerusalem. 25–28.

Gilan, A. 2013. "Pirates of the Mediterranean—A View from the Bronze Age." In Jaspert, N., and Kolditz, S., eds. *Seeraub im Mittelmeerraum: Piraterie, Korsarentum und Maritime Gewalt von der Antike bis zur Neuzeit.* Mittelmeerstudien 3. Padeborn. 49–66.

Gilboa, A. 2006–7. "Fragmenting the Sea Peoples, with an Emphasis on Cyprus, Syria and Egypt: A Tel Dor Perspective." In Harrison, T. P., ed. *Cyprus, the Sea Peoples and the Eastern Mediterranean: Regional Perspectives of Continuity and Change.* Scripta Mediterranea 27–28. Toronto. 209–244.

Gitin, S., Mazar, A. and Stern, E., eds. 1998. *Mediterranean Peoples in Transition, Thirteenth to Early Tenth Centuries BCE.* Jerusalem.

Gjerstad, E. 1948. *The Swedish Cyprus Expedition, Vol. IV Part 2: The Cypro-Geometric, Cypro-Archaic and Cypro-Classical Periods.* Stockholm.

Goedicke, H. 1975. *The Report of Wenamun.* Baltimore: Johns Hopkins University Press.

Gordon, C. H. 1992. "The Mediterranean Synthesis." In Ward, W. A. and Joukowsky, M. S., eds. *The Crisis Years: The 12th Century B.C. from Beyond the Danube to the Tigris.* Dubuque. 188–196.

Gosse, P. 1932. *The History of Piracy.* New York.

Güterbock, H. G. 1967. "The Hittite Conquest of Cyprus Reconsidered." *Journal of Near Eastern Studies* 26: 73–81.

———. 1983. "The Hittites and the Aegean World: Part 1. The Ahhiyawa Problem Reconsidered." *American Journal of Archaeology* 87: 133–138.

———. 1992. "Survival of the Hittite Dynasty." In Ward, W A. and Joukowsky, M. S., eds. *The Crisis Years: The 12th Century B.C. from Beyond the Danube to the Tigris.* Dubuque. 53–55.

Habachi, L. 1980. "The Military Posts of Ramesses II on the Coastal Road and the Western Part of the Delta." *Bulletin de l'Institut Français d'Archéologie Orientale* 80: 13–30.

Hafford, W. B. 2001. *Merchants in the Late Bronze Age Eastern Mediterranean, Tools, Texts, and Trade.* Doctoral dissertation, University of Pennsylvania.

Haggis, D. C. and Nowicki, K. 1993. "Khalasmeno and Katalimata: Two Early Iron Age Settlements in Monastiraki, East Crete." *Hesperia* 62: 303–337.

Hall, W. E. 1890. *A Treatise on International Law,* 3rd ed. New York.

Hallo, W. W. 1992. "From Bronze Age to Iron Age in Western Asia, Defining the Problem." In Ward, W. A. and Joukowsky, M. S., eds. *The Crisis Years: The 12th Century B.C. from Beyond the Danube to the Tigris.* Dubuque. 1–9.

Halstead, P. 1992. "The Mycenaean Palatial Economy: Making the Most of the Gaps in the Evidence." *Proceedings of the Cambridge Philological Society* 38: 57–86.

Halverson, J. 1986. "The Succession Issue in the *Odyssey.*" *Greece & Rome* 33: 119–128.

Hankey, V. 1967. "Mycenaean Pottery in the Middle East: Notes on Finds since 1951." *Annual of the British School at Athens* 62: 107–147.

———. 1993. "Pottery as Evidence for Trade: The Levant from the Mouth of the River Orontes to the Egyptian Border." In Zerner, C, ed. *Proceedings of the International Conference, Wace and Blegen: Pottery as Evidence for Trade in the Aegean Bronze Age, 1939–1989.* Amsterdam. 101–108.

Harrell, K. 2014. "Man/Woman, Warrior/Maiden: The Lefkandi Toumba Female Burial Reconsidered." In Galanakis, Y., Wilkinson, T. and Bennet, J., eds. AΘYPMATA: Critical Essays on the Archaeology of the Eastern Mediterranean in Honour of E. Susan Sherratt. Oxford. 99–104.

Harrison, A. B. and Spencer, N. 2007. "After the Palace: The Early 'History' of Messenia." In Davis, J. L., ed. *Sandy Pylos: An Archaeological History from Nestor to Navarino*. Princeton. 147–162.

Harrison, T. P., ed. 2006–7. *Cyprus, the Sea Peoples and the Eastern Mediterranean: Regional Perspectives of Continuity and Change*. Scripta Mediterranea 27–28. Toronto.

Harrison, T. P. 2009. "Neo-Hittites in the 'Land of Palistin': Renewed Investigations at Tell Ta'yinat on the Plain of Antioch." *Near Eastern Archaeology* 72: 174–189.

Hasel, M. G. 1996. *Domination and Resistance: Egyptian Military Activity in the Southern Levant During the Late Bronze/Early Iron Age Transition*. Doctoral dissertation, University of Arizona.

Hawkins, J. D. 1988. "KuzI–Tešub and the 'Great Kings' of Karkamiš." *Anatolian Studies* 38: 99–108.

———. 2000. *Corpus of Hieroglyphic Luwian Inscriptions I: Inscriptions of the Iron Age*. Berlin.

———. 2009. "Cilicia, the Amuq, and Aleppo: New Light in a Dark Age." *Near Eastern Archaeology* 72: 164–173.

Heltzer, M. 1979. "Some Questions Concerning the Sherdana in Ugarit." *Israel Oriental Studies* 9: 9–16.

Hencken, H. O. 1967. *Tarquinia, Villanovans, and Early Etruscans* II. Bulletin (American School of Prehistoric Research) 23. Cambridge.

Higganbotham, C. R. 1996. "Elite Emulation and Governance in Ramesside Canaan." *Tel Aviv* 23: 154–169.

———. 2000. *Egyptianization and Elite Emulation in Ramesside Palestine: Governance and Accommodation on the Imperial Periphery*. Culture and History of the Ancient Near East 2. Leiden.

Hirschfeld, N. 2009. "The Many Ways between Late Bronze Age Aegeans and Levants." *BAAL Hors-Série* 6: 285–294.

Hitchcock, L. A. and Maeir, A. M. 2014. "Yo-Ho, Yo-Ho, a *Seren*'s Life for Me!" *World Archaeology* 20: 1–17.

———. 2016. "A Pirate's Life for Me: The Maritime Culture of the Sea Peoples." *Palestine Exploration Quarterly* 148: 245–264.

———. 2017. "Fifteen Men on a Dead *Seren*'s Chest: Yo Ho Ho and a Krater of Wine." In Batmaz A., Bedianashvili G., Michalewicz A. and Robinson A., eds. *Context and Connection: Essays on the Archaeology of the Ancient Near East in Honour of Antonio Sagona*. Leuven. Orientalia Lovaniensia Analecta. 147–159.

Höckmann, O. 2001. "The Kynos Sea-Fighters: Exception or Rule?" In Tzalas, H., ed. *TROPIS VI: 6th International Symposium on Ship Construction in Antiquity, Lamia 1996*. Athens. 223–234.

Hoffner, H. A. 1992. "The Last Days of Khattusha." In Ward, W. A. and Joukowsky, M. S., eds. *The Crisis Years: The 12th Century B.C. from Beyond the Danube to the Tigris*. Dubuque. 46–52.

———. 2009. *Letters from the Hittite Kingdom.* Writings from the Ancient World 15. Atlanta.

Höflmayer, F. 2016. "Radiocarbon Dating and Egyptian Chronology—From the 'Curve of Knowns' to Bayesian Modeling." *Oxford Handbooks Online.* DOI: 10.1093/oxfordhb/9780199935413.013.64.

Hoftijzer, J. and Van Soldt, W. H. 1998. "Texts from Ugarit Pertaining to Seafaring." In Wachsmann, S. *Seagoing Ships and Seamanship in the Bronze Age Levant.* College Station. 333–344.

Holland, L. B. 1929. "Mycenaean Plumes." *American Journal of Archaeology* 33: 173–205.

Hood, S. 1995. "The Bronze Age Context of Homer." In Carter, J. B. and Morris, S. P., eds. *The Ages of Homer: A Tribute to Emily Townsend Vermeule.* Austin. 25–32.

Hooker, J. T. 1987. "Titles and Functions in the Pylian State." In Killen, J., Melena, J. and Oliver, J. P., eds. *Studies in Mycenaean and Classical Greek: Presented to John Chadwick.* Salamanca. 257–268.

———. 2014 [1976]. *Mycenaean Greece.* Routledge Revivals. London.

Horrocks, G. 1980. "The Antiquity of the Greek Epic Tradition: Some New Evidence." *Proceedings of the Cambridge Philological Society* 26: 1–11.

Houwink ten Cate, P. H. J. 1994. "UrhI-Tessub Revisited." *Bibliotheca Orientalis* 51: 233–259.

Hulin, L. and White, D. 2002. "A Final Summary of the Evidence." In White, D., ed. *Marsa Matruh II: The Objects: The University of Pennsylvania Museum of Archaeology and Anthropology's Excavations on Bates's Island, Marsa Matruh, Egypt 1985–1989.* Prehistory Monographs 2. Philadelphia. 169–186.

Iacovou, M. 2005. "Cyprus at the Dawn of the First Millennium BC: Cultural Homogenization Versus the Tyranny of Ethnic Identifications." In Clarke, J., ed. *Archaeological Perspectives on the Transmission and Transformation of Culture in the Eastern Mediterranean.* Levant Supplementary Series 2. Oxford. 125–134.

———. 2006. "From the Mycenaean *QA-SI-RE-U* to the Cypriote *PA-SI-LE-WO-SE*: The *Basileus* in the Kingdoms of Cyprus." In Deger-Jalkotzy, S. and Lemos, I. S., eds. *Ancient Greece: From the Mycenaean Palaces to the Age of Homer.* Edinburgh Leventis Studies 3. Edinburgh. 315–335.

———. 2012. "External and Internal Migrations During the 12th Century BC: Setting the Stage for an Economically Successful Early Iron Age in Cyprus." In Iacovou, M., ed. *Cyprus and the Aegean in the Early Iron Age: The Legacy of Nicolas Coldstream.* Nicosia. 207–228.

Iakovidis, S. 1986. "Destruction Horizons at Late Bronze Age Mycenae." In Mylonas, G. E., ed. *Philia epē eis Geōrgion E. Mylōnan: Dia ta 60 etē tou Anaskaphikou tou Ergou.* Athens. 233–260.

Jackson, A. H. 1973. "Privateers in the Ancient Greek World." In Foot, M. R. D., ed. *War and Society: Historical Essays in Honour and Memory of J. R. Western, 1928–1971.* New York. 241–253.

Jackson, C. M. and Nicholson, P. T. 2010. "The Provenance of Some Glass Ingots from the Uluburun Shipwreck." *Journal of Archaeological Sciences* 37: 9–24.

Jamison, S. W. 1994. "Draupadí on the Walls of Troy: '*Iliad*' 3 from an Indic Perspective." *Classical Antiquity* 13: 5–16.

Janeway, B. 2006–7. "The Nature and Extent of Aegean Contact at Tell Ta'yinat and Vicinity in the Early Iron Age: Evidence of the Sea Peoples?" In Harrison, T. P., ed. *Cyprus, the Sea Peoples and the Eastern Mediterranean Regional Perspectives of Continuity and Change.* Scripta Mediterranea 27–28. Toronto. 123–146.

———. 2011. "Mycenaean bowls at 12th/11th century BC Tell Tayinat (Amuq Valley)." In Karageorghis, V. and Kouka, O., eds. *On Cooking Pots, Drinking Cups, Loomweights and Ethnicity in Bronze Age Cyprus and Neighbouring Regions.* Nicosia. 167–186.

———. 2017. *Sea Peoples of the Northern Levant? Aegean-Style Pottery from Early Iron Age Tell Tayinat.* Studies in the Archaeology and History of the Levant 7. Winona Lake.

Janko, R. 1982. *Homer, Hesiod and the Hymns: Diachronic Development in Epic Diction.* Cambridge.

———. 1992. *The Iliad: A Commentary* IV. Cambridge.

Janssen, J. 2004. *Grain Transport in the Ramesside Period: Papyrus Baldwin (BM EA 10061) and Papyrus Amiens.* Hieratic Papyri in the British Museum 8. London.

Jasink, A. M. and Marino, M. 1998. "The Homeric Poems as Oral Dictated Texts." *Classical Quarterly* 48: 1–13.

———. 2005, Sept. *The West Anatolian Origins of the Que Kingdom Dynasty.* Paper presented at the 6th International Congress of Hittitology, Rome.

Jones, D. 1988. *A Glossary of Ancient Egyptian Nautical Titles and Terms.* London.

———. 1995. *Boats.* Austin.

Jones, H. L., ed. 1924. *The Geography of Strabo.* London.

Jung, R. 2009. "Pirates of the Aegean: Italy—East Aegean—Cyprus at the End of the Second Millennium BCE." In Karageorghis, V. and Kouka, O., eds. *Cyprus and the East Aegean: Intercultural Contacts from 3000 to 500 BC.* Nicosia. 72–93.

———. 2017. "The Sea Peoples After Three Millennia: Possibilities and Limitations of Historical Reconstruction." In Fischer, P. M. and Bürge, T., eds. *'Sea Peoples' Up-to-Date: New Research on Transformation in the Eastern Mediterranean in the 13th–11th Centuries BCE.* Contributions to the Chronology of Eastern Mediterranean 35. Vienna: Austrian Academy of Sciences Press. 23–42.

Jung, R. and Mehofer, M. 2013. "Mycenaean Greece and Bronze Age Italy: Cooperation, Trade or War?" *Archäologisches Korrespondenzblatt* 43: 175–192.

Kahn, D. 2011. "The Campaign of Ramesses III Against Philistia." *Journal of Ancient Egyptian Interconnections* 3: 1–11.

Kamarinou, D. 2002. "On the Form of Mycenaean Ships." In Tzalas, H., ed. *TROPIS VII: 7th International Symposium on Ship Construction in Antiquity, Pylos 1999.* Athens. 445–460.

Kanta, A. 1980. *The Late Minoan III Period in Crete: A Survey of Sites, Pottery, and their Distribution.* Göteborg.

Kantor, H. J. 1947. *The Aegean and the Orient in the Second Millennium B.C.* Bloomington.

Karageorghis, V. 1985. "Chronique des Fouilles et Découvertes Archéologiques à Chypre en 1984." *Bulletin de Correspondance Hellénique* 109: 897–967.

———. 1992. "The Crisis Years: Cyprus." In Ward, W. A. and Joukowsky, M. S., eds. *The Crisis Years: The 12th Century B.C. from Beyond the Danube to the Tigris.* Dubuque. 79–86.

———. 2001. "Patterns of Fortified Settlements in the Aegean and Cyprus c. 1200 B.C." In Karageorghis, V. and Morris, C. E., eds. *Defensive Settlements of the Aegean and the Eastern Mediterranean after c. 1200 B.C.* Nicosia. 1–12.

Karageorghis, V. and Kouka, O., eds. 2011. *On Cooking Pots, Drinking Cups, Loomweights and Ethnicity in Bronze Age Cyprus and Neighbouring Regions: An International Archaeological Symposium held in Nicosia, November 6th–7th 2010.* Nicosia.

Karraker, C. H. 1953. *Piracy Was a Business.* Rindge.

Katary, S. L. D. 1989. *Land Tenure in the Ramesside Period.* London.

Keegan, J. 1993. *A History of Warfare.* New York.

Kelder, J. 2004–5. "The Chariots of Ahhiyawa." *Dacia: Revue d'Archéologie et d' Histoire Ancienne* 48–49: 151–160.

———. 2010. "The Egyptian Interest in Mycenaean Greece." *Jaarbericht 'Ex Oritente Lux'* 42: 125–140.

Killebrew, A. E. 2007. "The Canaanite Storage Jar Revisited." In White Crawford, S., Ben-Tor, A., Dessel, J. P., Dever, W. G., Mazar, A. and Aviram, J., eds. *Up to the Gates of Ekron: Essays on the Archaeology and History of the Eastern Mediterranean in Honor of Seymour Gitin.* Jerusalem. 166–188.

Killebrew, A. E. and Lehmann, G., eds. 2013. *The Philistines and Other Sea Peoples in Text and Archaeology.* Archaeology and Biblical Studies 15. Atlanta.

Killen, J. T. 1983. "PY An 1." *Minos* 18: 71–80.

King, P. J. 2009. "Wenamun Docks at Dor." In Aviram, J., Ben-Tor, A., Eph'al, I., Gitin, S. and Reich, R., eds. *Eretz-Israel: Archaeological, Historical and Geographical Studies.* Eretz-Israel 29: Ephraim Stern Volume. Jerusalem. 70*–77.*

Kirk, G. S. 1949. "Ships on Geometric Vases." *The Annual of the British School at Athens* 44: 93–153.

———. 1965. *Homer and the Epic.* Cambridge.

Kitchen, K. A. 1996. *Ramesside Inscriptions Translated and Annotated: Translations II.* Cambridge.

———. 1999. *Ramesside Inscriptions Translated and Annotated: Notes and Comments II: Ramesses II, Royal Inscriptions.* Cambridge.

———. 2003. *Ramesside Inscriptions Translated and Annotated: Translations: Volume IV: Merenptah and the Late Nineteenth Dynasty.* Cambridge.

———. 2007. "Egyptian and Related Chronologies—Look, No Sciences, No Pots!" In Bietak, M. and Czerny, E. eds. *The Synchronisation of Civilisations in the Eastern Mediterranean in the Second Millennium B.C.* Contributions to the Chronology of the Eastern Mediterranean 9. Vienna. 163–172.

———. 2008. *Ramesside Inscriptions Translated and Annotated: Translations: Volume V: Setnakht, Ramesses III, & Contemporaries.* Cambridge.

———. 2012. "Ramesses III and the Ramesside Period." In Cline, E. H. and O'Connor, D. *Ramesses III: The Life and Times of Egypt's Last Great Hero*. Ann Arbor. 1–26.

———. 2013. "Establishing Chronology in Pharaonic Egypt and the Ancient Near East: Interlocking Textual Sources Relating to c. 1600–664 BC." In Shortland, A. J. and Bronk Ramsey, C., eds. *Radiocarbon and the Chronologies of Ancient Egypt*. Oxford. 1–18.

Knapp, A. B. 1990. "Ethnicity, Entrepreneurship, and Exchange: Mediterranean Inter-Island Relations in the Late Bronze Age." *The Annual of the British School at Athens* 85: 115–153.

Knapp, A. B. and Manning, S. W. 2016. "Crisis in Context: The End of the Late Bronze Age in the Eastern Mediterranean." *American Journal of Archaeology* 120: 99–149.

Koehl, R. B. 2005. "Preliminary Observations on the Unpublished Mycenaean Pottery from Woolley's Dig-House at Tell Atchana (Ancient Alalakh)." In Laffineur, R. and Greco, E., eds. *Emporia: Aegeans in the Central and Eastern Mediterranean*. Aegaeum 25. Liège. 415–422.

———. 2010. "Mycenaean Pottery." In Yener, K. A., ed. *Tell Atchana, Ancient Alalakh I: The 2003–2004 Excavation Seasons*. Istanbul. 81–84.

———. 2013. "The Near Eastern Contribution to Aegean Wall Painting and Vice Versa." In Aruz, J., Graff, S. B. and Rakic, Y., eds. *Cultures in Contact. From Mesopotamia to the Mediterranean in the Second Millennium B.C.* New York. 170–179.

Kohlmeyer, K. 2000. *Der Tempel des Wettergottes von Aleppo*. Munster.

Kopanias, K. (forthcoming). "Deconstructing Achilles: The Stories about Piyamaradu and the Making of a Homeric Heros." In Pavuk, P., ed. *EUDAIMON: Studies in Honour of Prof. Jan Bouzek*. Prague.

Korres, G. S. 1989. "Representation of a Late Mycenaean Ship on the Pyxis from Tragana, Pylos." In Tzalas, H., ed. *TROPIS I: 1st International Symposium on Ship Construction in Antiquity, Piraeus 1985*. Athens. 177–202.

Kramer-Hajos, M. 2016. *Mycenaean Greece and the Aegean World: Palace and Province in the Late Bronze Age*. Cambridge.

Kuchman, L. 1977. "Egyptian Clay Anthropoid Coffins." *Serapis* 4: 11–22.

Kuentz, C. 1928–1934. *La Bataille de Qadech: Les Textes ('Poème de Pentaour' et 'Bulletin de Qadech') et les Bas-Reliefs*. Mémoires Publiés par les Membres de l'Institut Français d'Archéologie Orientale du Caire 55. Cairo.

Lackenbacher, S. and Malbran-Labat, F. 2005. "Ugarit et les Hittites dans les Archives de la 'Maison d'Urtenu.'" *Studi Micenei ed Egeo-Anatolici* 47: 227–240.

Lambrou-Phillipson, C. 1991. "Seafaring in the Bronze Age Mediterranean: The Parameters Involved in Maritime Travel." In Laffineur, R. and Basch, L., eds. *Thalassa: l'Egée Préhistorique et la Mer*. Aegaeum 7. Liège. 11–20.

———. 1993. "Ugarit: A Late Bronze Age Thalassocracy? The Evidence of the Textual Sources." Orientalia 62: 163–170.

Landström, B. 1970. *Ships of the Pharaohs: 4000 Years of Egyptian Shipbuilding*. Garden City.

Lantzas, K. 2015. "Reconsidering Collapse: Identity, Ideology, and Postcollapse Settlement in the Argolid." In Faulseit, R., ed. *Beyond Collapse: Archaeological Perspectives on Resilience, Revitalization, and Transformation in Complex Societies*. Center for Archaeological Investigations Occasional Paper 42. Carbondale. 459–485.

Lehmann, G. 1979. "Die Sikilaju: Ein Neues Zeugnis zu den Seevölker-Heerfahrten im Späten 13 Jh. V. Chr. (RS 34.129)." *Ugarit-Forschungen* 11: 481–494.

———. 2013. "Aegean-Style Pottery in Syria and Lebanon During Iron Age I." In Killebrew, A. E. and Lehmann, G., eds. *The Philistines and Other Sea Peoples in Text and Archaeology*. Archaeology and Biblical Studies 15. Atlanta. 265–328.

———. 2017. "The Late Bronze—Iron Age Transition and the Problem of the Sea Peoples Phenomenon in Cilicia." In Fischer, P. M. and Bürge, T., eds. *'Sea Peoples' Up-to-Date: New Research on Transformation in the Eastern Mediterranean in the 13th–11th Centuries BCE*. Contributions to the Chronology of Eastern Mediterranean 35. Vienna: Austrian Academy of Sciences Press. 229–256.

Lemos, I. S. 2006. "Athens and Lefkandi: A Tale of Two Sites." In Deger-Jalkotzy, S. and Lemos, I. S., eds. *Ancient Greece: From the Mycenaean Palaces to the Age of Homer*. Edinburgh Leventis Studies 3. Edinburgh. 505–530.

Lesko, L. H. 1992. "Egypt in the 12th Century B.C." In Ward, W. A. and Joukowsky, M. S., eds. *The Crisis Years: The 12th Century B.C. from Beyond the Danube to the Tigris*. Dubuque. 151–156.

Levaniouk, O. 2011. *Eve of the Festival: Making Myth in* Odyssey *19*. Hellenic Studies Series 46. Washington, DC.

Liverani, M. 1977. "Le Chêne de Sherdanu." *Vetus Testamentum* 27: 212–216.

Lòpez-Ruiz, C. 2009. "Mopsos and Cultural Exchange between Greeks and Locals in Cilicia." In Dill, U. and Walde, Ch., eds. *Antike Mythen*. Berlin. 382–396.

Loretz, O. 1995. "Les Sardanu et la fin d'Ougarit: A Propos des Documents d'Égypte, de Byblos et d'Ougarit Relatifs aux Shardana." In Yon, M., Sznycer, M. and Bordreuil, P., eds. *Le Pays d'Ougarit Autour de 1200 av. J.-C.: Histoire et Archéologie*. Paris. 125–136.

Lorton, D. 1974. "Terminology Related to the Laws of Warfare in dyn. XVIII." *Journal of the American Research Center in Egypt* 11: 53–68.

Maeir, A. M., ed. 2012. *Tell es-Safî—Gath: Report on the 1996–2005 Seasons*. Ägypten und Altes Testament 69. Wiesbaden.

Maeir, A. M. and Hitchcock, L. A. 2017. "The Appearance, Formation and Transformation of Philistine Culture: New Perspectives and New Finds." In Fischer, P. M. and Bürge, T., eds. *'Sea Peoples' Up-to-Date: New Research on Transformation in the Eastern Mediterranean in the 13th–11th Centuries BCE*. Contributions to the Chronology of Eastern Mediterranean 35. Vienna: Austrian Academy of Sciences Press. 149–162.

Maeir, A. M., Hitchcock, L. A. and Horwitz, L. K. 2013. "On the Constitution and Transformation of Philistine Identity." *Oxford Journal of Archaeology* 32: 1–38.

Malamat, A. 1971. "The Egyptian Decline in Canaan and the Sea-Peoples." In Mazar, B., ed. *The World History of the Jewish People III: Judges*. New Brunswick. 23–38.

Malkin, I. 2011. *A Small Greek World: Networks in the Ancient Mediterranean.* Greeks Overseas 1. Oxford.

Mallowan, M. E. L. 1966. *Nimrud and Its Remains* I. London.

Manassa, C. 2003. *The Great Karnak Inscription of Merneptah: Grand Strategy in the 13th Century BC.* Yale Egyptological Studies 5. New Haven.

———. 2013. *Imagining the Past: Historical Fiction in New Kingdom Egypt.* Oxford.

Maran, J. 2001. "Political and Religious Aspects of Architectural Change on the Upper Citadel of Tiryns: The Case of Building T." In Laffineur, R. and Hägg, R., eds. *POTNIA: Deities and Religion in the Aegean Bronze Age.* Liège. 113–122.

———. 2006. "Coming to Terms with the Past: Ideology and Power in Late Helladic IIIC." In Deger-Jalkotzy, S. and Lemos, I. S., eds. *Ancient Greece: From the Mycenaean Palaces to the Age of Homer.* Edinburgh Leventis Studies 3. Edinburgh. 123–150.

———. 2010. "Tiryns." In Cline, E. H., ed. *The Oxford Handbook of the Bronze Age Aegean (ca. 3000–1000 BC).* Oxford. 722–734.

Marinatos, S. 1974. *Excavations at Thera VI (1972 Season).* Vivliothēkē tēs en Athēnais Archaiologikēs Hetaireias 64. Athens.

Mark, S. E. 2000. *Homeric Seafaring.* Doctoral dissertation, Texas A&M University.

Maspero, G. 1881. "Notes sur Quelques Points de Grammaire et d'Histoire." *Zeitschrift für Ägyptische Sprache 19*: 116–131.

Master, D. M. 2005. "Iron I Chronology at Ashkelon: Preliminary Results of the Leon Levy Expedition." In Higham, T. and Levy, T. E., eds. *The Bible and Radiocarbon Dating: Archaeology, Text, and Science.* London. 337–348.

Master, D. M. and Aja, A. 2017. "The Philistine Cemetery of Ashkelon." *Bulletin of the American Schools of Oriental Research* 377: 135–159.

Master, D. M., Stager, L. E. and Yasur-Landau, A. 2011. "Chronological Observations at the Dawn of the Iron Age in Ashkelon." Ägypten und Levante 21: 261–280.

McFadden, G. H. and Sjöqvist, E. 1954. "A Late Cypriote III Tomb from Kourion Kaloriziki No. 40." *American Journal of Archaeology* 58: 131–142.

McGrail, S. 1996. "Navigational Techniques in Homer's *Odyssey*." In Tzalas, H., ed. *TROPIS IV: 4th International Symposium on Ship Construction in Antiquity, Athens 1991.* Athens. 311–320.

Mehofer, M. and Jung, R. 2017. "Weapons and Metals—Interregional Contacts between Italy and the Eastern Mediterranean during the Late Bronze Age." In Fischer, P. M. and Bürge, T., eds. *'Sea Peoples' Up-to-Date: New Research on Transformation in the Eastern Mediterranean in the 13th–11th Centuries BCE.* Contributions to the Chronology of Eastern Mediterranean 35. Vienna: Austrian Academy of Sciences Press. 389–400.

Meiberg, L. G. *Figural Motifs on Philistine Pottery and Their Connections to the Aegean World, Cyprus and Coastal Anatolia.* Doctoral dissertation, University of Pennsylvania.

Meier-Brügger, M. 2006. "The Rise and Descent of the Language of the Homeric Poems." In Deger-Jalkotzy, S. and Lemos, I. S., eds. *Ancient Greece: From the Mycenaean Palaces to the Age of Homer.* Edinburgh Leventis Studies 3. Edinburgh. 417–426.

Meijer, D. J. W. 2017. "The Archaeological Ramifications of 'Philistines' in Aleppo." In Fischer, P. M. and Bürge, T., eds. *Sea Peoples' Up-to-Date: New Research on Transformation in the Eastern Mediterranean in the 13th–11th Centuries BCE.* Contributions to the Chronology of Eastern Mediterranean 35. Vienna: Austrian Academy of Sciences Press. 257–262.

Menu, B. 1970. *Le Tégime Juridique des Terres et du Personnel Attaché à la Terre Dans le Papyrus Wilbour.* Lille.

Michailidou, A. and Voutsa, K. 2005. "Humans as a Commodity in Aegean and Oriental Societies." In Laffineur, R. and Greco, E., eds. *Emporia: Aegeans in the Central and Eastern Mediterranean.* Aegaeum 25. Liège. 17–28.

Middleton, G. D. 2010. *The Collapse of Palatial Society in LBA Greece and the Post-palatial Period.* BAR International Series 2110. Oxford.

———. 2015. "Telling Stories: The Mycenaean Origins of the Philistines." *Oxford Journal of Archaeology* 34: 45–65.

Millek, J. M. 2017. "Sea Peoples, Philistines, and the Destruction of Cities: A Critical Examination of Destruction Layers 'Caused' by the 'Sea Peoples.'" In Fischer, P. M. and Bürge, T., eds. *Sea Peoples' Up-to-Date: New Research on Transformation in the Eastern Mediterranean in the 13th–11th Centuries BCE.* Contributions to the Chronology of Eastern Mediterranean 35. Vienna: Austrian Academy of Sciences Press. 113–140.

Millet, N. B. 1987. "The First Appearance of the Loose-Footed Squaresail Rig in the Mediterranean." *Journal of the Society for the Study of Egyptian Antiquities* 17: 89–91.

Monro, D. B. 1886. *Homer's Odyssey.* Berkeley.

Monroe, C. M. 2009. *Scales of Fate: Trade, Tradition, and Transformation in the Eastern Mediterranean ca. 1350–1175 BCE.* Alter Orient und Altes Testament 357. Munster.

Moran, W. L. 1992. *The Amarna Letters.* Baltimore.

Morris, E. F. 2005. *The Architecture of Imperialism: Military Bases and the Evolution of Foreign Policy in Egypt's New Kingdom.* Probleme der Ägyptologie 22. Leiden.

Morris, S. P. 1989. "A Tale of Two Cities: The Miniature Frescoes from Thera and the Origins of Greek Poetry." *American Journal of Archaeology* 93: 511–535.

———. 2001. "Potnia Aswiya: Anatolian Contributions to Greek Religion." In Laffineur, R. and Hägg, R., eds. *POTNIA: Deities and Religion in the Aegean Bronze Age.* Liège. 423–434.

———. 2003. "Islands in the Sea: Aegean Polities as Levantine Neighbors." In Dever, W. G. and Gitin, S., eds. *Symbiosis, Symbolism, and the Power of the Past: Canaan, Ancient Israel, and Their Neighbors from the Late Bronze Age through Roman Palaestina.* Winona Lake. 3–16.

Moschos, I. 2009. "Evidence of Social Re-Organization and Reconstruction in Late Helladic IIIC Achaea and Modes of Contacts and Exchange via the Ionian and Adriatic Sea." In Borgna, E. and Cassola Guida, P., eds. *From the Aegean to the Adriatic: Social Organisations, Modes of Exchange and Interaction in Postpalatial Times (12th–11th B.C.).* Studi e Ricerche di Protostoria Mediterranea 8. Rome. 349–414.

Mountjoy, P. A. 1997. "The Destruction of the Palace at Pylos Reconsidered." *The Annual of the British School at Athens* 92: 109–137.

———. 1998. "The East Aegean-West Anatolian Interface in the Late Bronze Age: Mycenaeans and the Kingdom of Ahhiyawa." *Anatolian Studies* 48: 33–67.

———. 1999. *Regional Mycenaean Decorated Pottery*. Rahden.

———. 2005. "Mycenaean Connections with the Near East in LH IIIC: Ships and Sea Peoples." In Laffineur, R. and Greco, E., eds. *Emporia: Aegeans in the Central and Eastern Mediterranean*. Aegaeum 25. Liège. 423–431.

———. 2006. "Mycenaean Pictorial Pottery from Anatolia in the Transitional LH IIIB2–LH IIIC Early and the LH IIIC Phases." In Rystedt, E. and Wells, B., eds. *Pictorial Pursuits: Figurative Painting on Mycenaean and Geometric Pottery*. Stockholm. 107–122.

———. 2007. "A Definition of LH IIIC Middle." In Deger-Jalkotzy, S. and Zavadil, M., eds. *LH IIIC Chronology and Synchronisms II: LH IIIC Middle*. Vienna. 221–242.

———. 2010. "A Note on the Mixed Origins of Some Philistine Pottery." *Bulletin of the American Schools of Oriental Research* 359: 1–12.

———. 2011. "A Bronze Age Ship from Ashkelon with Particular Reference to the Bronze Age Ship from Bademgediği Tepe." *American Journal of Archaeology* 115: 483–488.

———. 2013. "The Late LH IIIB and LH IIIC Early Pottery of the East Aegean-West Anatolian Interface." In Killebrew, A. E. and Lehmann, G., eds. *The Philistines and Other Sea Peoples in Text and Archaeology*. Archaeology and Biblical Studies 15. Atlanta. 563–584.

———. 2014. "The East Aegean-West Anatolian Interface in the 12th Century BC: Some Aspects Arising from the Mycenaean Pottery." In Stampolidis, N. Ch., Maner, Ç. and Kopanias, K., eds. *Nostoi: Indigenous Culture, Migration and Integration in the Aegean Islands and Western Anatolia During the Late Bronze and Early Iron Ages*. Koç University Press 58. Istanbul. 37–80.

———. 2017. "The Sea Peoples: A View from the Pottery." In Fischer, P. M. and Bürge, T., eds. *'Sea Peoples' Up-to-Date: New Research on Transformation in the Eastern Mediterranean in the 13th–11th Centuries BCE*. Contributions to the Chronology of Eastern Mediterranean 35. Vienna: Austrian Academy of Sciences Press. 355–378.

Mountjoy, P. A. and Gowland, R. 2005. "The End of the Bronze Age at Enkomi, Cyprus: The Problem of Level IIIB." *The Annual of the British School at Athens* 100: 125–214.

Muhly, J. D. 2003. "Greece and Anatolia in the Early Iron Age: The Archaeological Evidence and the Literary Tradition." In Dever, W. G. and Gitin, S., eds. *Symbiosis, Symbolism, and the Power of the Past: Canaan, Ancient Israel, and Their Neighbors from the Late Bronze Age through Roman Palaestina*. Winona Lake. 23–36.

———. 2010. "History of Research." In Cline, E. H., ed. *The Oxford Handbook of the Bronze Age Aegean (ca. 3000–1000 BC)*. Oxford. 3–10.

Murray, A. S., Smith, A. H. and Walters, H. B. 1900. *Excavations in Cyprus: Bequest of Miss E. T. Turner to the British Museum*. London.

Nagy, G. 1995. "An Evolutionary Model for the Making of Homeric Poetry." In Carter, J. B. and Morris, S. P., eds. *The Ages of Homer: A Tribute to Emily Townsend Vermeule*. Austin. 163–180.

———. 1996a. *Homeric Questions*. Austin.

———. 1996b. *Poetry as Performance: Homer and Beyond*. Cambridge.

———. 2001. "Homeric Poetry and Problems of Multiformity: The 'Panathenaic Bottleneck.'" *Classical Philology* 96: 109–119.

———. 2007. "Homer and Greek Myth." In Woodard, R. D., ed. *The Cambridge Companion to Greek Mythology*. Cambridge. 52–82.

———. 2013. *The Ancient Greek Hero in 24 Hours*. Cambridge.

———. 2015a. "A Cretan Odyssey, Part 2." https://classical-inquiries.chs.harvard. edu/a-cretan-odyssey-part-2/.

———. 2015b. "East of the Achaeans: Making Up for a Missed Opportunity While Reading Hittite Texts." https://classical-inquiries.chs.harvard.edu/east-of-the-achaeans-making-up-for-a-missed-opportunity-while-reading-hittite-texts/.

Nelson, H. H. 1929. *The Epigraphic Survey of the Great Temple of Medinet Habu (Seasons 1924–25 to 1927–28)*. Oriental Institute Communications 5. Chicago.

———. 1943. "The Naval Battle Pictured at Medinet Habu." *Journal of Near Eastern Studies* 2: 40–55.

Nibbi, A. 1972. *The Sea Peoples: A Re-Examination of the Egyptian Sources*. Oxford.

———. 1975. *The Sea Peoples and Egypt*. Park Ridge.

Niemeier, W.-D. 1998. "The Mycenaeans in Western Anatolia and the Problem of the Origins of the Sea Peoples." In Gitin, S., Mazar, A. and Stern, E., eds. *Mediterranean Peoples in Transition, Thirteenth to Early Tenth Centuries BCE*. Jerusalem. 17–65.

Niemeier, W.-D. and Niemeier, B. 1998. "Minoan Frescoes in the Eastern Mediterranean." In Cline, E. H. and Harris-Cline, D., eds. *The Aegean and the Orient in the Second Millennium*. Aegaeum 18. Liège. 69–98.

Nikolaidou, M. and Kokkinidou, D. 2007. "Epos, History, Metahistory in Aegean Bronze Age Studies." In Morris, S. P. and Laffineur, R., eds. *EPOS: Reconsidering Greek Epic and Aegean Bronze Age Archaeology*. Aegaeum 28. Liège. 35–48.

Nims, C. F. 1976. "Ramesseum Sources of the Medinet Habu Reliefs." In Johnson, J. H. and Wente, E. F., eds. *Studies in Honor of George R. Hughes*. Chicago. 169–175.

Nowicki, K. 1987. "Topography of Refuge Settlement in Crete." *Jahrbuch des Romisch-Germanischen Zentralmuseums* 34: 213–234.

———. 1994. "A Dark Age Refuge Centre Near Pefki, East Crete." *The Annual of the British School at Athens* 89: 235–268.

———. 2000. *Defensible Sites in Crete c. 1200–800 B.C. (LM IIIB/IIIC Through Early Geometric)*. Aegaeum 21. Liège.

———. 2001. "Sea-Raiders and Refugees." In Karageorghis, V. and Morris, C. E., eds. *Defensive Settlements of the Aegean and the Eastern Mediterranean after c. 1200*. Nicosia. 23–39.

———. 2002. "From Late Minoan IIIC Refuge Settlements to Geometric Acropoleis: Architecture and Social Organization of Dark Age Villages and Towns in Crete." In Luce, J.-M., ed. *Habitat et Urbanisme dans le Monde Grec de la Fin des Palais Mycéniens à la Prise de Milet*. Pallas 58. Toulouse. 149–174.

———. 2011. "Settlement in Crisis: The End of the LM/LH IIIB and Early IIIC in Crete and Other South Aegean Islands." In Mazarakis Ainian, A., ed. *The Dark Age Revisited*. Volos. 435–450.

Nuñez, F. J. 2017. "The Impact of the Sea Peoples in the Central and Northern Levant in Perspective." In Fischer, P. M. and Bürge, T., eds. *'Sea Peoples' Up-to-Date: New Research on Transformation in the Eastern Mediterranean in the 13th–11th Centuries BCE*. Contributions to the Chronology of Eastern Mediterranean 35. Vienna: Austrian Academy of Sciences Press. 263–284.

O'Connor, D. 2000. "The Sea Peoples and the Egyptian Sources." In Oren, E. D., ed. *The Sea Peoples and Their World: A Reassessment*. University Museum Monographs 108. Philadelphia. 85–102.

Olsen, B. A. 2014. *Women in Mycenaean Greece: The Linear B tablets from Pylos and Knossos*. London.

Oren, E. D. 1973. *The Northern Cemetery of Beth Shan*. Leiden.

———, ed. 2000. *The Sea Peoples and Their World: A Reassessment*. University Museum Monographs 108. Philadelphia.

Ormerod, H. A. 1924. *Piracy in the Ancient World: An Essay in Mediterranean History*. London.

Page, D. L. 1959. *History and the Homeric Iliad*. Sather Classical Lectures 31. Berkeley.

Palaima, T. G. 1991. "Maritime Matters in the Linear B Texts." In Laffineur, R. and Basch, L., eds. *Thalassa: l'Egée Préhistorique et la Mer*. Aegaeum 7. Liège. 273–310.

———. 1995a. "The Last Days of the Pylos Polity." In Laffineur, R. and Niemeier, W.-D., eds. *Politeia: Society and State in the Aegean Bronze Age*. Aegaeum 12. Liège. 623–633.

———. 1995b. "The Nature of the Mycenaean *Wanax*: Non-Indo-European Origins and Priestly Functions." In Rehak, P., ed. *The Role of the Ruler in the Prehistoric Aegean*. Aegaeum 11. Liège. 119–139.

———. 2007. "Mycenaean Society and Kingship: Cui bono? A Counter-Speculative View." In Morris, S. P. and Laffineur, R., eds. *EPOS: Reconsidering Greek Epic and Aegean Bronze Age Archaeology*. Aegaeum 28. Liège. 129–140.

Palmer, L. R. 1980. *Mycenaeans and Minoans: Aegean Prehistory in the Light of the Linear B Tablets*. Westport.

Papadimitriou, N. 2015. "Aegean and Cypriot Ceramic Trade Overseas During the 2nd Millennium BCE." In Mynářová, J., Onderka, P. and Pavúk, P., eds. *There and Back Again—the Crossroads II*. Prague. 423–446.

Papadopoulos, A. 2006. "Cities Under Siege? A Look at Bronze Age Iconography." In Day, J., ed. *SOMA 2004 Symposium on Mediterranean Archaeology*. BAR International Series 1514. Oxford. 131–137.

———. 2009. "Warriors, Hunters, and Ships in the Late Helladic IIIC Aegean: Changes in the Iconography of Warfare?" In Bachhuber, C. and Roberts, R. G., eds. *Forces of Transformation: The End of the Bronze Age in the Mediterranean.* BANEA Themes from the Ancient Near East 1. Oxford. 69–77.

Parkinson, R. B. and Schofield, L. 1995. "Images of Mycenaeans: A Recently Acquired Painted Papyrus from El-Amarna." In Davies, W. V. and Schofield, L., eds. *Egypt, the Aegean and the Levant: Interconnections in the Second Millennium B.C.* London. 125–126.

Parry, M. 1930. "Studies in the Epic Technique of Oral Verse-Making I: Homer and the Homeric Style." *Harvard Studies in Classical Philology* 41: 73–147.

Peden, A. J. 1994. *Egyptian Historical Inscriptions of the Twentieth Dynasty.* Documenta Mundi 3. Jonsered.

Peltenburg, E. 2012. "King Kušmešuša and the Decentralised Political Structure of Late Bronze Age Cyprus." In Cadogan, G., Iacovou, M., Kopaka, K. and Whitley, J., eds. *Parallel Lives: Ancient Island Societies in Crete and Cyprus.* British School at Athens Studies 20. London. 119–140.

Petrakis, V. P. 2004. "Ship Representations on Late Helladic III C Pictorial Pottery: Some Notes." *Inferno* 9: 1–6.

———. 2011. "Politics of the Sea in the Late Bronze Age II–III Aegean: Iconographic Preferences and Textual Perspectives." In Vavouranakis, G., ed. *The Seascape in Aegean Prehistory.* Monographs of the Danish Institute at Athens 14. Athens. 185–229.

Petrie, W. M. F. 1905. *Ehnaysia, 1904.* London.

———. 1933. "Egyptian Shipping (Continued)." *Ancient Egypt* 3–4: 65–75.

Pfoh, E. 2016. *Syria-Palestine in the Late Bronze Age: An Anthropology of Politics and Power.* London: Routledge.

Pirenne, H. 1940. *Economic and Social History of Medieval Europe.* New York.

Pomey, P. 2009. "On the Use of Design in Ancient Mediterranean Ship Construction." In Nowacki, H. and Lefévre, W., eds. *Creating Shapes in Civil and Naval Architecture: A Cross-Disciplinary Comparison.* History of Science and Medicine Library 11. Leiden. 49–63.

Ponchia, S. 2011. "Patterns of Relationships in the Syro-Hittite Area." In Strobel, K., ed. *Empires after the Empire: Anatolia, Syria and Assyria after Suppiluliuma (ca.1200–800/700 B.C.).* Eothen 17. Florence. 281–308.

Popham, M., Touloupa, E. and Sackett, L. H. 1982. "The Hero of Lefkandi." *Antiquity* 56: 169–174.

Prior, C. A. 2013. "Radiocarbon Age Analysis of the Gurob Ship-Cart Model." In Wachsmann, S. *The Gurob Ship-Cart Model and its Mediterranean Context.* College Station. 239–242.

Pritchard, J. B. 1943. *Palestinian Figurines in Relation to Certain Goddesses Known Through Literature.* American Oriental Series 24. New Haven.

Pulak, Ç. 1998. "The Uluburun Shipwreck: An Overview." *The International Journal of Nautical Archaeology* 27: 188–224.

———. 2005. "Who Were the Mycenaeans Aboard the Uluburun Ship?" In Laffineur, R. and Greco, E., eds. *Emporia: Aegeans in the Central and Eastern Mediterranean.* Aegaeum 25. Liège. 295–310.

Qviller, B. 1981. "The Dynamics of the Homeric Society." *Symbolae Osloenses* 56: 109–155.

Raaflaub, K. A. 2006. "Historical Approaches to Homer." In Deger-Jalkotzy, S. and Lemos, I. S., eds. *Ancient Greece: From the Mycenaean Palaces to the Age of Homer*. Edinburgh Leventis Studies 3. Edinburgh. 449–462.

Raban, A. 1989. "The Medinet Habu Ships: Another Interpretation." *International Journal of Nautical Archaeology* 18: 163–171.

Raban, A. and Stieglitz, R. 1991. "The Sea Peoples and their Contributions to Civilization." *Biblical Archaeology Review* 17: 34–42.

Rainey, A. F. 1982. "Toponymic Problems." *Tel Aviv* 9: 130–136.

Redford, D. B. 1984. *Akhenaten: The Heretic King*. Princeton.

——. 1992. *Egypt, Canaan, and Israel in Ancient Times*. Princeton.

——. 2000. "Egypt and Western Asia in the Late New Kingdom: An Overview." In Oren, E. D., ed. *The Sea Peoples and Their World: A Reassessment*. University Museum Monographs 108. Philadelphia. 1–20.

——. 2006-7. "The Tjeker." In Harrison, T. P., ed. *Cyprus, the Sea Peoples and the Eastern Mediterranean Regional Perspectives of Continuity and Change*. Scripta Mediterranea 27–28. Toronto. 9–14.

——. 2007. "Some Toponyms and Personal Names Relating to the Sea Peoples." In Hawass, Z. A., ed. *The Archaeology and Art of Ancient Egypt: Essays in Honor of David B. O'Connor*. Annales du Service des Antiquités de l'Egypte 36. Cairo. 299–302.

Reece, S. 1994. "The Cretan Odyssey: A Lie Truer Than Truth." *American Journal of Philology* 115: 157–173.

Rehak, P. and Younger, J. G. 1998. "Review of Aegean Prehistory VII: Neopalatial, Final Palatial, and Postpalatial Crete." *American Journal of Archaeology* 102: 91–173.

Richard, T. T. 2010. "Reconsidering the Letter of Marque: Utilizing Private Security Providers Against Piracy." *Public Contract Law Journal* 39: 411–464.

Ritner, R. K. 2009. *The Libyan Anarchy: Inscriptions from Egypt's Third Intermediate Period*. Writings from the Ancient World 21. Atlanta.

Roberts, O. T. P. 1991. "The Development of the Brail into a Viable Sail Control for Aegean Boats of the Bronze Age." In Laffineur, R. and Basch, L., eds. *Thalassa: l'Egée Préhistorique et la Mer*. Aegaeum 7. Liège. 55–64.

——. 1995. "An Explanation of Ancient Windward Sailing—Some Other Considerations." *International Journal of Nautical Archaeology* 24: 307–315.

Roberts, R. G. 2009. "Identity, Choice and the Year 8 Reliefs of Ramesses III at Medinet Habu." In Bachhuber, C. and Roberts, R. G., eds. *Forces of Transformation: The End of the Bronze Age in the Mediterranean*. BANEA Themes from the Ancient Near East 1. Oxford. 60–68.

Rutter, J. B. 1992. "Cultural Novelties in the Post-palatial Aegean World: Indices of Vitality or Decline?" In Ward, W. A. and Joukowsky, M. S., eds. *The Crisis Years: The 12th Century B.C. from Beyond the Danube to the Tigris*. Dubuque. 61–78.

Samaras, V. 2015. "Piracy in the Aegean During the Postpalatial Period and the Early Iron Age." In Babbi, A., Bubenheimer-Erhart, F., Marin-Ahulera, B. and Muhl, S., eds. *The Mediterranean Mirror: Cultural Contacts in the Mediterranean Sea*

*Between 1200 and 750 B.C.* Römisch-Germanisches Zentralmuseum Tagungen 20. Mainz. 189–204.

Sandars, N. K. 1985. *The Sea Peoples: Warriors of the Ancient Mediterranean.* London.

Sasson, J. 1966. "Canaanite Maritime Involvement in the Second Millennium B.C." *Journal of the American Oriental Society* 86: 126–138.

Sauvage, C. 2012. *Routes Maritimes et Systèmes d'Echanges Internationaux au Bronze Récent en Méditerranée Orientale.* Travaux de la Maison de l'Orient et de la Méditerranée 61. Lyon.

Säve-Söderbergh, T. 1946. *The Navy of the Eighteenth Egyptian Dynasty.* Uppsala.

———. 1957. *Four Eighteenth Dynasty Tombs.* Private Tombs at Thebes 1. Oxford.

Schaeffer. C. F. A. 1952. *Enkomi-Alasia.* Paris.

Schilardi, D. U. 1984. "The LH IIIC Period at the Koukounaries Acropolis, Paros." In MacGillivray, J. A. and Barber, R. L. N., eds. *The Prehistoric Cyclades: Contributions to a Workshop on Cycladic Chronology.* Edinburgh. 184–206.

———. 1992. "Paros and the Cyclades after the Fall of the Mycenaean Palaces." In Olivier, J. P., ed. *Mykenaïka: Actes du IXe Colloque International sur les Textes Mycéniens et Égéens.* Paris. 621–693.

———. 1999. "The Mycenaean Horseman (?) of Koukounaries." In Betancourt, P., Karageorghis, V., Laffineur, R. and Niemeier, W.-D., eds. *Meletemata: Studies in Aegean Archaeology Presented to Malcolm H. Wiener.* Aegaeum 20. Liège. 751–756.

Schofield, L. and Parkinson, R. B. 1994. "Of Helmets and Heretics: A Possible Egyptian Representation of Mycenaean Warriors on a Papyrus from el-Amarna." *The Annual of the British School at Athens* 89: 157–170.

Schulman, A. R. 1962. *Military Rank, Title, and Organization in the Egyptian New Kingdom.* Doctoral dissertation, University of Pennsylvania.

———. 1968. "A Private Triumph in Brooklyn, Hildesheim, and Berlin." *Journal of the American Research Center in Egypt* 7: 27–35.

Sethe, K. 1909. *Urkunden der 18. Dynastie.* Urkunden des Ägyptischen Altertums 4. Leipzig.

Sharon, I. and Gilboa, A. 2013. "Dor in the Early Iron Age." In Killebrew, A. E. and Lehmann, G., eds. *The Philistines and Other Sea Peoples in Text and Archaeology.* Archaeology and Biblical Studies 15. Atlanta. 393–468.

Shaw, J. W. 1981. "Excavations at Kommos (Crete) during 1979." *Hesperia* 50: 211–251.

Shaw, M. C. 1980. "Painted 'Ikria' at Mycenae?" *American Journal of Archaeology* 84: 167–179.

———. 2001. "Symbols of Naval Power at the Palace at Pylos: The Evidence from the Frescoes." In Böhm, S. and von Eickstedt, K.-V., eds. *Ithakē: Festschrift für Jörg Schäfer zum 75.* Würzburg. 37–43.

Shear, I. M. 1998. "Bellerophon Tablets from the Mycenaean World? A Tale of Seven Bronze Hinges." *Journal of Hellenic Studies* 118: 187–189.

Shelmerdine, C. W. 1997. "Review of Aegean Prehistory VI: The Palatial Bronze Age of the Southern and Central Greek Mainland." *American Journal of Archaeology* 101: 537–585.

———. 1999. "Pylian Polemics: The Latest Evidence on Military Matters." In Laffineur, R., ed. *Polemos: Le Contexte Guerrier en Égée à l'âge du Bronze*. Aegaeum 19. Liège. 403–410.

Sherratt, A. and Sherratt, E. S. 1991. "From Luxuries to Commodities: The Nature of Bronze Age Trading Systems." In Gale, N. H., ed. *Bronze Age Trade in the Mediterranean: Papers Presented at the Conference Held at Rewley House, Oxford, in December 1989*. Studies in Mediterranean Archaeology 90. Jonsered. 351–384.

———. 1998. "Small Worlds: Interaction and Identity in the Ancient Mediterranean." In Cline, E. H. and Harris-Cline, D., eds. *The Aegean and the Orient in the Second Millennium*. Aegaeum 18. Liège. 329–342.

Sherratt, E. S. 1990. "Reading the Texts: Archaeology and the Homeric Question." *Antiquity* 64: 807–824.

———. 2000. "Circulation of Metals and the End of the Bronze Age in the Eastern Mediterranean." In Pare, Ch., ed. *Metals Make the World Go Round: The Supply and Circulation of Metals in Bronze Age Europe*. Oxford. 82–98.

———. 2010. "The Trojan War: History or Bricolage?" *Bulletin of the Institute of Classical Studies* 53: 1–18.

Sherratt, E. S. and Crouwel, J. H. 1987. "Mycenaean Pottery from Cilicia in Oxford." *Oxford Journal of Archaeology* 6: 325–352.

Sherratt, E. S. and Mazar, A. 2013. "'Mycenaean IIIC' and Related Pottery from Beth Shean." In Killebrew, A. E. and Lehmann, G., eds. *The Philistines and Other Sea Peoples in Text and Archaeology*. Archaeology and Biblical Studies 15. Atlanta. 349–392.

Siddall, R. 2013. "Analysis of the Pigments from the Gurob Ship-Cart Model." In Wachsmann, S., *The Gurob Ship-Cart Model and its Mediterranean Context*. College Station. 243–247.

Singer, I. 1983. "Western Anatolia in the Thirteenth Century B.C. According to the Hittite Sources." *Anatolian Studies* 33: 205–217.

———. 1985. "The Beginning of Philistine Settlement in Canaan and the Northern Boundary of Philistia." *Tel Aviv* 12: 109–122.

———. 2000. "New Evidence on the End of the Hittite Empire." In Oren, E. D., ed. *The Sea Peoples and Their World: A Reassessment*. University Museum Monographs 108. Philadelphia. 21–34.

———. 2006. "Ships Bound for Lukka: A New Interpretation of the Companion Letters RS 94.2530 and RS 94.2523." *Altorientalische Forschungen* 33: 242–262.

———. 2009. "The Luwian-Phoenician Bilingual from Çineköy and its Historical Implications." In Aviram, J., Ben-Tor, A., Eph'al, I., Gitin, S. and Reich, R., eds. *Eretz-Israel: Archaeological, Historical and Geographical Studies*. Eretz-Israel 29: Ephraim Stern Volume. Jerusalem. 147–152 (in Hebrew, with English summary on 287).

———. 2011. "A Political History of Ugarit." In Singer, I. *The Calm Before the Storm: Selected Writings of Itamar Singer on the Late Bronze Age in Anatolia and the Levant*. Writings from the Ancient World 1. Atlanta. 19–146.

———. 2013a. "The Philistines in the Bible: A Short Rejoinder to a New Perspective." In Killebrew, A. E. and Lehmann, G., eds. *The Philistines and Other Sea Peoples in Text and Archaeology*. Archaeology and Biblical Studies 15. Atlanta. 19–28.

————. 2013b. "Old Country Ethonyms in New Countries of the Sea Peoples Diaspora." In Koehl, R. B., ed. *AMILLA: The Quest for Excellence: Studies in Honor of Günter Kopcke*. Prehistory Monographs 43. Philadelphia. 321–334.

Smith, S. T. 1991 "A Model for Egyptian Imperialism in Nubia." *Göttinger Miszellen* 122: 77–102.

————. 1995. *Askut in Nubia: The Economics and Ideology of Egyptian Imperialism in the Second Millennium B.C.* London.

Snape, S. R. 1997. "Ramesses II's Forgotten Frontier." *Egyptian Archaeology* 11: 23–24.

————. 1998. "Review of S. T. Smith, Askut in Nubia: The Economics and Ideology of Egyptian Imperialism in the Second Millennium B.C." *Journal of the Economic and Social History of the Orient* 41: 503–505.

————. 2000. "Imported pottery at Zawiyet Umm el-Rakham: Preliminary report." *Bulletin de Liaison due Groupe International d'Étude de la Céramique Égyptienne* 21: 17–21.

————. 2010. "Vor der Kaserne: External Supply and Self-Sufficiency at Zawiyet Umm el-Rakham." In Bietak, M., Czerny, E. and Forstner-Müller, I., eds. *Cities and Urbanism in Ancient Egypt*. Untersuchungen der Zweigstelle Kairo des Österreichischen Archäologischen Institutes 35. Vienna. 271–288.

Snodgrass, A.M. 1991. "Bronze Age Exchange: A Minimalist Position." In Gale, N. H., ed. *Bronze Age Trade in the Mediterranean: Papers Presented at the Conference Held at Rewley House, Oxford, in December 1989*. Studies in Mediterranean Archaeology 90. Jonsered. 15–20.

Sølver, C. V. 1936. "Egyptian Shipping of About 1500 B.C." *Mariner's Mirror* 22: 430–469.

Spalinger, A. J. 2002. *The Transformation of an Ancient Egyptian Narrative: P. Sallier III and the Battle of Kadesh*. Göttinger Orientforschungen: Ägypten 40. Wiesbaden.

————. 2005. *War in Ancient Egypt: The New Kingdom*. Malden.

Spiegelberg, W. 1896. *Rechnungen aus der Zeit Setis I*. Strassburg.

Stadelmann, R. 1967. *Syrisch-Palästinensische Gottheiten in Ägypten*. Probleme der Ägyptologie 5. Leiden.

Stager, L. E. 1991. *Ashkelon Discovered: From Canaanites and Philistines to Romans and Moslems*. Washington, DC.

————. 1995. "The Impact of the Sea Peoples in Canaan (1185–1050 B.C.E)." In Levy, T. E., ed. *The Archaeology of Society in the Holy Land*. London. 332–348.

Stager, L. E. and Mountjoy, P. A. 2007. "A Pictorial Krater from Philistine Ashkelon." In White Crawford, S. and Ben-Tor, A., eds. *Up to the Gates of Ekron: Essays on the Archaeology and History of the Eastern Mediterranean in Honor of Seymour Gitin*. Jerusalem. 50–61.

Stager, L. E., Schloen, J. D. and Master, D. M. 2008. *Ashkelon 1: Introduction and Overview*. Winona Lake.

Stampolidis, N. Ch. and Kotsonas, A. 2006. "Phoenicians in Crete." In Deger-Jalkotzy, S. and Lemos, I. S., eds. *Ancient Greece: From the Mycenaean Palaces to the Age of Homer*. Edinburgh Leventis Studies 3. Edinburgh. 337–361.

Starkey, D. J. 1990. *British Privateering Enterprise in the 18th Century.* Exeter.

Stern, E. 2013. *The Material Culture of the Northern Sea Peoples in Israel.* Studies in the Archaeology and History of the Levant 5. Winona Lake.

Stone, B. J. 1995. "The Philistines and Acculturation: Culture Change and Ethnic Continuity in the Iron Age." *Bulletin of the American Schools of Oriental Research* 298: 7–32.

Sweeney, D. and Yasur-Landau, A. 1999. "Following the Path of the Sea Persons: The Women in the Medinet Habu Reliefs." *Tel Aviv* 26: 116–145.

Tandy, D. W. 1997. *Warriors into Traders: The Power of the Market in Early Greece.* Classics and Contemporary Thought 5. Berkeley.

Tartaron, T. F. 2013. *Maritime Networks in the Mycenaean World.* Cambridge.

Thomas, S. 2003. "Imports at Zawiyet Umm el-Rakham." In Hawass, Z. and Brock, L. P., eds. *Egyptology at the Dawn of the Twenty-First Century.* Cairo. 522–529.

Tilley, A. F. and Johnstone, P. 1976. "A Minoan Naval Triumph?" *International Journal of Nautical Archaeology and Underwater Exploration* 5: 285–292.

Toffolo, M., Fantalkin, A., Lemos, I. S., Felsch, R. C. S., Niemeier, W.-D., Sanders, G. D. R., Finkelstein, I. and Boaretto, E. 2013. "Towards an Absolute Chronology for the Aegean Iron Age: New Radiocarbon Dates from Lefkandi, Kalapodi and Corinth." *PLOS One* 8: 1–11.

Tomlinson, J. E., Rutter, J. B. and Hoffman, S. M. A. 2010. "Mycenaean and Cypriot Late Bronze Age Ceramic Imports to Kommos: An Investigation by Neutron Activation Analysis." *Hesperia* 79: 191–231.

Tritsch, F. J. 1968. "Tirynthia Semata." *Kadmos* 7: 24–137.

Tsountas, Ch. 1886. "Graptē Stēlē ek Mykēnōn." *Ephēmeris Archaiologikē* 4: 1–22.

Tsountas, Ch. and Manatt, J. I. 1897. *The Mycenaean Age: A Study of the Monuments and Culture of Pre-Homeric Greece.* London.

Tubb, J. N. 2000. "Sea Peoples in the Jordan Valley." In Oren, E. D., ed. *The Sea Peoples and Their World: A Reassessment.* University Museum Monographs 108. Philadelphia. 181–196.

Tzachili, I. 1999. "Before Sailing: The Making of Sails in the Second Millennium B.C." In Betancourt, P., Karageorghis, V., Laffineur, R. and Niemeier, W.-D., eds. *Meletemata: Studies in Aegean Archaeology Presented to Malcolm H. Wiener.* Aegaeum 20. Liège. 857–862.

Uehlinger, C. 1988. "Der Amun-Tempel Ramses' III. in p3-Kn'n, seine Südpalästinischen Tempelgüter und der Übergang von der Ägypter- zur Philisterherrschaft: Ein Hinweis auf Einige Wenig Beachtete Skarabäen." *Zeitschrift des Deutschen Palästina-Vereins* 104: 6–25.

Ünlü, E. 2005. "Locally Produced and Painted Late Bronze to Iron Age Transitional Period Pottery of Tarsus-Gözlükule." In Özyar, A., ed. *Field Seasons 2001–2003 of the Tarsus-Gözlükule Interdisciplinary Research Project.* Istanbul. 145–168.

Vagnetti, L. and Lo Schiavo, F. 1989. "Late Bronze Age Long Distance Trade in the Mediterranean: The Role of the Cypriots." In Peltenburg, E. J., ed. *Early Society in Cyprus.* Edinburgh. 217–243.

Van de Mieroop, M. 2009. *The Eastern Mediterranean in the Age of Ramesses II.* Malden.

Van Soldt, W. 2010. "Ugarit as a Hittite Vassal State." *Altoriental Forschungen* 37: 198–207.

Van Wees, H. 1992. *Status Warriors: War, Violence and Society in Homer and History*. Dutch Monographs on Ancient History and Archaeology 9. Amsterdam.

Venturi, F. 2011. "The North Syrian Plateau Before and After the Fall of the Hittite Empire: New Evidence from Tell Afis." In Strobel, K., ed. *Empires after the Empire: Anatolia, Syria and Assyria after Suppiluliuma (ca.1200–800/700 B.C.)*. Eothen 17. Florence. 139–166.

———. 2013. "The Transition from Late Bronze Age to Early Iron Age at Tell Afis, Syria phases VII–III." In: Yener, A., ed. *Across the Border: Late Bronze-Iron Age Relations between Syria and Anatolia*. Ancient Near Eastern Studies Supplement Series 42. Leuven. 227–262.

Vercoutter, J. 1954. *Essai sur les Relations Entre Égyptiens et Préhellènes*. Paris.

Vermeule, E. T. 1964. *Greece in the Bronze Age*. Chicago.

———. 1987. "Baby Aegisthus and the Bronze Age." *Proceedings of the Cambridge Philological Society* 33: 122–152.

Vermeule, E. T. and Karageorghis, V. 1982. *Mycenaean Pictorial Vase Painting*. Cambridge.

Vinson, S. 1993. "The Earliest Representations of Brailed Sails." *Journal of the American Research Center in Egypt* 30: 133–150.

———. 1994. *Egyptian Boats and Ships*. Buckinghamshire.

Vlachopoulos, A. 2007. "Mythos, Logos and Eikon: Motifs of Early Greek Poetry in the Wall Paintings of Xeste 3." In Morris, S. P. and Laffineur, R., eds. *EPOS: Reconsidering Greek Epic and Aegean Bronze Age Archaeology*. Aegaeum 28. Liège. 107–118.

Wachsmann, S. 1981. "The Ships of the Sea Peoples." *International Journal of Nautical Archaeology* 10: 187–220.

———. 1982. "The Ships of the Sea Peoples (*IJNA*, 10.3: 187–220): Additional Notes." *International Journal of Nautical Archaeology* 11: 297–304.

———. 1987. *Aegeans in Theban Tombs*. Orientalia Lovaniensia Analecta 20. Leuven.

———. 1998. *Seagoing Ships and Seamanship in the Bronze Age Levant*. College Station.

———. 1999. "The Pylos Rower Tablets Reconsidered." In Tzalas, H., ed. *TROPIS V: 5th International Symposium on Ship Construction in Antiquity, Nauplia 1993*. Athens. 491–504.

———. 2000. "To the Sea of the Philistines." In Oren, E. D., ed. *The Sea Peoples and Their World: A Reassessment*. University Museum Monographs 108. Philadelphia. 103–143.

———. 2013. *The Gurob Ship-Cart Model and Its Mediterranean Context*. College Station.

Wainright, G. A. 1939. "Some Sea Peoples and Others in the Hittite Archives." *Journal of Egyptian Archaeology* 25: 148–153.

———. 1961. "Some Sea Peoples." *Journal of Egyptian Archaeology* 47: 71–90.

Walberg, G. 1995. "The Midea Megaron and Changes in Mycenaean ideology." *Aegean Archaeology* 2: 87–91.

Wardle, K. A. and Wardle, D. 2003. "Prehistoric Thermon: Pottery of the Late Bronze and Early Iron Age." In N. Kyparissl–Apostolika and M. Papakonstantinou, eds. *The Periphery of the Mycenaean World*. Athens. 147–56.

Watkins, C. 1986. "The Language of the Trojans." In Mellink, M. J., ed. *Troy and the Trojan War*. Bryn Mawr Archaeological Monographs. 45–62.

Watrous, L. V. 1985. "Late Bronze Age Kommos: Imported Pottery as Evidence for Foreign Contact." In Shaw, J. W. and Shaw, M. C., eds. *A Great Minoan Triangle in Southcentral Crete: Kommos, Hagia Triadha, Phaistos*. Toronto. 7–11.

———. 1992. *Kommos III: The Late Bronze Age Pottery*. Princeton.

Wedde, M. 1999. "War at Sea: The Mycenaean and Early Iron Age Oared Galley." In Laffineur, R., ed. *Polemos: Le Contexte Guerrier en Égée à l'âge du Bronze*. Aegaeum 19. Liège. 465–476.

———. 2000. *Toward a Hermeneutics of Aegean Bronze Age Ship Imagery*. Peleus: Studien zur Archäologie und Geschichte Griechenlands und Zyperns 6. Mannheim.

———. 2005. "The Mycenaean Galley in Context: From Fact to *Idée Fixe*." In Laffineur, R. and Greco, E., eds. *Emporia: Aegeans in the Central and Eastern Mediterranean*. Aegaeum 25. Liège. 29–38.

———. 2006. "Pictorial Evidence for Partial System Survival in the Greek Bronze to Iron Age Transition." In Rystedt, E. and Wells, B., eds *Pictorial Pursuits: Figurative Painting on Mycenaean and Geometric Pottery*. Stockholm. 255–269.

Weinstein, J. M. 1989. "The Bronze Age Shipwreck at Ulu Burun: 1986 Campaign III: The Gold Scarab of Nefertiti from Ulu Burun: Its Implications for Egyptian History and Egyptian-Aegean Relations." *American Journal of Archaeology* 93: 17–29.

West, M. L. 1988. "The Rise of the Greek Epic." *Journal of Hellenic Studies* 108: 151–172.

———. 2012. "Towards a Chronology of Early Greek Epic." In Andersen, Ø. and Haug, D. T. T., eds. *Relative Chronology in Early Greek Epic Poetry*. Cambridge. 224–241.

White, D. B. 1986. "Excavations on Bates's Island, Marsa Matruh, 1985." *Journal of the American Research Center in Egypt* 23: 51–84.

———. 1999. "Water, Wood, Dung and Eggs: Reciprocity in Trade Along the LBA Marmarican Coast." In Betancourt, P., Karageorghis, V., Laffineur, R. and Niemeier, W.-D., eds. *Meletemata: Studies in Aegean Archaeology Presented to Malcolm H. Wiener*. Aegaeum 20. Liège. 931–935.

———. 2002. *Marsa Matruh: The University of Pennsylvania Museum of Archaeology and Anthropology's Excavations on Bates's Island, Marsa Matruh, Egypt, 1985–1989*. Prehistory Monographs 1. Philadelphia.

White, D. B. and White, A. P. 1996. "Coastal Sites of Northeast Africa: The Case Against Bronze Age Ports." *Journal of the American Research Center in Egypt* 33: 11–30.

Whitley, J. 1991. "Social Diversity in Dark Age Greece." *The Annual of the British School at Athens* 86: 341–365.

Whittaker, H. 2017. "The Sea Peoples and the Collapse of Mycenaean Palatial Rule." In Fischer, P. M. and Bürge, T., eds. *'Sea Peoples' Up-to-Date: New Research on*

*Transformation in the Eastern Mediterranean in the 13th–11th Centuries BCE.* Contributions to the Chronology of Eastern Mediterranean 35. Vienna: Austrian Academy of Sciences Press. 75–84.

Wilson, J. A. 1974a. "The Journey of Wenamun to Phoenicia." In Pritchard, J. B., ed. *Ancient Near Eastern Texts Relating to the Old Testament.* Princeton. 26–28.

———. 1974b. "Egyptian Historical Texts." In Pritchard, J. B., ed. *Ancient Near Eastern Texts Relating to the Old Testament.* Princeton. 227–263.

Wright, G. E. 1959. "Philistine Coffins and Mercenaries." *The Biblical Archaeologist* 22: 54–66.

———. 1966. "Fresh Evidence for the Philistine Story." *The Biblical Archaeologist* 29: 69–86.

Yakubovich, I. 2015a. "Phoenician and Luwian in Early Iron Age Cilicia." *Anatolian Studies* 65: 35–53.

———. 2015b: "Adanawa or Ahhiyawa? Reply to the Addendum by J.D. Hawkins." *Anatolian Studies* 65: 56–58.

Yasur-Landau, A. 2003. "Why Can't We Find the Origin of the Philistines? In Search of the Source of a Peripheral Aegean Culture." In Kyparissl–Apostolika, N. and Papakonstantinou, M., eds. *The Periphery of the Mycenaean World.* Athens. 587–598.

———. 2010. *The Philistines and the Aegean Migration at the End of the Late Bronze Age.* Cambridge.

———. 2011. "Deep Change in Domestic Behavioural Patterns and Theoretical Aspects of Interregional Interactions in the 12th Century Levant." In Karageorghis, V. and Kouka, O., eds. *On Cooking Pots, Drinking Cups, Loomweights and Ethnicity in Bronze Age Cyprus and Neighbouring Regions.* Nicosia. 245–256.

———. 2012a. "The Role of the Canaanite Population in the Aegean Migration to the Southern Levant in the Late 2nd Millennium BC." In Maran, J. and Stockhammer, P. W., eds. *Materiality and Social Practice: Transformative Capacities of Intercultural Encounters.* Oxford: 190–197.

———. 2012b. "The 'Feathered Helmets' of the Sea Peoples: Joining the Iconographic and Archaeological Evidence." *Talanta* 44: 27–40.

———. 2012c. "Chariots, Spears and Wagons: Anatolian and Aegean Elements in the Medinet Habu Land Battle Relief." In Galil, G., Maeir, A., Gilboa, A. and Kahn, D., eds. *The Ancient Near East in the 12th–10th Centuries BCE: Culture and History.* Münster. 27–40.

Yon, M. 1992. "The End of the Kingdom of Ugarit." In Ward, W. A. and Joukowsky, M. S., eds. *The Crisis Years: The 12th Century B.C. from Beyond the Danube to the Tigris.* Dubuque. 111–122.

Yonge, C. D., ed. 1854. *Athenaeus, The Deipnosophists.* London.

Youssef, A. A.-H., Leblanc, C. and Maher, M. 1977. *Le Ramesseum IV: Les Batailles de Tounip et de Dapour.* Cairo.

Yoyotte, P. J. 1949. "Les Stèles de Ramsès II a Tanis: Première Partie." *Kémi* 10: 65–75.

Yurco, F. J. 1999. "Sea Peoples." In Bard, K. A. and Shubert, S. B., eds. *The Encyclopedia of the Archaeology of Ancient Egypt.* London. 876–879.

Zaccagnini, C. 1983. "Patterns of Mobility among Ancient Near Eastern Craftsmen." *Journal of Near Eastern Studies* 42: 245–264.

Zangger, E., Timpson, M. E., Yazvenko, S. B., Kuhnke, F. and Knauss, J. 1997. "The Pylos Regional Archaeological Project: Part II: Landscape Evolution and Site Preservation." *Hesperia* 66: 549–641.

Ziskind, J. R. 1974. "Sea Loans at Ugarit." *Journal of the American Oriental Society* 94: 134–137.

Zukerman, A. 2010. "On Aegean Involvement in Trade with the Near East During the Late Bronze Age." *Ugarit-Forschungen* 42: 887–901.

# Index

Abu Simbel, 77, 101, 104
Abydos, 101–102, 104; boat, 119
Achilles, 112, 137, 152, 163 n2
Adana, 41–44
Adoption Papyrus, 159
Aegean list, 45
Tell Afis, 56
aḫa, 131–32, *133*, 135
Aḫḫiya. *See* Aḫḫiyawa
Aḫḫiyawa, 5, 8, 25, 31, 41, 48–49,
    54–55, 74, 80, 140–141, 167 n1; as
    Aḫḫiya, 31; as Ḫiyawa, 42–44, 82,
    92, 141; location of, 41–42; Que and,
    43; raids and piracy and, 31, 47–49;
    status of, 25, 46–47; Troy and, 47
el–Ahwat, 22, 165 n35
Akhenaten, 26, 28, 30, 74
Akhetaten. *See* el–Amarna
Akko, 22
Akrotiri. *See* Thera
Alaksandu, 5, 47
Alalaḫ, 27, 92, 141
Alašiya, 17, 34–35, 52, 55, 66, 80–82,
    139, 141; enemies from, 34, 80, 82,
    141; raids and piracy and, 30–31, 33,
    35, 72, 74, 80, 130–131; ships of,
    80–81. *See also* Cyprus
Aleppo, 91; Temple of the Storm God
    at, 91–92

Alexandria, 70–71, 77
el–Amarna, 48, 105; chronology and,
    13; Mycenaean ceramics and, 19. *See
    also* Amarna letters
Amarna letters, 26, 30, 46; copper in,
    52; gold in, 26; Mycenaeans in, 52;
    raids and piracy in, 30–31, 33, 35,
    72, 74, 80, 130–131; Sherden in, 166
    n28; Ulu Burun shipwreck and, 29
Amarynthos. *See* Euboea
Amenhotep III, 30, 132; and the
    Aegean, 44–45. *See also* Aegean list
Amenhotep IV. *See* Akhenaten
Amenhotep son of Hapu, 30, 72, 130
Amenope. *See* Onomasticon of
    Amenope
Ammiṭṭamru II, 54
'Ammurapi, 42, 139–142
Amnisos. *See* Aegean list
Amor. *See* Amurru
'Amuq, 56–57, 91–92, 141
Amurru, 46–48, 54, 68, 81, 141–42; Sea
    Peoples and, 66, 101, 141. *See also*
    Šaušgamuwa
anthropoid coffin, 92–94
Antioch. *See* 'Amuq
Apollodorus, 48–49
Apšuna, 141
Argolid, 19, 58

Arsuz, 44
Ashdod: in the Onomasticon of
    Amenope, 22; Philistines and, 16,
    21–22
Ashkelon: hedgehog helmets from,
    89, 91, 94; in the Onomasticon of
    Amenope, 21–22; Mopsos and, 43–44;
    Philistines and, 16, 21–22; possible
    ship representation from, 89, 129
Askut, 171 n24
Aššuwa, 48, 53
Aššuwan League. *See* Aššuwa
Assyria, 11, 22, 25–26, 28, 46–47;
    Aḫḫiyawa and, 43, 48; Neo–
    Assyrian, 29
Aswan Stele, 70, 130, 154
Tell Atchana. *See* Alalaḫ
Athenaeus, 43–44
Athribis Stele, 73, 75–76, 131
Attarissya, 31–32, 42

b3r–ship, 132, *133*
Babylonia, 11, 25–26, 28, 46–47, 55;
    *See also* cuneiform
Bademgediği Tepe, 97; ship
    representation from, 97, *98*, 100–
    101, 108, 128, 143
basileus, 113, 115
Battle Krater, *2*, 105–106
Berbati Valley, 19
Beth Shean, 13, 92–94, 159, 164 n5,
    172 n36. *See also* anthropoid coffins
big–man society, 114–15, 145
bireme, 145
boar's tusk helmet, 48, 101, 104, *105*,
    *106*, 108, 110–111; Odysseus and,
    104, 111, 153–54
Boğazköi. *See* Ḫattuša
boom-footed squaresail, 118–21, 175
    n36, 176 n64
brailed rig, 117–23, *126*, *129*, *130*, 174
    n5, 176 n64; at Medinet Habu, *63*,
    122, *123*, *128*, 150; origin of, 125–127
Byblos, 21, 140
Byblos ships, 117, 119

Canaan, 16–18, 21–22, 43, 46, 57, 69,
    77, 92, 94, 158, 165 n20
Cape Gelidonya shipwreck, 52–53
Carmel coast, 22; ship graffiti from,
    129, *130*
Chania, 110
chiefdom, 115. *See also* big–man
    society
Chios, 53
Cilicia, 82; Aḫḫiyawa and, 41–44;
    foreigners at, 56–57, 169 n65
Çineköy: inscription from, 42–44
Crete, 13, 41, 45, 47, 50, 87; as Keftiu,
    45, 52, 104; in the *Odyssey*, 1, 4,
    54, 81, 90, 120–121; maritime trade
    networks and, 51, 72, 83, 111, 121;
    raids and piracy and, 54, 80–81, 83;
    refuge settlements on, 9, 58. *See also*
    warrior burial
crow's nest, 124; side–mounted, *124*,
    125; top–mounted, *63*, 122, *123*, 125,
    *126*, 127, *128*, 129, *133*, *135*
cuneiform, 25–26. *See also* Amarna
    letters
Cyclopean. *See* Cyclopes
Cyclopes, 1, 49–50; in the *Odyssey*, 163
    n8
Cypriot. *See* Cyprus
Cypro–Aegean, 19, 21, 92, 108,
    141
Cyprus, 9, 11, 28–29, 38, 41, 51–52,
    56, 71–72, 83, 109–10, 119;
    Aegean migrants or Mycenaean
    colonies and, 51–53, 80, 83,
    115–16, 144; Helladic galley and,
    144–45; in the *Odyssey*, 109–10;
    Mycenaean and Aegean–style
    pottery and, 18–19, 21, 56, 83, 164
    n5; raids and piracy and, 30–31, 51,
    80–81; warrior burials and, 110–13,
    115. *See also* Alašiya. *See also*
    Enkomi

Dakhla Oasis: ship representations from,
    147

Danuna, 43–44, 76; at Medinet Habu, 46, 67–69, 76; in the Amarna archive, 46. *See also* Sea Peoples
Dapur: Ramesses II and, 73, 101
Deir el–Bahri: Punt reliefs from, 117
Dendra, 105
Denyen. *See* Danuna
dieres, 145
Dimini, 58
Djahi, 62–64, 66
Dodecanese, 52, 84–85, 97, 99, 164 n17. *See also* East Aegean–West Anatolian Interface
Donation Stele of Djedptahiuefankh, 159
Dor: and the Sea Peoples, 20–22, 169 n64; in the Tale of Wen–Amon, 20–22

*East Aegean–West Anatolian Interface*, 9, 11, 41, 56, 97, 108–109, 129, 142; defined, 164 n17; Odysseus and, 109
Ekron: Philistines and, 16; ship representations from, 119, *129*
Ekwesh: Achaeans and, 49, 74–75, 109; and Merneptah, 73–76
Enkomi, 105, 120; feather–hatted representations from, 87, *88*, 95, 99, 108, 159; ship graffiti from, 129
Euboea, 58, 111; feather–hatted representation from, 87. *See also* Lefkandi feather-hatted warriors. *See* feathered headdress

Faneromeni Cave, 87
Tell el–Far'ah (S): possible feather–hatted representation from, *88*, 94, 159
feathered headdress, 33, 84–85, 97, 107–108, 143; at Ashkelon, 89, 91, 94; at Bademgediği Tepe, 97, *98*, 100, 108; at Beth Shean, 92, *93*, 94; at Enkomi, 87, *88*, 95, 99, 108, 159; at Kynos, *99*, 100–101; at Liman Tepe, *98*; at Medinet Habu, 62, *63*,

65, 67–68, 84, *87*, *89*, *93*, *103*, 104; at Mycenae, *3*, *85*, *86*, 104; at Tell Ta'yinat, 90, *91*, 94; on Kos, 84, 97, 108; on the Greek mainland, 86–87; possible representation from Tell el–Far'ah (S), *88*, 94. *See also* Sea Peoples

galley subculture, 142–45
Gath, 16–17
Gaza: in the Onomasticon of Amenope, 22; Philistines and, 16, 22
Gazi ship representation from, 136, 176 n64
Gelidonya. *See* Cape Gelidonya shipwreck
el–Gharbaniyat: Ramesside fort at, 77
Gla, 49, 57
Great Harris Papyrus, 69, 75–76, 132–33, 154–55
Great Karnak Inscription, 73–76, 131, 154
Gurob ship–cart model, 145–147, 158

Hala Sultan Tekke, 120
Halikarnassos, 53
Hama, 91
Hatshepsut: Punt expedition of, 117
Ḥatti. *See* Hittite
Ḥattuša, 5, 79, 81–82; Mycenaean warrior from, 47–48, *107*, 108
Ḥattušili III, 46–47, 81–82, 146
hedgehog helmet. *See* feathered headdress
Herakleopolis. *See* Temple of Heryshef
Herakles: seaborne raid on Troy by, 30, 137–139
Herodotus, 43–44
Heroön. *See* Toumba
Hittite, 5, 14, 17, 23, 26, 29, 44, 48–49, 55, 61, 66, 68, 74–75, 101, 154, 163 n13; and Aḫḫiyawa, 5, 30–31, 38, 41–42, 46–48, 54, 82, 140–41; and Homer, 5; and the sea, 30, 34, 79–82, 138–41, 146

Ḥiyawa. *See* Aḫḫiyawa
Horemheb, 119

Iklaina, 117
Ilios. *See* Troy
Iniwia, 124
Interface. *See East Aegean–West
    Anatolian Interface*
Iolkos: feather–hatted representation
    from, 86

Tell Kabri, 27, 166 n7
Kadesh. *See* Qidš
Kallithea, 105
Karadunia. *See* Babylonia
Karatepe, 43–44
Karkemiš, 140–41, 163–64 n13; at
    Medinet Habu, 17, 55, 66
Karnak, 26, 101; Annals of Thutmose
    III at, 45; Poem of Ramesses II at,
    102, 104
Kaş. *See* Ulu Burun shipwreck
Kastelli Pediada, 110
Kazanli Höyük, 56
Keftiu. *See* Crete
Kehek. *See* Libyans
keimelia, 110–11
Kenamun: ship from the tomb of, *124,*
    132
Kilise Tepe, 19, 56
Kinet Höyük, 56
Kition, 120
klea andron, 152
Knidos, 53
Knossos, 29, 45, 104, 110–13, 115;
    Linear B tablets from, 50, 53
Kom el–Hetan. *See* Aegean list
Kommos, 38, 51, 119
Kos, 128, 176 n63; feather–hatted
    representations from, 84, 97, 108
Koukounaries. *See* Paros
Kourion–Kaloriziki, 111–12
Kunulua. *See* Tell Taʻyinat
Kušmešuša, 52
Kydonia. *See* Aegean list

Kynos, 97; ship representations from,
    *99,* 100–101, 122, *123,* 124, 127,
    *128,* 129, 136, 143
Kythera. *See* Aegean list

Lebanon, 1, 56
Lefkandi, 58, 111–13
Lemnos, 53
Libu. *See* Libyans
Libya, 14, 49, and Ramesses II, 75; and
    Ramesses III, 14, 67, 75, 170 n14; in
    the *Odyssey*, 1, 110
Libyans, 70–71; and Merneptah, 9, 49,
    73–74, 77, 110; and Ramesses II, 77;
    and Ramesses III, 62, 67, 155, 165
    n37
Liman Tepe: rower sherd from, 97, *98,*
    100, 128, 143
Linear B tablets, 50–51, 58, 113, 152–
    53; captive women in, 8, 53. . *See
    also* Mycenaean Greece. *See also*
    Rower Tablets
Livanates. *See* Kynos
Lukka, 31, 34, 42, 49, 80, 131; in the
    Amarna archive, 30–33, 35, 37, 72,
    74, 80, 130–31; and Merneptah, 74,
    76; and Ramesses II, 74, 154 land of,
    42, 82, 139–41
Lukki. *See* Lukka
Luxor, 26, 45, 101–102, 104
Lycia, 29, 31, 42, 49–50, 82, 140

Maa–Paleokastro, 83
Madduwatta, 30–31, 42, 49, 80
Malta, 19
Marsa Matruh, 71–72, 120
Medinet Habu, *7,* 9, 14, 23, 46, 64–69,
    75–76, 84, 86, *89,* 92, *93, 102,* 104;
    land battle relief from, *62,* 63, *87;*
    naval battle relief from, 34, *63,*
    100–101, 103, 122, *123,* 124–25,
    127, *128,* 129, *133,* 134, *135,* 136,
    147, 149, 158–59; Sea Peoples
    inscriptions from, 46, 67–69, 75–76,
    89, 99, 132, 136, 141, 154

Memphis, 70
Merneptah, 8–9, 14, 49, 71–77, 80, 109–10, 130, 154, 165 n37
Meshwesh. *See* Libyans
Messenia, 45, 58; depopulation of, 58–59
Midea, 49, 57–58
Miletos, 41, 47, 53
Millawanda. *See* Miletos
Tel Miqne. *See* Ekron
Mittani, 25, 47
mnš–ship, 132, *133*, 135
Mopsos, 5, 43–44, 89
Mukasa. *See* Mopsos
Mukiš, 141
Muršili II, 47, 55
Muwatalli II, 47, 54, 74–75, 154
Mycenae, 2–3, 5, 41, 45, 49, 57–58, 105–106, 108; feather–hatted representations from, *3, 85, 86*, 104; shaft graves at, 2, 4, 93–94, 105
Mycenaean Greece, 5, 8, 18–19, 28–29, 31–32, 41–42, 45–51, 75, 88, 100–101, 106, 110, 108, 115–16, 141, 151–54, 165 n20; chariots from, 41–42, 88, 115, 144; collapse of, 5, 48, 57–60, 83, 113–16, 143–45; international exchange and, 19, 38, 48, 50–53, 92; pottery from or in imitation of, 18–22, 51–52, 71, 83–84, 92, 104, 136, 164 n5, 169 n65, 174 n48; ships and sailing in, 51–53, 97, *98, 99*, 117–18, 122, *123*, 136–39, 141, 143–46; warriors and warfare in, *2, 3*, 48, *85*,100–101, 104, 107–108. *See also* Aegean List. *See also* Aḫḫiyawa . *See also* Linear B

Nahal Me'arot. *See* Carmel coast
Nauplion. *See* Aegean list
Nebamun: ship from the tomb of, *125*, 127
Neferhotep: Abydos boat from the tomb of, 119

Nubia, 14, 28, 45, 92, 94, 171 n24
nuraghe. *See* Sardinia

oared galley, 118
Onomasticon of Amenope, 16, 21–22, 69
Orchomenos, 58

Palistin, 56, 91–92, 141; feather–hatted representation from, 90, *91*, 94
Pantanassa, 111
Papyrus Anastasi I, 158
Papyrus Anastasi II, 73, 75, 77, 135, 154
Papyrus Harris I. *See* Great Harris Papyrus
Paros, 60, 83
Peleset. *See* Philistines
pentekontor, 136, 138, 142, 145; in the *Iliad*, 136–38; in the *Odyssey*, 137–38
Perati, 113
Phaiakia, 1, 109, 143, 147–48; pentekontors and, 137–38
Phaiakians. *See* Phaiakia
Phaistos. *See* Aegean list
Philistines, 14, 16–23, 33, 43, 57, 75, 90–94, 108, 129, 141, 165 n18, 165 n20, 165 n22, 165 n37; 165 n39; at Deir el–Medineh, 68–69, 76; at Medinet Habu, 66–69, 76, *89*; in the Great Harris Papyrus, 69, 76; in the Onomasticon of Amenope, 21–22; ship representations by, 89, *129*
Phoenicia, 7, 9, 21–22, 42–43, 51–52, 56, 110, 140, 145, 169 n64
Phoenician. *See* Phoenicia
piracy, 6, 8–9, 28–39, 52, 71–72, 80, 83–84, 90, 109, 118, 127, 130, 136, 140, 145–47, 158, 166 n28
pirate. *See* Piracy
Piyamaradu, 46–47
Polybius, 134
Portes: Helmet base from, 84
privateer, 35–36, 130, 158

prw–nfr, 135
Punt, 117, 119
Puranda. *See* Bademgediği Tepe
Pyla–*Kokkinokremos, 19*
Pylos, 49–50, 104–105, 117, 119, 136, 138, 152; captive women at, 53; collapse of, 8, 57–60. . *See also* Linear B tablets. *See also* Rower Tablets
Pyrgos Livanaton. *See* Kynos

qa-si-re-u. *See* basileus
Qidš, 19; Battle of, 23, 74–75, 101–102, 154
qrr–ship, 133
Que. *See* Aḫḫiyawa

ra-wi-ja-ja, 8, 53
Ramesses II, 8–9, 23, 32, 33, 48, 70, 72, 74–75, 77, 81–82, 101–102, 127, 130, 132, 134–35, 141, 146, 154–55, 158, 160
Ramesses III, 8–9, 14, 16–17, 23, 37, 46, 55, 61–69, 71, 75–76, 80, 89, 94, 101–102, 122, 130, 132–133, 150, 154–55, 160, 165 n37
Ramesseum, 101–102
Ras Shamra. *See* Ugarit
refuge settlements, 82; in the Cyclades, 59–60, 83; on Crete, 9, 82, 110; on Cyprus, 9, 31, 83
Rekhmire, 104, 175 n36
Rhodes, 41, 45, 109
Rower Tablets, 8, 58–60, 138, 143. *See also* Linear B tablets

Tell es–Safi. *See* Gath
Salamis, 48
Samos, 100
Saqqara, 125–27, 135–36
Sardinia, 19, 120; Sherden and, 22. *See also* el–Ahwat
Šaušgamuwa, 46–48
Šaušgamuwa Treaty. *See* Šaušgamuwa
scaraboid, 127, 172 n36

seal, 11, 28, 105, 115; cylinder, 28, 53, 119; possible feather–hatted representations on, 87–88, 94–95, 159
Seraglio. *See* Kos
Shardana. *See* Sherden
Shasu, 77
Shekelesh: and Merneptah, 73–76, 80; and Ramesses III, 66–69, 75–76, 80
Sherden, 6–10, 23, 34, 70, 72, 103–104, 107, 130, 136, 154, 158–59, *160,* 161, 165 n37, 166 n28; and Akko, 22; and Merneptah, 73–77, 135; and Ramesses II, 9, 23, 32, 34, 70, 75–76, 82, 101–102, 104, 127, 130–32, 135, 154–55; and Sardinia, 22; at Medinet Habu, *7,* 23, 63, 68, 76, 101, *102, 103,* 104; in the Great Harris Papyrus, 69, 75–76, 155; in the Onomasticon of Amenope, 21–22; in the Wilbour Papyrus, 155–58, 178 n13; in Ugaritic texts, 130–31; ships of, 131–32, 134–35, 145, 160–61
Shoshenq I, 71
Šikala. *See* Sikil
Sikil, 20, 80; Ugaritic captive and, 79–82. *See also* Tjekker
Skyros: ship representation from, 122, 129, 147
Soleb, 45
Spermeru, 159
Strabo, 43, 49, 121
Sudan, 45
Šuppiluliuma I, 54
Šuppiluliuma II, 79–82

Tell Ta'yinat. *See* Palistin
Taita, 92. *See also* Palistin
Tale of Wen–Amon, 20–22
Tanaya, 44–45
Tanis II Rhetorical Stele, 32–34, 70–71, 130, 154; ship terminology on, 131, 135; warship determinative from, 132, *133*
Tawagalawa Letter, 46–47

Temple of Heryshef: Sherden–related stelae from, 159, *160*

Teresh: and Merneptah, 73–76; and Ramesses III, 68–69, 75–76

Thebes (Egypt), 26, 52, 62–63, 68, 75, 104, 124–25, 150, 175 n36

Thebes (Greece), 41, 45, 49–50, 58, 152

Thera, 4, *105*, 106, 117, 119–20, 153

Thermon, 87

Thrace, 41

Thutmosis III, 44–45, 131

Tiryns, 29, 49–50, 57–58, 169 n77; feather–hatted representations from, 86–87; Tiye, 45

Tjehenu, 71, 77

Tjekker, 80, 169 n64; at Medinet Habu, 66–69, 76, 89; in the Great Harris Papyrus, 76; in the Onomasticon of Amenope, 22; in the Tale of Wen–Amon, 20. . *See also* Sikil

Tjemeh, 71

Tragana: ship representation from, 136, *147*

transcultural, 17, 87, 165 n22

triakontor, 138, 142

Troy, 1–2, 5, 14, 30, 41, 43, 47, 54, 109, 112, 137–38, 143, 153, 163 n9; in

the *Iliad*, 30, 112–13, 137–38; in the *Odyssey*, 1, 25, 109, 148–49

Tudhaliya IV, 46–48

Ugarit, 8, 23, 26, 46, 52, 54, 82, 127, 138–42; Ahhiyawa and, 42, 51, 82, 140, 177 n76; destruction of, 13, 55–56, 61; maritime trade networks and, 38, 51, 120, 130; raids and piracy and, 30–31, 51, 79–81, 139–42, 144

Ulu Burun shipwreck, 27–29, 37, 120, 140

Walistin. *See* Palistin

wanax, 41, 59–60, 113, 116

warrior burial, 9, 104, 110–13, 115, 144, 173 n27

Warrior Stele, *85*

Warrior Vase, *3*, 85, 87, 101, 104, 108

Wen–Amon. *See* Tale of Wen–Amon

Weshesh: at Medinet Habu, 66, 68, 76; in the Great Harris Papyrus, 69, 76, 165

Wilbour Papyrus, 155–56, 158, 178 n13

Wiluša. *See* Troy

Zawiyet Umm el–Rakham, 70–72, 77, 120

# About the Author

**Jeffrey P. Emanuel** is associate director of Academic Technology and CHS fellow in Aegean archaeology and prehistory at Harvard University. His historical and archaeological research focuses on the Aegean and Eastern Mediterranean in the Late Bronze and Early Iron Ages (Late Helladic IIIB–C), with emphases on the intersection between myth, history, and archaeology; and on maritime affairs, including piracy, ship construction, technological and cultural transmission, and the development of naval warfare. In his academic technology role, he leads in the study, implementation, and support of digital methods in teaching and research, with an emphasis on the humanities and social sciences. He studied Classical Archaeology at the University of Georgia and Social and Cultural Anthropology and Archaeology at Harvard University.